Battling to the End

STUDIES IN VIOLENCE, MIMESIS, AND CULTURE SERIES

Battling to the End

Conversations with Benoît Chantre

René Girard
Translated by Mary Baker

Michigan State University Press · *East Lansing*

Copyright © 2010 by Michigan State University
Achever Clausewitz © Editions Carnets Nord, 2007

⊗ The paper used in this publication meets the minimum requirements of ANSI/
NISO Z39.48-1992 (R 1997) (Permanence of Paper).

Michigan State University Press
East Lansing, Michigan 48823-5245

Printed and bound in the United States of America.

16 15 14 13 12 11 10   1 2 3 4 5 6 7 8 9 10

LIBRARY OF CONGRESS CATALOGING-IN-PUBLICATION DATA

Girard, René, 1923-
  [Achever Clausewitz. English]
  Battling to the end / René Girard.
     p. cm. — (Studies in violence, mimesis, and culture series)
  Translation of Achever Clausewitz, published: Paris : Carnets nord, 2007.
  Based on discussions with Benoît Chantre.
  Includes index.
  ISBN 978-0-87013-877-5 (pbk. : alk. paper)
1. War.   2. Clausewitz, Carl von, 1780–1831.   3. Strategy.
4. Military art and science.   5. Girard, René, 1923—Interviews.
I. Chantre, Benoît.   II. Title.
  U21.2.G52513 2010
  355.02–dc22

                                                  2009031985

Book and cover design by Sharp Des!gns, Inc., Lansing, MI
Cover photo is from istock.com.

g green press INITIATIVE Michigan State University Press is a member of the Green Press Initiative and is committed to developing and encouraging ecologically
responsible publishing practices. For more information about the Green Press Initiative and the use of recycled paper in book publishing, please visit
www.greenpressinitiative.org.

Visit Michigan State University Press on the World Wide Web at:
www.msupress.msu.edu

Contents

A Note on the Translation

Mary Baker is the primary translator of *Achever Clausewitz*. She captured beautifully the rapid back and forth of ideas between René Girard and Benoît Chantre, producing the primary manuscript. Andrew McKenna, Professor of French at Loyola University, was a graduate student of Girard at Johns Hopkins University in the sixties. He has been the publishers' go-to person for reviewing manuscripts on mimetic theory for the last 30 years; he is also the former editor of *Contagion* (1996–2006). No one (except perhaps Martha Girard herself) has listened longer and more carefully to Girard work through the mimetic theory in both English and French. McKenna was invaluable in suggesting how sentences in *Achever Clausewitz* would sound if Girard wrote them in English. I made the final decisions on when to adopt McKenna's suggestions and, because Mary Baker lives in Japan, I provided the standard English translations for the references.

William A. Johnsen
Series Editor
Studies in Violence, Mimesis, and Culture Series

Introduction

This is a peculiar kind of book. It claims to be a study of Germany and French-German relations over the last two centuries. At the same time, it says things that have never before been said with the violence and clarity they require. Its subject is the *possibility* of an end to Europe, the Western world and the world as a whole. Today, this possibility has become real. This is an apocalyptic book.

Until now, my entire work has been presented as a discussion of archaic religion through comparative anthropology. Its goal was to shed light on what is known as the process of hominization, the fascinating passage from animality to humanity that occurred thousands of years ago. My hypothesis is mimetic: because humans imitate one another more than animals, they have had to find a means of dealing with contagious similarity, which could lead to the pure and simple disappearance of their society. The mechanism that reintroduces difference into a situation in which everyone has come to resemble everyone else is sacrifice. Humanity results from sacrifice; we are thus the children of religion. What I call after Freud the founding murder, in other words, the immolation of a sacrificial victim that is both guilty of disorder and able to restore order, is constantly re-enacted in the rituals at the origin of our institutions. Since the dawn of humanity, millions of innocent victims have been killed in this way in order to enable their fellow humans to live together, or at least not to destroy one another. This is the implacable logic of the sacred, which myths dissimulate less and less as humans become increasingly self-aware. The decisive point in this evolution is Christian revelation, a kind of divine expiation in which God through his Son could be seen as asking for forgiveness from humans for having revealed the mechanisms of their violence so late. Rituals had slowly educated them; from then on, humans had to do without.

Christianity demystifies religion. Demystification, which is good in the absolute, has proven bad in the relative, for we were not prepared to shoulder its consequences. We are not Christian enough. The paradox can be put in a different way: Christianity is the only religion that has foreseen its own failure. This prescience is known as the apocalypse. Indeed, it is in the apocalyptic texts that the word of God is most forceful, repudiating mistakes that are entirely the fault of humans, who are less and less inclined to acknowledge the mechanisms of their violence. The longer we persist in our error, the stronger God's voice will emerge from the devastation. This is why no one wants to read the apocalyptic texts that abound in the Synoptic Gospels and Pauline Epistles. This is also why no one wants to recognize that these texts rise up before us because we have disregarded Revelation. Once in our history *the truth about the identity of all humans* was spoken, and no one wanted to hear it; instead we hang ever more frantically onto our false differences.

Two world wars, the invention of the atomic bomb, several genocides, and an imminent ecological disaster have not sufficed to convince humanity, and Christians above all, that the apocalyptic texts might not be predictions but certainly do concern the disaster that is underway. What needs to be done to get them a hearing? I have been accused of repeating myself too often, of turning my theory into a fetish, of using it to explain everything. Yet it has described mechanisms that recent discoveries in neuroscience confirm: imitation is the initial and essential means of learning; it is not something acquired later on. We can escape mimetism only by understanding the laws that govern it. Only by understanding the dangers of imitation can we conceive of authentic identification with the Other. However, we are becoming aware of the primacy of moral relationship at the very time when the atomization of humanity is being realized, and when violence has increased in intensity and unpredictability.

Today, violence has been unleashed across the whole world, creating what the apocalyptic texts predicted: confusion between disasters caused by nature and those caused by humans, between the natural and the man-made: global warming and rising waters are no longer metaphors today. Violence, which produced the sacred, no longer produces anything but itself. I am not the one repeating myself: reality is beginning to resemble a truth that was not invented, since it was described 2000 years ago. The fact that reality now confirms this truth is what our unhealthy obsession with contradiction and innovation neither can nor wants to understand. The paradox is that by always getting closer to Alpha, we are going towards Omega; that by better understanding the origin, we can see every day a little better that the origin is coming closer. The fetters put in place by the founding murder but unshackled by the Passion, are now liberating planet-wide violence, and we cannot refasten the bindings because we now know that scapegoats are innocent. The Passion unveiled the sacrificial origin of humanity once and for all. It dismantled the sacred and revealed its violence.

However, Christ *also* confirmed the divine that is within all religions. The incredible paradox, which no one can accept, is that the Passion has freed violence at the same time as holiness. The sacred, which has been "returning" for 2000 years, is thus not an archaic form of the sacred, but a sacred that has been "satanized" by the awareness we have of it, and that indicates, through its very excesses, the imminence of the Second Coming. Thus, what we are seeking to describe as occurring at the beginning applies increasingly to events in progress. This *more and more* is the law of relations among us as violence grows in the world, this time at the risk of destroying it. Heraclitus wrote that Polemos, war, "is father of all and king of all."[1]

This law of human relations was reformulated in an office of the Berlin Military Academy a few years after Napoleon's fall. The reformulation took the shape of the trend to extremes, the inability of politics to contain reciprocal, in other words, mimetic, increase of violence. Its author, Carl von Clausewitz (1780–1831), was working on a book that he left unfinished when he died. It was perhaps the greatest book ever written on war, a treatise that the English, Germans, French, Italians, Russians and Chinese have read and reread from the end of the nineteenth century until the present day. Clausewitz's posthumous treatise, *On War,* claims to be a work on strategy. It discusses what was at the time the most recent example of the trend to extremes, which had occurred, as always, unbeknownst to those involved. The trend then destroyed Europe and now threatens the world.

Clausewitz spoke to us about his specialty as if it were not related to everything that is going on around us, when in fact it has huge implications far beyond his discourse. He formulated and helped to identify what might be called "Prussianism" in its most disturbing form, but without considering the consequences of the trend to extremes, which did not frighten him enough. Clausewitz's thought applies to French-German relations as a whole, from Prussia's defeat in 1806 to France's collapse in 1940. His book was written for the period when European wars escalated mimetically until they resulted in disaster. It would thus be perfectly hypocritical to see *On War* as only a technical book. What happens when we reach the extremes that Clausewitz glimpses before hiding them behind strategic considerations? He does not tell us. This is the question we have to ask today.

Let us dare to say that we, the French and Germans, are responsible for the devastation that is underway because our extremes have become the whole world. We set the spark to the tinder. If we had been told 30 years ago that Islamism would replace the Cold War, we would have laughed. If we had said 30 years ago that military and environmental events were foretold in the Gospel or that the apocalypse began at Verdun, people would have taken us for Jehovah's Witnesses. Yet war has been the only engine of technological progress. Its disappearance as an institution, which goes hand in hand with conscription and total mobilization, has drenched the world in blood and fire. By continuing to not want to see, we are encouraging the escalation towards the worst.

Clausewitz had a stunning intuition about history's suddenly accelerated course, but he immediately disguised it, and tried to give his book the tone of a technical, scholarly treatise. We therefore have to *complete* Clausewitz by taking up the route he interrupted and following it right to the end. For this, we have gone to the texts that no one seems to read: that of Clausewitz first, and then the apocalyptic texts. Through the former, the relevance of the latter becomes apparent with greater force.

We shall not turn the author of *On War* into a scapegoat, as did in their time Stalin and Liddell Hart, one of his most famous commentators. We shall also not be content with the timidity with which Raymond Aron tried to rehabilitate him. The reason the text is not yet fully understood is perhaps because it has been attacked and defended too often. It is as if we have not yet wanted to understand the central intuition that it seeks to hide. This constant denial is interesting. Clausewitz was *possessed,* like all the great writers of resentment. It was because he wanted to be more rational than the strategists who preceded him that he suddenly put his finger on an aspect of reality that is absolutely irrational. Then he retreated and tried to shut his eyes.

Completing the interpretation of *On War* is to say that its meaning is religious and that only a religious interpretation has a chance of reaching what is essential in it. Clausewitz conceives relations among men as mimetic in spite of the fact that his philosophical approach was that of Enlightenment rationalism. He provided all the means for showing that the world is tending more and more to extremes, and yet his imagination always thwarted and limited his intuitions. Clausewitz and his commentators were hampered by their rationalism. This is as good a proof as any that a different kind of rationality is needed to understand the reality of what he glimpsed. Ours is the first society that knows it can completely destroy itself. Yet we lack the belief that could bear up under this knowledge.

It is not theologians who set us on the track of the new rationality; that was done by an armchair strategist who died at the age of 51 from the misunderstanding surrounding his work. He was a military theorist whom France, England and the Soviet Union detested, a feisty writer who left no one indifferent. The theses themselves have no future. Yet there is a sub-current running beneath them that needs to be read aloud, for it can reveal a hidden reality, however imperfect we find certain formulations. *Durch diese Wechselwirkung wieder das Streben nach dem Äussersten*,[2] "by this reciprocal action, the movement towards the *outside shadows*." Without realizing it, Clausewitz discovered not only the apocalyptic formula but also the fact that it is bound up with mimetic rivalry. Where can this truth be understood in a world that continues to close its eyes to the incalculable consequences of mimetic rivalry? Not only was Clausewitz right, in opposition to Hegel and all modern wisdom, but what he was right about has terrible implications for humanity. This warmonger alone saw certain things. To turn him into a devil would be to slumber on a volcano.

Like Hölderlin, I think that Christ alone allows us to face this reality without sinking into madness. The apocalypse does not announce the end of the world; it creates hope. If we suddenly *see* reality, we do not experience the absolute despair of an unthinking modernity, but rediscover a world where things have meaning. Hope is possible only if we dare to think about the danger at hand, but this requires opposing both nihilists, for whom everything is only language, and "realists," who reject the idea that intelligence can attain truth: heads of state, bankers and soldiers who claim to be saving us when in fact they are plunging us deeper into devastation each day.

By accepting crucifixion, Christ brought to light what had been "hidden since the foundation of the world," in other words, the foundation itself, the unanimous murder that appeared in broad daylight for the first time on the cross. In order to function, archaic religions need to hide their founding murder, which was being repeated continually in ritual sacrifices, thereby protecting human societies from their own violence. By revealing the founding murder, Christianity destroyed the ignorance and superstition that are indispensable to such religions. It thus made possible an advance in knowledge that was until then unimaginable.

Freed of sacrificial constraints, the human mind invented science, technology and all the best and worst of culture. Our civilization is the most creative and powerful ever known, but also the most fragile and threatened because it no longer has the safety rails of archaic religion. Without sacrifice in the broad sense, it could destroy itself if it does not take care, which clearly it is not doing.

Was Paul a megalomaniac when he said in the First Epistle to the Corinthians that "None of the rulers of this age understood this; for if they had, they would not have crucified the Lord of glory"? I do not think so. The "rulers of this age," and all that Paul calls "Powers" and "Principalities," were state structures based on the founding murder, which was effective because hidden. In the context, the leading power was the Roman Empire, which was essentially evil in the absolute but indispensable in the relative, and better than the total destruction about which the Christian revelation warns us. Once again, this does not mean that Christian revelation is bad. It is wholly good, but we are unable to come to terms with it.

A scapegoat remains effective as long as we believe in its guilt. Having a scapegoat means not knowing that we have one. Learning that we have a scapegoat is to lose it forever and to expose ourselves to mimetic conflicts with no possible resolution. This is the implacable law of the escalation to extremes. The protective system of scapegoats is finally destroyed by the Crucifixion narratives as they reveal Jesus' innocence, and, little by little, that of all analogous victims. The process of education away from violent sacrifice is thus underway, but it is going very slowly, making advances that are almost always unconscious. It is only today that it has had increasingly remarkable results in terms of our comfort, but has also proved ever more dangerous for the future of life on Earth.

To make the Revelation wholly good, and not threatening at all, humans have only to adopt the behavior recommended by Christ: abstain completely from retaliation, and renounce the escalation to extremes. Indeed, if the escalation to extremes continues a little longer, it will lead straight to the extinction of all life on the planet. This is the possibility that Raymond Aron glimpsed when reading Clausewitz. He then wrote an impressive work to expel apocalyptic logic from his mind and persuade himself at all cost that the worst could be avoided, that "deterrence" would always triumph. This budding religious clairvoyance is infinitely superior to what most people are capable of, but insufficient. We have to take the interpretation of the text further. The interpretation has to be *finished*.

Since the beginning of the "novelistic conversion"[3] in *Deceit, Desire, and the Novel,* all of my books have been more or less explicit apologies of Christianity. I would like this one to be even more explicit. What we are saying will become more understandable with time because, unquestionably, we are accelerating swiftly towards the destruction of the world. Christianity is a founding murder in reverse, which illuminates what has to remain hidden to produce ritual, sacrificial religions. Paul compared it to food for adults, in contrast with food for children, which is what archaic religions were. Nietzsche himself sometimes had intuitions of this kind regarding the Greeks' "infantile" character. However, to make the situation even more perverse, Christian revelation is the paradoxical victim of the knowledge that it provides. Absurdly, it is conflated with myth, which it clearly is not, and doubly misunderstood by both its enemies and partisans, who tend to confuse it with one of the archaic religions that it demystifies. Yet all demystification comes from Christianity. Even better: the only true religion is the one that demystifies archaic religions.

Christ came to take the victim's place. He placed himself at the heart of the system to reveal its hidden workings. The "second Adam," to use Saint Paul's expression, revealed to us how the "first" came to be. The Passion teaches us that humanity results from sacrifice, is born with religion. Only religion has been able to contain the conflicts that would have otherwise destroyed the first groups of humans. However, the Revelation has not destroyed religion. Mimetic theory does not seek to demonstrate that myth is null, but to shed light on the *fundamental discontinuity and continuity between the Passion and archaic religion.* Christ's divinity which precedes the Crucifixion introduces a radical rupture with the archaic, but Christ's resurrection is in complete continuity with all forms of religion that preceded it. The way out of archaic religion comes at this price. A good theory about humanity must be based on a good theory about God.

Indeed, what do people in thrall to the sacrificial mechanism confusedly think if not that He who organized the "thing," namely, the lynching of the victim, is living? For, after having set all against all, He reconciles everyone. He is resuscitated because they are not dead. People in the process of being educated, who are not yet fully human, can become so only by measuring themselves against the divine, and there comes a time when God can reveal himself fully to them. It is understandable that Christ frightened the Apostles. However, He is also the only Model, the one that places man at just the right distance from the divine. Christ came to reveal that his kingdom was not of this world, but that humans, once they have understood the mechanisms of their own violence, can have an accurate intuition of what is beyond it. We can all participate in the divinity of Christ so long as we renounce our own violence. However, we now know, in part thanks to Clausewitz, that humans will not renounce it. The paradox is thus that we are starting to grasp the Gospel message at the very moment when the escalation to extremes is becoming the unique law of history.

Christian revelation has confirmed all religions in its relation to the divine that is rejected by the modern world. It *confirms* what religions have glimpsed. In a way, it is because Christ accepted the mold of false resurrections that he is truly risen. The beneficiaries of archaic resurrections that re-established peace and order were in a real relation to the divine. There was something Christian in all myths. However, by revealing the victims' innocence, the Passion makes positive what was still negative in myths: we now know that victims are never guilty. Satan thus becomes the name of a sacred that is revealed and utterly devalued through Christ's intervention. This is why Vatican II accomplished a decisive action: it eliminated God's violence but not the reality of evil.

At present, the "wise" and the "discerning," which I suppose refers to academics, are furiously redoubling their attacks on Christianity and once again congratulating themselves on its forthcoming demise. These unfortunates do not see that their skepticism itself is a by-product of Christian religion. While it is good to get rid of the sacrificial idiocies of the past in order to accelerate progress, eliminating obstacles to humanity's "forward march" and facilitating the invention and production of what will make our lives more prosperous and comfortable (at least in the West), it is nonetheless true that sacrificial stupidity was also what prevented us from perfecting ways of killing one another. Paradoxically, "stupid sacrifice" is what we are most in need of at present.

The only Christians who still talk about the apocalypse are fundamentalists, but they have a completely mythological conception of it. They think that the violence of the end of time will come from God himself. They cannot do without a cruel God. Strangely, they do not see that the violence we ourselves are in the process of amassing and that is looming over our own heads is entirely sufficient to trigger the worst. They have no sense of humor.

This book is based on long discussions with Benoît Chantre, and has been entirely reworked and rewritten by him. We established the definitive version together. We follow Clausewitz's text very closely. Conversation's blessings include surprises and new connections. Little by little, we came to see that various authors, poets and exceptional people were crucial to our discussion. A whole constellation of writers and thinkers finally merged with our thinking. I consider this a little like the communion of saints. The enormous problems that we have raised based on a single text have highlighted these people, and the central thinker has seemed to us to be the poet Hölderlin. He was an exact contemporary of Clausewitz and Hegel, and undeniably saw that at the heart of European conflicts the world's future would depend on the face-off between the Passion and archaic religion, between Christ and the Greeks.

This apocalyptic moment thus serves as a link between a specific theme in Clausewitz's treatise and considerations on the destiny of Europe. We use analytical tools borrowed from anthropology, history, literary history, psychology, philosophy and theology, and argue, at the time of the delicate constructing of European unity, for authentic dialogue between France and Germany because the mysterious hatred between these two countries has been the alpha and omega of Europe.

In our discussions, we constantly point out that relationship resides at the heart of reciprocity and that reconciliation *reveals* the negative meaning that war gives to relationship. These are the "signs of the times" that the future can be deciphered from the present: the prophet, like the strategist, has a responsibility to know how to read clues to the future. However, violence is a terrible adversary, especially since it always wins. Desiring war, which Clausewitz says is the typical attitude of the defender, against those who desire peace, in other words, desiring lies and domination, can thus become a spiritual attitude. Does not Christ himself invite us to be more cunning than the serpent? We are thus more at war than ever, at a time when war itself no longer exists. We have to fight a violence that can no longer be controlled or mastered. Yet what if triumph were not the most important thing? What if the battle were worth more than the victory?

The primacy of victory is the triumph of the weak. The primacy of battle, by contrast, is the prelude to the only conversion that matters. This is the heroic attitude that we have sought to redefine. It alone can link violence and reconciliation, or, more precisely, make tangible both the possibility of the end of the world *and* reconciliation among all members of humanity. We cannot escape this ambivalence. More than ever, I am convinced that history has meaning, and that its meaning is terrifying.

> But where danger threatens
> That which saves from it also grows.[4]

René Girard

CHAPTER 1

The Escalation to Extremes[1]

"WAR IS NOTHING BUT A DUEL ON A LARGER SCALE."[2]

Benoît Chantre: René Girard, your work is based on literary criticism, the study of religion in archaic societies, and an anthropological rereading of the Gospels and the Jewish prophetic tradition. Nothing, in principle, destined you to become interested in the writings of a Prussian general who died in Berlin in 1831 amidst relative indifference. What sparked your interest in Carl von Clausewitz?

René Girard: It happened relatively recently, through the discovery of an abridged American edition of his treatise, *On War,* and the sudden realization that the Prussian general, as you call him, had intuitions very similar to my own. His ideas enabled me to finally articulate the broad lines of my mimetic theory in its relation to history, particularly that of the last two centuries. Of course I do discuss war in my books, especially in *Violence and the Sacred,*[3] but from a strictly anthropological point of view. I could not approach it theoretically, as have done all the great strategists, such as Sun Tzu, Mao Zedong, Machiavelli, Guibert, Saxe, and Jomini. I think that Clausewitz stands alone among such theorists because he was at the turning point of two eras of war and bears witness to a new situation with respect to violence. In this regard, his approach is much more profound and much less technical than that of the others. Thus it was only very recently that I began to see the *end of war* as a subject in itself. The last days of an institution whose purpose was to control and restrain violence corroborates my central hypothesis, namely, that for about three centuries all rituals and institutions have been crumbling. War, through its rules and codes, also helped to create meaning by establishing new equilibria over an ever growing geographical area. It has generally ceased to play this role since the end of World War II. How did the system suddenly disintegrate? How has political rationality finally become powerless? These questions are vital.

I quickly obtained a complete French translation.[4] The further I advanced in my reading of Clausewitz's treatise, the more I was fascinated by the fact that the tragedy of the modern world was laid out in those dense and sometimes dry pages, which purport to speak only of military theory. Naturally, I had skimmed through Raymond Aron's book, *Clausewitz: Philosopher of War,*[5] when it appeared in the 1970s, but at the time I was too absorbed in my own research to really pay attention. I see now that it was also because Aron's *rationalist* reading prevented me from exploring Clausewitz's text, which says something completely different from what Aron tried to make it say. Aron's brilliant essay is now dated, and he cannot be blamed for that. It was a product of the time, the Cold War, when people still believed in nuclear deterrence and thought that foreign policy had meaning; that meaning has now largely disappeared. This is why I am convinced that we have entered an era when anthropology will become a more relevant tool than political science. We will have to radically change our interpretation of events, stop thinking as products of the Enlightenment, and finally envisage the radical nature of violence; this will produce a quite different kind of rationality, as required by events. This makes reading Clausewitz pertinent today. I trust that others will continue the work for which our conversation will hopefully lay the foundations.

BC: If you don't mind, let's briefly situate *On War* historically before discussing it. Carl von Clausewitz (1780–1831) was a Prussian officer, son of a military man, and spent most of his time with soldiers. Like all his colleagues, he was proud of his country's recent rise in power, having experienced as a disaster the defeat by Napoleon's army at Jena in 1806. This crushing defeat (King Frederick William III fled into eastern Prussia while the French armies occupied the whole country) revived in officers' minds the humiliation felt at Valmy, when on September 20, 1792, Frederick William II, the successor of his uncle Frederick the Great (Voltaire's friend) saw the Duke of Brunswick order a retreat in the face of a new phenomenon: an army of volunteers supporting a professional army (the alliance of the "culs-blancs" and the "bleuets"), which was to launch the revolutionary expansion across Europe.

RG: Let's not forget that Clausewitz was in the Duke of Brunswick's army at the Battle of Valmy. I read somewhere that apparently he immediately saw the importance of that battle, which was in fact nothing more than a cannonade. Yet this was when the French army became revolutionary: instead of fleeing in panic, as they had done two or three times before, the French stood firm. The Duke of Brunswick was the one who retreated, but without any major losses. I think that all historians agree on this. They also agree about the extraordinary importance of the event because it was from that point on that the Revolutionary Army became effective. The volunteers from Marseilles, who had come to join professional soldiers at Valmy, were not content with simply giving France a national anthem: they announced a new era, that of total mobilization. Indeed, Jena was one of Napoleon's fastest victories: he toppled the adversary in three minutes.

BC: Clausewitz was very quick to see the newness of a populace in arms and the novelty of military conscription. Note that the principle of revolutionary expansion was adopted in the November 17, 1792 Convention. It precedes the policy of the Committee of Public Safety ("no freedom for the enemies of freedom," proclaimed Saint-Just), which, beginning in March 1793, enabled the Revolutionary Army to occupy Belgium and the Rhineland. The clinging to its conquests, which was to provide some of the Revolution's decisive acquisitions, determined Napoleon's policy and his rush to establish a continental embargo from Russia to Spain to counter England and its hegemonic commercial aims.

RG: These events have to be kept in mind in order to understand why Jena was so traumatic in 1806. Prussia, which had been experiencing the military pride of an upstart, saw its system of political centralization destroyed by a single blow. Everything had to be rebuilt and set on new foundations. Clausewitz, who deserted his country from 1811 to 1814 and joined the Tsar's army because of the temporary alliance between the King of Prussia and Napoleon, lived until the end of his days in the hope of a reform, which was initially led by Scharnhorst. The reform became impossible owing to Frederick William III's reactionary policy after the Congress of Vienna. No constitution was adopted in Prussia. The philosophical dreams of Frederick the Great, the "enlightened despot" of the eighteenth century, were utterly abandoned.

It has been said that Clausewitz inspired Kutusov's strategy. However, he ended his career rather sadly, as Director of the Berlin Military Academy, where he was kept from teaching towards the end. His colleagues never forgave him for being right about pursuing the war, especially since the engagement proved legitimate. Clausewitz was unable to play the political role he would have liked. Consequently he drew lessons from the exceptional military events, and meditated until his death on the unfinished treatise that his wife published posthumously. It seems that Clausewitz considered only the first chapter of Book 1 to be finished. As a result, often it is only the first pages that are quoted, the ones taken from Chapter 1 of Book 1 "On the Nature of War," which summarize the book as a whole.

BC: The first chapter, entitled "What is War?," is in fact fundamental. It is the chapter that Clausewitz reworked a few years before his death, in 1831, and in which Raymond Aron tried to see a desire to rethink everything in a more political, less warlike sense. Aron went so far as to say that there is a break between Chapter 1 of Book 1 and the rest of the treatise, and that Chapter 1 is a whole unto itself.

RG: As I am sure you agree, this poses major problems. We have to examine this insistence on a "break." It is as if Raymond Aron did not want to see the unity of the work, which, from my point of view, the later rewriting did not challenge. Indeed, I think that the tone of the treatise is recognizable right from the beginning in Chapter 1. The tone, and the tension in it throughout the treatise, is essential.

BC: He begins with a definition of war...

RG: ... as a duel.[6]

BC: Let's quote him:

> I shall not begin by expounding a pedantic, literary definition of war, but go straight to the heart of the matter, to the duel. War is nothing but a duel on a larger scale. Countless duels go to make up war, but a picture of it as a whole can be formed by imagining a pair of wrestlers. Each tries through physical force to compel the other to do his will; his *immediate* aim is to *throw* his opponent in order to make him incapable of further resistance.
>
> *War is thus an act of force to compel our enemy to do our will.*[7]

RG: We will return to the definition, but note that it is followed by a comment that is not intended to reassure the reader:

> Kind-hearted people might of course think there was some ingenious way to disarm or defeat an enemy without too much bloodshed, and might imagine this is the true goal of the art of war. Pleasant as it sounds, it is a fallacy that

must be exposed: war is such a dangerous business that the mistakes which come from kindness are the very worst.[8]

What is Clausewitz telling us? Two things: first that he was living at a time when what has been called a "gentleman's war," namely that of the eighteenth century, had been abandoned; and second that the indirect approach is a mistake proceeding from kindness of heart. The latter affirmation proves, unsurprisingly, that Clausewitz was ignorant of Chinese strategy, which aims specifically at winning battles before they are begun. However, it is also a clear judgment on his part: the foundation of indirect strategy (that of maneuvers rather than battle) is often an admission of weakness. Intelligence must thus serve force, since it is no longer a question of controlling it:

> The maximum use of force is in no way incompatible with the simultaneous use of the intellect. If one side uses force without compunction, undeterred by the bloodshed it involves, while the other side refrains, the first will gain the upper hand. That side will force the other to follow suit; each will drive its opponent toward extremes, and the only limiting factors are the counterpoises inherent in war.[9]

This leads to his striking definition of a duel as a "trend to extremes," which immediately suggested to me what I call mimetic conflict. The realities of war entail that "hostile feelings" (battle lust) always ends up overwhelming "hostile intentions" (the reasoned decision to fight).

> Even the most civilized of peoples, in short, can be fired with passionate hatred of each other. . . . The thesis, then, must be repeated: war is an act of force, and *there is no logical limit to the application of that force.*[10] Each side, therefore, compels its opponent to follow suit; a reciprocal action is started which must lead, in theory, to extremes. This is the *first case of interaction and the first "extreme"* we meet with.[11]

It was this passage in Clausewitz's text that really gripped me. Suddenly I had the impression that he held the key to understanding the tragedy of the modern world. I am now convinced that Clausewitz is a major author, but for reasons that are very different than those alleged by Raymond Aron. I have to admit that his definition of a duel both fascinates and frightens me because it is consistent with my analyses and applies them to history with a force that I had not imagined.

BC: Unlimited application of force is the first reciprocal action that Clausewitz mentions in his definition of a duel. After that, there are two other types of reciprocity that result in two trends to extremes: the "aim to disarm the enemy" (shared exponentially by both camps) and "maximum exertion of strength" (the increasingly shared desire to destroy).

RG: Suddenly, in section 11, Clausewitz seems to contradict this first apocalyptic definition. Or, rather, he seems to assert that this conception of war (which he did not hesitate to call "optimistic") implies such tension and takes the imagination to such extremes that we finally lose sense of what is real. This is very surprising. We suddenly come back down from ideas to reality, from the violent reciprocity of the duel to the peaceful reciprocity of what Clausewitz called "armed observation."[12] From this point on, Clausewitz tries to fill the cracks that he had opened. The "trend to extremes"[13] is subsequently defined as a "logical fantasy," a pure concept that does not correspond to historical reality. Note in passing that it seems as if Clausewitz regrets it. He thus separates the concept from reality for theoretical reasons that would enable "absolute war" to subsume all conflicts, from the most warlike to the most political: the idea of war as a duel thus becomes a point of reference. All the ambivalence of Clausewitz's thinking is in evidence here. Clausewitz does not say that reality is separate from the concept, but that real wars *tend towards that point*.

Raymond Aron, however, based his demonstration on the fact that "absolute war" is *nothing but a concept*. This introduces an unbridgeable abyss between the concept of war as a duel and real war. He was writing in 1976 and we had just begun the last decade of the Cold War, the era in which politics managed to hold in check a nuclear apocalypse. Aron reflected ideas of his own time, not Clausewitz's thinking. Aron stoked the dying embers of Enlightenment rationality, which was certainly admirable, but unrealistic.

BC: Yet Raymond Aron did follow the text closely. It is as if in Clausewitz's thought the human mind was unable to imagine the worst, to take the art of war to its "perfect" state, and reciprocal action therefore had to be thought of in the space and time of "real" wars.

RG: Indeed. The brutal passage from one extreme to the other, from concepts to reality, from violent reciprocity to peaceful reciprocity is quite mysterious. However, I am not at all convinced by Raymond Aron's interpretation of it. We could also say that in Clausewitz's time the conditions were not ripe for the "trend to extremes," that he was not facing an apocalypse, but that we are tending more and more towards that absolute state of affairs which we find in his first definition of war. We could say that humans are in a sense not yet able to match real war with its concept, but that they will succeed some day. This is one possible interpretation of the text. This is what I immediately felt, which is why I have the strange impression that Clausewitz, after his brief and frightening apocalyptic epiphany, returned, sobered, to ordinary, grim reality:

> But move from the abstract to the real world, and the whole thing looks quite different. In the abstract world, optimism was all-powerful and forced us to assume that both parties to the conflict not only sought perfection but attained it. Would this ever be the case in practice? Yes, it would if: (a) war were a wholly isolated act, occurring suddenly and not produced by previous events in the political world; (b) it consisted of a single decisive act or a set of simultaneous ones; (c) the decision achieved was complete and perfect in itself, uninfluenced by any previous estimate of the political situation it would bring about.[14]

First, however, "war is never an isolated act,"[15] because the adversary is known, we already have certain views about him, and he is not considered an abstraction. Second,

> War does not consist of a single short blow.... [T]he interaction of the two sides tends to fall short of maximum effort. Their full resources will therefore not be mobilized immediately.[16]

Further on, Clausewitz notes that the "very nature" of the forces involved (military power, terrain, and alliances) and the use that is made of them "means they cannot all be deployed at the same moment," and that therefore "the very nature of war impedes the *simultaneous concentration of all forces.*" He adds,

> The fact in itself cannot be grounds for making any but a maximum effort to obtain the first decision ... But it is contrary to human nature to make an extreme effort, and the tendency therefore is always to plead that a decision may be possible later on.[17]

What then happens? The adversary simply *imitates* the other side:

> The tendency toward extremes is once again reduced by this interaction.[18]

Finally, and this is the third point, war does not lead to an absolute decision, but always to a relative result. Calculation of probabilities thus replaces
apocalyptic imagination: we act on the basis of what we know from "the
enemy's character, from his institutions, the state of his affairs and his general
situation."[19]

BC: Can't we conclude from this that, in real war, it is the adversary's
differences that have to be imagined, whereas in "theoretical" war, in which
reality would match the concept and where the "tendency toward extremes"
would prevail, the differences would shade off in a way that is favorable to
both unity of time and unity of place?

RG: That's it exactly. The "trend to extremes" is indeed imaginable
only "theoretically," in other words, when the adversaries are rigorously
similar. Let's say, framing the idea in terms of mimetic theory, that the
conditions of *undifferentiation*[20] did not yet obtain in Clausewitz's time,
but that they will perhaps one day. This explains the obligation to identify laws that apply in real wars, where "the political object now comes
to the fore again." Clearly, Clausewitz is straining here; he is trying to
go against his own nature, and to reassure the reader in a way. Aron
used Clausewitz's corrections of the first chapter to try to reconstruct
the rest of the treatise as Clausewitz *would have written it* if he had not
died of cholera in 1831. You have to admit that this is striking. All of
Raymond Aron's humanist faith is in evidence here, but also the limits of
his argumentation.

This is why we have to return to the text, to section 11 of Chapter 1 in
particular, where Clausewitz writes that once we have gone past the "logical
fantasy" of the trend to extremes, the "political object now comes to the fore
again." Clausewitz is thus trying in his revised text to imagine war as contained by politics, but it is clear that war regains the upper hand, so to speak.
Take the first and last paragraphs of the section, and see the difference in tone.
First, the return of politics:

> A subject which we last considered in Section 2 now forces itself on us
> again, namely the *political object of the war*. Hitherto it had been rather
> overshadowed by the law of extremes, the will to overcome the enemy
> and make him powerless. But as this law begins to lose its force and as
> this determination wanes, the political aim will reassert itself. If it is all
> a calculation of probabilities based on given individuals and conditions,
> the *political object*, which was the *original motive*, must become an essential
> factor in the equation.[21]

"The less involved the population" the more the political object reappears,[22] in other words, in Clausewitz's terms, when "hostile intention" dominates "hostile feeling." However, the problem is in fact that "the recent wars,"[23] namely, the Napoleonic Wars and the "total war" that they launched, in which all of a nation's "masses" were mobilized with a view to war alone, had changed the rules of the game. The trend to extremes thus returns, in the unforeseen face-off between two nationalistic hatreds:

> The same political object can elicit *differing* reactions from different peoples, and even from the same people at different times. . . . Between two peoples and two states there can be such tensions, such a mass of flammable material, that the slightest quarrel can produce a wholly disproportionate effect—a real explosion.[24]

The formulation is not anodyne. Let us go now to the conclusion of the section:

> Generally speaking, a military objective that matches the political object in scale will, if the latter is reduced, be reduced in proportion; this will be all the more so as the political object increases its predominance. Thus it follows that without any inconsistency wars can have all degrees of importance and intensity, ranging from a war of extermination down to simple armed observation.[25]

What does this mean if not that the political object is weak when the masses are indifferent, and that it is strong when they are not? In other words, that politics follow in war's footsteps? Despite Raymond Aron's rationalism, passions do indeed rule the world, and the revolutionary and Napoleonic Wars released them. A principle of war, which had until then been latent and contained, was released, or perhaps we should say "almost released," for real wars were not *yet* exact replicas of the concept. The Congress of Vienna led to relative stability in Europe until the war of 1870 and the explosive events in 1914. I say "relative stability" because the colonial massacres, organization of the proletariat as a "fighting class" and social Darwinism's influence on thinking set the stage for a global catastrophe in the twentieth century. War leads to war, even when, from Jena to Moscow, Napoleon was always desperately seeking peace, mobilizing more of his country each time, each time raising more troops. What if that was the "World Spirit" that Hegel saw pass under his window in Jena? What if it was less the writing of the universal into history than

the twilight of Europe, not a theodicy of the Spirit, but a formidable
undifferentiation in progress. This is why Clausewitz both intrigues and
frightens me.

Reciprocal Action and the Mimetic Principle

BC: Perhaps we can say that if politics follows on the heels of war, we have
to think of reciprocal action *both as what provokes the trend to extremes and as
that which suspends it?* If so, then perhaps the independent engine of history is
imitation of a model who becomes an imitator in turn, which leads to escalated conflict between two rivals, in other words, the reciprocal action that
you call "double mediation" in your books?

RG: You are right to identify reciprocal action with the mimetic principle.
Violent imitation, *which makes adversaries more and more alike,* is at the root of
all myths and cultures. This seems to be the principle that Clausewitz saw
reappearing. The implications of this remark are enormous. You are taking a
big leap, but it is possible. "Reciprocal action" (*Wechselwirkung*)[26] is obviously
a concept borrowed from Kant's table of categories,[27] but it can be transposed
into the domain of intersubjectivity, more precisely, into that of mimetic
anthropology, based on the relations of reciprocal imitation among humans.

Mimetic theory contradicts the thesis of human autonomy. It tends to
relativize the very possibility of introspection: going into oneself always means
finding the other, the mediator, the person who orients my desires without
my being aware of it. When we are speaking of military automatisms and
interactions between opposing armies, such tools work well. With respect to
total war and totalitarian regimes in the twentieth century, we have spoken of
"militarization of civil life." This is a terrible reality and proves that something
new has indeed happened. The Napoleonic Wars were the jolt that caused this
change in European societies. I even think that this militarization is one of
the factors of undifferentiation that is in its process of completion, now that
we have turned the page on regulated, codified conflicts. Terrorism is the culmination of what Clausewitz identified and theorized about as the "partisans'
war": its efficiency comes from the primacy of defending over attacking. It is
always justified as being only a response to aggression, and is thus based on
reciprocity. Reciprocal action and the mimetic principle concern the same
reality, even though Clausewitz, strangely, never spoke of imitation. Moreover,
in the next section he notes that "what we are talking about is not the progress
made by one side or the other but the progress of military action as a whole."[28]

War is a total social phenomenon. In this respect, Clausewitz's analysis is a precursor of Durkheim's sociology. Clausewitz has things to teach us about "mass" violence and contagion.

I'm going back to your comment, which seems to me to be very accurate, about the fact that reciprocal action *simultaneously provokes and suspends* the escalation to extremes. This is indeed one of the consequences of imitation, namely, to have these two opposite effects. This ambivalence is fundamental, and helps to see interaction as a principle unique to humans. Reciprocal action will trigger the escalation to extremes if the unity of time and space is realized, which is what Clausewitz means when he writes about an "isolated act," a "unique" and "complete" decision whose results are absolute.

However, reciprocal action is also what can suspend the escalation to extremes and act as the hidden engine of "real war" as opposed to "absolute war": we enter into the play of various computations regarding the adversary's intentions, calculation of probabilities, etc. Reciprocal action is thus at once exchange, trade and violent reciprocity. As Clausewitz writes in section 13, "If action would bring advantage to one side, the other's interest must be to wait."[29] Real war is thus different from absolute war because it takes into account the dimensions of space and time: location, climate, various "frictions," fatigue, etc. It follows that the two adversaries will not move towards the extremes and will not respond to each other in the same way at the same time and in the same place. To what extent is such postponed combat a victory of the political or what Clausewitz called "armed observation"? That is what requires scrutiny.

BC: At this point in Clausewitz's argument, he introduces the "principle of polarity," which is also known as the zero-sum game: "the victory of one side excludes the victory of the other."[30] This is what Clausewitz called war of the "first kind" in his note from 1827, which indicated where he thought the treatise needed to be reworked: "The objective is to *overthrow the enemy*, to render him politically helpless or militarily impotent, thus forcing him to sign whatever peace we please."[31] War of overthrow clearly waters down the apocalyptic tone of "absolute war."

RG: Naturally, we will have to come back to Clausewitz's last corrections, which were attempts to soften the concept by rubbing it against reality. We have to try to understand his intentions. Note in passing that it is always Napoleon who is behind the idea of overthrow and "total war." Clausewitz is incredibly obsessed by Napoleon, who functions precisely as what I call a model-obstacle: a model that is attractive and repulsive at the same time, and is the source of the mental pathologies that Dostoevsky has described so well.

Clausewitz is not alone here. For example, consider the two kings of Spain, Charles IV and his son Ferdinand, at Napoleon's feet in Bayonne, destroying each other before the person who was then dominating Europe. It is a display of hysteria that could almost have come out of *The Possessed*. Napoleon was extraordinarily strong, and seemed to dominate every situation. There was talk of his "clemency" at Jena after his victory over Frederick William III in 1806. In fact, the emperor was trying to win Prussia's good favor, even after he had entered Berlin and the King had fled to Königsberg. He avoided acting like a tyrant and capitalized on his victory. He was thus both detested and admired by the Prussians, with whom he soon made an alliance against Russia. This is very important: such ambivalence is an essential part of a *model*. First attracted by the genius of the man he called the "god of war," Clausewitz later violently rejected him, and joined the Tsar's armies after the defeat at Jena. The entourage of the King of Prussia later reproached him for this, but would he have been Clausewitz if he had remained in Prussia? Napoleon's proximity and the very idea of collaborating with him against Russia might have driven him crazy. He finished his career in Berlin, where he worked on his treatise until his death. We must not lose sight of the profound resentment he must have felt as a man who could not play the political and military roles to which he aspired.

I do not know how he would have reacted if he had read Victor Hugo. It is interesting to compare their attitudes. Clausewitz had a vehement passion for Napoleon; he was, to use my own concepts, in a relationship of *internal mediation* with the emperor, while Hugo had a much less intense relation with him. Internal mediation supposes the nearness of the model in time and space, which was precisely the case of Clausewitz with respect to Napoleon. Hugo was only four years old in 1806 and was not at Jena. In this respect, Clausewitz is more profound and interesting from my point of view, because he is much more mimetic. He thought *against* Napoleon, in both senses of the word. See how fruitful resentment can be, and how it can make one "theorize."

Clausewitz predicted totalitarianism: the potential for that pathology resided in the way that he wanted to *respond* to Napoleon. There is something very deep in the reality of resentment, the modern passion *par excellence,* as Stendhal and Tocqueville saw, as did Nietzsche in a way, even though he was aiming at the wrong target. I am also thinking about Part Two of Dostoevsky's *Notes from Underground*. All these people are extraordinarily similar. What this makes us see about Clausewitz is his Napoleonic side, but he also gave us the means to see something completely different. Yet his analyses of "reciprocal action" are so enlightening only because mimetism is gnawing away at him.

It is therefore true that reciprocal action both *provokes and suspends* the trend to extremes. It provokes it when both adversaries behave in the same way, and *respond immediately* by each modeling his tactics, strategy and policy on those of the other.[32] By contrast, if each is speculating on the intentions of the other, advancing, withdrawing, hesitating, taking into account time, space, fog, fatigue and all the constant interactions that define real war, reciprocal action then suspends the trend to extremes. Individuals are always interacting with one another, both within an army (which explains Clausewitz's long analyses defining the qualities of a war leader, to which we will return below), and of course between opposing armies. Reciprocal action can thus be a source of both undifferentiation and of differences, a path to war and a road to peace. If it *provokes and accelerates* the trend to extremes, the "friction" of space and time disappear, and the situation strangely resembles what I call the "sacrificial crisis" in my theory of archaic societies. If, on the contrary, reciprocal action *suspends* the trend to extremes, it aims to produce meaning and new differences. However, for reasons that I have tried to describe many times in my books, everything seems to indicate that violent imitation is the rule today, not the imitation that slows and suspends the flow, but the one that accelerates it. Ongoing conflicts provide many disquieting examples of this. We are beginning to see that the reduction of a conflict is only apparent, and leaves open the possibility of its even more violent return.

Clausewitz's realism provides him with a glimpse of the mimetic principle at the heart of human interactions. He did not advance a theory about it because he needed to talk about attacking and defending, tactics, strategy, and policy; he needed to justify his presence at the Military Academy. Whence the importance of focusing on his first chapter, which is fascinating because it is so contradictory. In it, Clausewitz drew the lessons of his reflections. The chapter is a whole in itself, but not because it contradicts the rest. All the rest comes out more readily than Aron thinks. I am persuaded that Clausewitz is more important for anthropology than for political science. This is why I find in his thought the potential for what has always interested me *as an anthropologist*: theories about the continuous, not the discontinuous; about undifferentiation, not differences. For example, in section 14 we find:

> If this continuity were really to exist in the campaign its effect would again
> be to drive everything to extremes. Not only would such ceaseless activ-
> ity arouse men's feelings and inject them with more passion and elemental

strength, but events would follow more closely on each other and be governed by a stricter causal chain. Each individual action would be more
important, and consequently more dangerous.[33]

We should not be misled by his use of the conditional here. The threat of
the escalation to extremes, which is one with the *continuity* of war, is always
latent behind the discontinuities of real wars (maneuvers, hesitation, nego-
tiation, halts, etc.). Clausewitz must thus have felt that "reciprocal action,"
understood as an accelerated oscillation of like to like, which I call the mimetic
principle or principle of reciprocity, is all the more dangerous when it appears
uncloaked in the light of day. When differences between adversaries alternate
with increasing rapidity, such as in the passing back and forth of *kudos,* the
sign of victory among the Greeks that I mention in *Violence and the Sacred,*[34] in
other words, when the belief of adversaries in their difference from each other
produces the alternation of defeats and victories and approaches reciprocity,
then we are nearing what I call the sacrificial crisis. This is the critical point
when the group borders on chaos. Put nuclear weapons in the hands of the
belligerents, and it will no longer be just the group, but the whole planet.

I thus define reciprocity as the sum of non-reciprocal moments. It can be
seen only by someone who is outside the conflict because *from the inside you
must always believe in your difference* and respond more and more quickly and
forcefully. From the outside, the adversaries look like what they are: simple
doubles. This is when war resembles its concept, when *there is a unity of alternation and reciprocity,* an accelerated oscillation of differences, and a kind of
shift to abstraction. This "logical fantasy" clearly mesmerizes Clausewitz; it
is undeniable. It is as if while meditating on the defeat at Jena in 1806, when
he wanted to *respond* to Napoleon by enrolling in the Tsar's armies, he made
an essential discovery. I therefore want to reverse your earlier remark and
say that reciprocal action, which *used to suspend* the escalation to extremes
in the time of "the wars of gentlemen," accelerates it now that it is no longer
hidden. *The mimetic principle is no longer hidden but appears in broad daylight,*
and Clausewitz was a key witness to this. Christianity played a crucial role in
this revelation, even though it has worked like a time bomb: the Gospel texts
"prophesy" a reality that will increasingly be that of our own history. Because
the mimetic principle can be seen and differences are vacillating with increasing rapidity, we can see from our vantage point that history has speeded up
over the last three centuries. It is impossible to understand Clausewitz if we
overlook this dimension of reciprocal action, which is present from the beginning of his treatise.

ATTACK AND DEFENSE: SUSPENDED POLARITY

BC: It is striking how your analyses in *Violence and the Sacred* overlap with Clausewitz's first intuition that, in a way, "real wars" mask "absolute war," towards which they are constantly tending. This is like the alternation of victories and defeats that masks reciprocity and towards which that very alternation of reprisals is tending with every reprisal and counter-reprisal. In your theory, as in that of Clausewitz, it is as if one polarity masks another more terrible one, and the succession of zero-sum games leads, through acceleration of reciprocity, to the "extermination" of the adversary.

RG: Indeed, the polarity is not simple but quite complex. An attack by one adversary does not necessarily lead to the defeat of the other. This explains the need to study the relationship of attack to defense, and brings us to sections 16 and 17 of Chapter 1 of Book 1. The attacker often secures only a *temporary* victory over the defender. Clausewitz concluded that "Polarity, then, does not lie in attack or defense, but in the object both seek to achieve: the decision."[35] Napoleon constantly had to attack and to mobilize more and more forces. The defender, by contrast, can prepare a decisive counter-attack that is more deadly than the attack. This is the point, and the only point, where polarity applies. This point is absolutely fundamental, and here we are touching on Clausewitz's second great intuition, which takes the form of a paradox: *the attacker wants peace but the defender wants war.*

Jacques Bainville's book *Napoleon* is full of remarks by Napoleon that support this interpretation. For example, on the eve of the Russian campaign, the emperor said:

> But although I do not wish for war, and am far from wishing to be the Don Quixote of Poland, I have at least the right to insist on Russia remaining loyal to the alliance.[36]

Napoleon thus embarked on a slippery slope that forced him to control a whole continent with an iron fist in order to maintain his strategy of establishing an embargo against England. Alexander I secretly wanted war and to return to trading with the English, so he broke the Tilsit agreements, and Kutusov let Moscow burn in order to prepare the defeat of the Grande Armée. In order to understand this, we have to skip to Chapter 7 of Book 6, entitled "Interaction between Attack and Defense":

Consider in the abstract how war originates. Essentially, the concept of war does not originate with the attack, because the ultimate object of attack is not fighting: rather, it is possession. The idea of war originates with the defense, which does have fighting as its immediate object, since fighting and parrying obviously amount to the same thing. ... It is thus in the nature of the case that the side that first introduces the element of war, whose point of view brings two parties into existence, is also the side that establishes the initial laws of war. That side is the defense.[37]

The defender is thus the one who begins and finishes the war. By the nature of its fortresses, armies and command, the defending side determines what the attack will be. It has the choice of terrain and the support of the people, and benefits from the fatigue experienced by the attacking side, whose initial momentum gradually weakens. Finally, it decides when to counter-attack. It thus controls the game, in accordance with the rule that it is always easier to keep than to take. From this we can conclude that the concept of defense *encompasses* that of attack, and that it is the most apt to make real war consistent with the concept of war. Clausewitz repeatedly writes "*beati sunt possidentes.*" Note that this is quite consistent with mimetic theory: the model (the side that will have to defend itself) is the one in possession of something that the adversary tries to take (or take back). It is thus the one that dominates and *ultimately* dictates its rules to the other. The escalation to extremes also involves what I have called double mediation because it is always difficult to know who attacks first: in a way, it is always the one that does not attack. This is exactly the same as in some criminal cases where the victim, much more than the accused, is the real guilty party. When violence is involved, wrongs are always shared. Alexander I fascinates Napoleon as much as Napoleon fascinates him.

The *mimesis* of appropriation, which dictates the attacker's behavior, nonetheless implies a *response,* and that will be the counter-attack, a means of defense. There will then also be defenses on the side that has to ward off the counter-attack. Clausewitz provided a clear description of this. Yet it is still the "initial" defender that dominates. This, and only this, is the point at which the principle of polarity applies: absolute polarity prepared by relative polarities. We should speak less of the risk of self-destruction and more of the triumph of violence when we consider the primacy of defense over attack. Violence will increasingly dominate: this is the principle of the superiority of defense. Thus, Clausewitz did not advocate total war, as Liddell Hart, his most critical commentator in the twentieth century, thought.[38] Instead, he showed that the defender "dictates the rules" to the attacker, which is very different, though the result is the same. In this regard, Clausewitz sees very clearly that *modern wars are as violent as they are only because they are "reciprocal"*: mobilization involves more and more people until it is "total," as Ernst Jünger wrote of the 1914 war.

And history did not take long to prove Clausewitz right. It was because he was "responding" to the humiliations inflicted by the Treaty of Versailles and the occupation of Rhineland that Hitler was able to mobilize a whole people. Likewise, it was because he was "responding" to the German invasion that Stalin achieved a decisive victory over Hitler. It was because he was "responding" to the United States that Bin Laden planned 9/11 and subsequent events. The primacy of a defensive position is consistent with the appearance in a conflict of the principle of reciprocity as a suspended polarity in the sense that victory will not be immediate, but will be total *later*. The one who believes he can control violence by setting up defenses is in fact controlled by violence. This is very important. It means that reciprocal action both provokes and suspends the escalation to extremes at the same time. It is perhaps a characteristic of the escalation to extremes to grow *gradually,* in a manner much more formidable than in the case of an immediate counter-attack, which can lead quickly to negotiations. This is the paradox that Clausewitz gives us the means to study: that of a non-immediate immediacy, of a polarity that is more threatening because it is suspended. Bainville certainly felt this, even though he did not talk about it in the way we are doing now:

> It took quite a fortnight for Paris to know what was happening in St. Petersburg. The age of the telegraphic ultimatum, of instantaneous mobilizations, of the irreparable brought to pass within a few hours, had not yet dawned. Each of the emperors pursued his "evolution" far from the other, and before the final impact came nearly two years went by.[39]

Yet the battle, *because it was suspended,* was only more terrible. It prefigured another Russian campaign in the twentieth century, when Hitler reproduced the same mistakes as Napoleon. At that time, Stalin placed large portraits of the Tsar and Kutusov in his office. The old Russia thus resurfaced from beneath the upheavals of communism. Mimetic theory, as it is corroborated here by reciprocal action, obliges us to see history on a larger scale and as involving very long alternations. Napoleon was not yet entirely in "the age of the telegraphic ultimatum." He still had a foot in the time of eighteenth century wars, but the accelerated era was also *already there,* and Clausewitz was one of the first to see it, at a time when suspended conflicts no longer dissimulated the underlying principle of reciprocity. Violence is never lost on violence. It cannot be eliminated. This is the fundamental reality that we need to understand.

This also contains a major discovery in anthropology: *aggression does not exist*. Among animals, there is predation, and there is doubtless genetic rivalry for females. However, among humans, the fact that no one ever feels they are the aggressor is because everything is always reciprocal. The slightest little difference, in one direction or another, can trigger the escalation to extremes. *The aggressor has always already been attacked.* Why are relations of rivalry never seen as symmetrical? Because people always have the impression that the other is the first to attack, that they are never the ones who begin, though in a way they are *always* the ones. Individualism is a formidable lie. We make others understand that we recognize the signs of aggressiveness which they manifest, and they in turn interpret our posture as aggression. And so on. There comes a time when conflict breaks out, and the initiator places himself in a weak position. The differences are so small at the beginning, and fade away so quickly that they are not perceived as reciprocal to each other, but as always unique to themselves. To think, as Clausewitz seems to have done in Chapter 1, about war as "the continuation of policy by other means" is thus to *lose sight of the intuition of war as a duel,* in other words, to deny the notion of aggression and response to aggression. It is to forget reciprocal action that both accelerates and suspends the escalation to extremes, which only suspends it in order to further accelerate it later.

Humans are thus always immersed in order and disorder, in war and peace. It is becoming more and more difficult to draw a line between the two realities that, until the French Revolution, were codified and ritualized. There are no differences anymore. Reciprocal action is so amplified by globalization, the planetary reciprocity in which the slightest event can have repercussions on the other side of the globe, that violence is always a length ahead of our movements. Violence steals a march on politics, and technology escapes our control, as Heidegger showed. Therefore we have to study the conditions for this escalation to extremes, from Napoleon to Bin Laden, in which attacking and defending have been promoted to the rank of the unique engine of history. This is why Clausewitz is fascinating, both attracts and repels, and frightens. Victory can no longer be relative; it can be only total. The principle of polarity is the very movement of suspended catastrophe. When Clausewitz speaks of the possibility of a "war of extermination," we have to understand it in the sense that the twentieth century has given to it. In this respect, one polarity masks the other, or rather, the "polarity" of which Clausewitz speaks masks the polarization that I try to describe in *Violence and the Sacred*. In the past, it focused on a victim whose destruction made a return to order possible. Today, it is of a piece with the escalation to extremes because there can no longer be unanimity about the guilt of victims.

For Clausewitz, this polarity means the return to peace, in the sense in which "eternal peace" can mean that of the cemetery. This is why we must always see reciprocity behind alternation, "absolute war" behind "real war," even though reciprocity and absolute war are apparently only abstractions. After all, the apocalypse is nothing more than an abstraction made real, reality made consistent with its concept, and we have to have the lucidity to say that humanity itself tends towards annihilation. This is the implacable law of the duel, spelled out in the primacy of defense over attack. In this respect, humans are different from animals, for the latter succeed in containing their violence in what ethnologists call networks of dominance. Humans cannot control reciprocity because they imitate one another too much and their resemblance to one another increases and accelerates.

We have to imagine that *for these very reasons* the first human groups self-destructed. However, those groups were small and did not interact with the rest of the world. The apocalypse is a real threat today on a planetary level because the principle of reciprocity has been unmasked and the abstraction has become concrete. This is what Clausewitz immediately saw, before taking refuge in a description of the rules of war as if we were still in the eighteenth century, as if war were still an institution. However, seeing states as adversaries, *which is a means of dissimulating the notion of duel,* was already outdated in his time. This announced the unleashing of violence.

Clausewitz does and does not say this. He is ambivalent. However, Sophocles too was ambivalent when he discovered reciprocity in *Oedipus the King* and tried to make us believe that Oedipus was actually a little bit guilty. No, Oedipus was innocent. The guilty party was the group. Violence looks terribly frightening when we have understood its laws and grasped that it is reciprocal and will thus *return*. How did small archaic societies deal with it? They found a solution: they invented sacrifice without knowing it, unconsciously, by channeling their violence onto a sacrificial victim, and necessarily unaware of the arbitrariness of their choice. In order to escape crisis, they always had to turn their reciprocal violence into polarizing convergence of all against one. Every time, the outside point of view (which sees reciprocity) and the inside point of view (which *wants to see* only differences) had to coincide but remain separate. Then all would turn against a single individual.

War of extermination

BC: Is there some way out of the crisis at a time when, according to you, the mimetic mechanism is spiraling out of control at the global level and there can be no sacrificial resolution? Unless the sacrificial resolution...

RG: ...coincides with the disappearance of humanity itself. Yes, that is a *possibility*. This is something that the genocides in the twentieth century and massacres of civilian populations have been telling us. This is the polarization that is masked by the polarities of war, the relative victories that always lead to other more violent wars. Of course, there were genocides in ancient history, and entire civilizations disappeared, but that happened in a sort of eternal return of religion with an apparently inexhaustible power of renewal that no longer operates today. I have a lot of trouble formulating the intuition that I feel is nonetheless very important: once unbridled, the principle of reciprocity no longer plays the unconscious role it used to play. Do we not now destroy simply to destroy? Violence now seems deliberate, and the escalation to extremes is served by science and politics.

Is this a principle of death that will finally wear itself out and open onto something else? Or is it destiny? I do not know. However, what I can say is that *we can see the growing futility of violence, which is now unable to fabricate the slightest myth to justify and hide itself.* This is indeed the escalation towards undifferentiation that Clausewitz glimpsed behind the law of the duel. Today's massacres of civilians are thus simply sacrificial failures, proof that it is impossible to eliminate violence through violence, to expel reciprocity violently. Convergence onto scapegoats has become impossible, and mimetic rivalries are unleashed contagiously with no possibility of warding them off.

Conflict resolution often fails when two groups "tend towards extremes." We saw this in the Yugoslavian tragedy and in Rwanda. We have much to fear today from the confrontations between the Shiites and Sunnis in Iraq and Lebanon, and hanging Saddam Hussein has only accelerated the process. From this point of view, Bush is the very caricature of what is lacking in politicians, who are incapable of thinking apocalyptically. He has succeeded in only one thing: demolishing a form of co-existence more or less maintained between brothers who have always been enemies. The worst is now likely in the Middle East, where Shiites and Sunnis are escalating to extremes. The escalation could just as well take place between Arab countries and the Western world.

Note that it has already begun: the exchange of attacks and American "interventions" can only accelerate, as each side responds to the other.

Violence will continue on its way. A conflict between the United States and China will follow: everything is in place, though it will not necessarily occur on the military level at first. This is why Clausewitz finally took refuge in politics, and hid his original intuitions. The escalation to extremes is a completely irrational phenomenon that only Christianity explains because over 2000 years ago it revealed the inanity of sacrifice, and regardless of those who still like to believe in its usefulness. Christ took away humanity's sacrificial crutches and left us before a terrible choice: either believe in violence, or not; Christianity is non-belief.

BC: What you are saying proves to those who reject your theory that it is not as abstract and "systematic" as they would like to think, but on the contrary bears concretely on events that are occurring right now. It could be a key to understanding certain historical phenomena, for example, what Ernst Nolte and François Furet glimpse, sometimes using concepts close to your own, though they do not take their explanations to their logical conclusion.

RG: Indeed, we should mention *The European Civil War* by Ernst Nolte[40] and *The Passing of an Illusion* by François Furet.[41] These two historical analyses provide excellent descriptions of situations to which I think mimetic theory provides the key. Ernst Nolte speaks constantly about what I call "model-obstacles"[42] with respect to the mimetism that closely links Bolshevism and Nazism, and which he argues makes Nazism a mimetic response to Bolshevism. This is precisely what mimetic theory calls a model-obstacle, and it is a crucial historical discovery. Yet Nolte lacks the anthropological point of view, which would help him formulate his intuition better. François Furet, who unlike Nolte has no nationalistic assumptions, is much more convincing when he goes back to the 1914 war to try to understand the mechanism.

However, we actually have to go back several thousand years. This is the effort we have to make to discover what violence is all about. This is why there is an anthropological interpretation of original sin: original sin is vengeance, never-ending vengeance. It begins with the murder of the rival. Religion is what enables us to live with original sin, which is why a society without religion will destroy itself. Vengeance does not exist among animals; they never place themselves in such danger. Only the conjunction of intelligence and violence makes it possible to speak of original sin and it justifies the idea of a real difference between animals and humans. This constitutes the greatness of all religions, with the exception of Christianity, which abolishes the provisional function of sacrifice. Sooner or later, either humanity will renounce violence without sacrifice or it will destroy the planet. Humanity will be either in a state of grace or in mortal sin. Thus, we can say that religion may have invented sacrifice, but Christianity takes it away. Here, Pascal is fundamental when he reaffirms that original sin is what defines man:

> Certainly nothing shocks us more harshly than this doctrine. And yet with-
> out this most incomprehensible of all mysteries, we are incomprehensible to
> ourselves. The knot of our condition takes its twists and turns in this abyss,
> so that man is more unintelligible without this mystery than this mystery is
> unintelligible to man.[43]

We absolutely need Pascal. He saw and immediately understood the "abysses" of foundation. He considered Descartes to be "useless and uncertain" precisely because he thought he could base something on the *cogito* and "deduce" the heavens and stars. Yet no one ever begins anything, except by grace. To sin means to think that one can begin something *oneself*. We never start anything; we always respond. The other has always decided for me and forces me to answer. The group always decides for the individual. This is the law of religion. What is "modern" exists only in the obstinate rejection of this obvious social truth, in clinging to its individualism. Durkheim is very great when he sees this. I am thus only restating his thesis and adding what I, along with Gabriel Tarde, though in a more radical manner, consider to be the engine behind construction of the social, namely, imitation.

However, Tarde never discovered the violent nature of mimetism. We also have to point out the other face of human relations: violent *mimesis*. We have to show that it is at the root of all institutions, which are based on the scapegoat mechanism. There is a point when mimetic violence, in which each imitates the other and becomes the other's rival for acquisition of increasingly symbolic objects, is so widespread in a group beginning to emerge that the group unconsciously avoids self-destruction by polarizing its violence around an individual who is a little more noticeable or disturbing. *Mimesis* is thus both the cause of the crisis and the means of resolving it. The victim is always made divine after the sacrifice. The myth is thus the *lie* that hides the founding lynching, which speaks to us about the gods, but *never about the victims that the gods used to be*. Rituals then repeat the initial sacrifice (the first victim leads to substitute victims: children, men, animals, various offerings), and repetition of rituals gives birth to institutions, which are the only means that humanity has found to postpone the apocalypse. This is why peaceful *mimesis* is possible only in the framework of an established institution that was founded long before. It is based on learning and maintaining cultural codes.

Foundation is never a solitary action; it is always done *with others.* This is the rule of unanimity, and *this unanimity is violent.* An institution's role is to make us to forget this. Pascal saw this clearly when he evoked the ruse of the "honest man" defending the "greatness of establishment." Only a group can found something, an individual never can. This is very important. However, I should in fact say that only groups *could have founded* something because the mechanism no longer works. We have seen the sterility of the "merging groups" that fascinated Sartre with respect to revolution. Violence lost its effectiveness long ago, but we are only barely beginning to realize it. Only ethical relations could still found something, but they are literally overcome by events, by the mimetic enthusiasm of individuals who believe they are free and cling frantically to their false differences. The enthusiasm is contagious, and has destroyed our moral frameworks, which themselves had ancient ritual origins. This is the engine of wars of extermination.

BC: You have just said something very important: mimetic enthusiasm is contagious. In *Violence and the Sacred,* you analyzed the plague that ravaged the city of Thebes and found it a clear sign of a loss of differences. The "undifferentiation" led to the designation of a scapegoat who, once expelled, brought calm and order back to the city. Does this mimetic interpretation of an epidemic apply to the catastrophes threatening us today?

RG: That interpretation would be possible except for one thing: a sacrificial resolution is no longer feasible. Sacrifice no longer works now that Christianity has revealed the mechanism of unanimity. Archaic religions were based on a complete absence of criticism regarding this unanimity. This is why in one of his Talmudic readings Levinas says that if everyone agrees that an accused should be convicted, then he should be released right away, for he must be innocent.

As for the rest, a plague epidemic always symbolizes a group's imminent demise and the advent of violent general reciprocity in which each is the rival of the other. Plague is a symbol and symptom of the loss of differences. Sophocles could not have found a better image in *Oedipus the King* to reveal the genesis of all institutions: the point where violence spreads through the group like a virus that only "vaccination" by sacrifice can stop. The scapegoat, the one used to bring unity back to a group that is threatened by its own violence, is called *pharmakos* in Greek: both remedy and poison, guilty of disorder and restorer of order. It is this ambivalence of the sacred that stops violence for a time.

Terrorist wars and looming pandemics recall the plague in Thebes. The devastating nature of bird flu virus H5N1, which is a mutant that can kill hundreds of turkeys in only a few hours, spreads through bird migrations, but especially thanks to air traffic. It is a pandemic that could cause hundreds of thousands of deaths in a few days, and is a phenomenon typical of the undifferentiation now coursing across the planet. We can counter it with vaccines, so long as we *share them,* and do not limit them to rich nations, seeing how porous borders have become between countries, and between all differences in general.

Pandemics tell us something about human relations, which can now be reduced to what might be called "global trade." Clausewitz glimpses this when he says that there are no differences in nature, only in degree, between trade and war. It is no accident that terrorist acts often take place in trains and planes. Terror is inherent to all reciprocity. Ancient archaic fears resurface today with new faces, but no sacrifice will save us from them. It is thus urgent to develop strategies to deal with this unpredictable violence that no institution today can control. However, the strategies can no longer be military or political. A new ethic is required in this time of catastrophe; catastrophe urgently has to be integrated into rational thought.

Our conversation will not provide any ready-made solutions. I hope only that it will help to explain the concrete stakes of what mimetic theory brings to light as we look upon the last two centuries, and especially upon French-German relations since Napoleon. Those 200 years have been one of the most virulent mimetic foci of the modern age and therefore merit analysis in these terms. Clausewitz's text is crucial to understanding them. In what political, philosophical and spiritual context was it written? Why did it remain unfinished? How was it received and how has it been read? All of these questions are important. I cannot provide scholarly answers to them, so I am counting on studying the text with you so as to understand its merits and dangers, and finally gain a new understanding of it from within a new form of rationality.

Clausewitz's treatise was composed outside of any dialogue or debate, in the solitude of an interior exile; it announces the imminent dictatorship of violence. In Clausewitz's writing, war is made sacred in a way, which is valid only when it is violent enough to take on its essential form. This is a strange thing for a man who passionately hated Napoleon: he suspected that the Empire would be nothing more than a happy parenthesis in the fading of war that distressed him. His was a strange embodiment of Enlightenment thinking, a line of thought that both informed and undermined Prussian militarism. We are indeed looking at a military religion since Clausewitz glimpsed the *tragic struggle of doubles,* which can be seen in all myths, even though sacrifice and divinization of victims hid the mechanism for a time.

We need to show the relevance of this text, so we will confront Clausewitz's work with that of contemporary and other authors. Raymond Aron was right to expand the analysis of Clausewitz's text beyond the purely military sphere, but we will take that approach further. We have to abandon the vicious circle of violence, the eternal return of a sacred that is less and less controlled by rites and is now merging into violence. We have to work amidst this unfettered mimetism; there is no other way. We have therefore to return to this exit out of religion that is only offered from within the demythified religion, namely, Christianity.

CHAPTER 2

Clausewitz and Hegel

The Duel and Alternation of Opposites

Benoît Chantre: When you said that for Clausewitz Napoleon incarnated something other than the manifestation of Spirit in history, you suggested that Clausewitz was in opposition to Hegel, his exact contemporary. The worldwide rise of undifferentiation supports your thesis. It is a powerful intuition, so I would like us to go back to the triangle that links Napoleon as an ambivalent model to his two greatest interpreters, both of whom were at Jena in 1806 and died in Berlin in 1831.

René Girard: You are asking me to take to its logical conclusion an intuition that came to me while we were speaking. That would require philosophical knowledge that I lack. I am probably opposing Hegelianism, much more than Hegel himself. However, it is essential to compare these two figures, even though Clausewitz was not a philosopher—this has to be kept in mind. Hegel's *Phenomenology of Mind* introduced an impressive philosophical illusion that we are finally managing to discard. It came out in 1807, the year after the Prussians were defeated by Napoleon. Hegel, who admired the ideals of the French Revolution and had followed the events in Paris when he was at the Tübingen Seminary with Schelling and Hölderlin, saw that Napoleon's actions were the paradoxical manifestation of those ideals in space and time. Napoleon both invaded and liberated the Germans, in a way (perhaps the worst way). Thus we have the famous quotation according to which, when he was working in Jena, Hegel saw the World-Soul pass on horseback under his window.[1] The legend misleads us, for Hegel is also the thinker who distrusted the Enlightenment, the *Aufklärung,* in which he was raised. We therefore have to try to avoid the commonplaces about his thought that always come to mind.

BC: Indeed, note that in 1820, when Hegel writes in the Preface to *The Philosophy of Right,* that "What is rational is actual and what is actual is rational,"[2] the reality in question was not the reality that we can perceive but the unity of essence and existence. The phrase thus has nothing to do with the "meaning of history" that Hegel supposedly claimed to understand and to have seen Napoleon as incarnating. Hegelianism has masked the tragic sense inhabiting Hegelian philosophy, both with respect to self-sacrifice, in which an individual risks his or her biological life to manifest the Spirit, and with respect to the absolute Spirit itself. We should not forget that Hegel spoke of a "Golgotha of Absolute Spirit."[3]

RG: Indeed, for him there was only one Incarnation: that of God in history. According to him, only that "divine mediation" has made the emergence of true rationality possible. All of Hegel's dialectic is therefore based on the Revelation. Here too we have to leave behind the sempiternal schema of "thesis, antithesis, synthesis." Hegelian dialectic has little to do with that. It went from the Spirit to alienation, and then out of alienation through a transcendence or elevation (*Aufhebung*) that is the reconciliation of the two opposing terms. Dialectic presents a position, then the "negation" of that position, and finally a "negation of the negation." To open up to the other, to get outside of oneself through alienation, is to prepare a *return to oneself* that provides true access to the real, access to real rationality free of any subjectivity. As we can see, this is a philosophical echo of Christ's death and resurrection. All the power, but also all the ambivalence, of Hegel's philosophy lies in this parallel.

From the Christian revelation, Hegel took the need for a double reconciliation, a double *Aufhebung:* that of humans among one another, and that of humanity with God. Peace and salvation would thus be two conjoined movements. Hegel thought that churches had failed to regulate the interplay of human will, so he assigned the task to the State, the "concrete universal" that has nothing to do with specific states. The rational universality of the State is supposed to become a worldwide organization, but *in the meantime* individual states will continue to wage war. The series of wars is an essential contingency of history.

However, if for Hegel war was *only* a contingency that could not be reduced to reason, it cannot be denied that he thought of it in a very deep way. Dialectic is not first and foremost the reconciliation of humans with one another; it is simply the same thing as the *duel,* the struggle for recognition, and the "opposing identities."

BC: We are at the heart of our topic. Yet we could think that, if there is no relationship between them, extreme positions are caught in a useless tug-of-war that will never end. To use another metaphor, the pendulum swings between two *abstractions,* two mutually exclusive positions that become equivalent owing to the very movement of the weight. Judgment divides, it breaks the relationship.

RG: Hegel saw this clearly when he was being taught about the philosophers of the Enlightenment at Tübingen and was told that their theories were the opposite of religion, just as reason was the opposite of faith. Hegelian rationalism thus attempts to ward off dialectic and bring reason out from behind its mirages of omnipotence. He borrowed reconciliation from Christianity; reconciliation is the only thing that can circumvent abstraction and bring salvation and peace to humanity. However, what Hegel did not see, and this is where I come to your question, *is that the oscillation of contradictory positions, which become equivalent, can very well go to extremes.* Adversaries can very well become hostile, and alternation can lead to reciprocity. Hegelian thought has tragic aspects, but no catastrophic ones. It thus goes from dialectic to reconciliation, from reciprocity to relationship, in a very confident manner, often by seeming to forget where it in fact comes from.

Yet it comes from religion, sacrifice, and Christ's death and resurrection. In other words, if we take an anthropological point of view, it comes from the definitive destruction of all sacrificial protections. Hegel had forgotten how Christ had suffered in his flesh. Though he began with Christian anthropology, Hegel abandons it along the way. Of course the Spirit is Spirit only because it is objectively realized, but for Hegel this takes place in an indeterminate place beyond history. In this sense, we could say that, long before Marx, Clausewitz put dialectic "back on its feet" by rejecting a separation between essential and contingent history. At the very time when Hegel was thinking about possible consistency between human reason and the *Logos,* Clausewitz is telling us that this is really a duel and the oscillation of antagonists leads straight to modern warfare, that the alternation can go to extremes and pass into reciprocity. *From then on it will be impossible to integrate it into a theodicy of the Spirit.* This is where I think lies the great opposition between these two thinkers.

BC: What you are saying is important for understanding how your thinking is anchored in a given context. The escalation of false differences, which you have described as a "sacrificial crisis" in your work on archaic religion, allows us to introduce with respect to the conflict of "opposing identities" a specific philosophical context: that of Hegel's reception in France at the end of the 1930s.

RG: This is why when *Deceit, Desire, and the Novel* was first published in French in 1961, many wanted to see me as the successor of Kojève, the great commentator on Hegel. I was seen as presenting a new version of Hegelian thought, which is why it was often said that mimetic desire was only a reformulation of the desire for recognition in Hegel's theory. This was to suggest that my ideas were obsolete and referred to stale debates. Naturally, I fought back like a demon, but I cannot deny that Hegel was in the background.

Kojève's influence was huge in France. His classes at the École pratique des hautes études[4] were attended by Raymond Aron, Georges Bataille and Jacques Lacan, and much was made of the theme of desire in Hegel's *The Phenomenology of Spirit*. What everyone was familiar with in Kojève's work was the notion of the master-slave dialectic, through which Hegel conceptualized the desire for recognition. At the time, everyone was talking about the "self-consciousness" that only comes about through "consciousness of the other." A slave had to recognize his or her master. There was thus something true in the idea that the dialectic influenced my reading of novels, and what I call "novelistic truth." Like Hegel, I was saying that we desire things less than we desire for ourselves the desire that others have for things; I was talking about *a desire for the other's desire,* in a way.

However, my interpretation of this dialectic was different from everyone else's. I could not even tell you how Hegel influenced the way I formulated my thoughts. Perhaps it was the idea of expressing mimetic influences in terms of desire. Daring to define Don Quixote's chivalry in this way was a major step. There is also what Hegel calls "evil infinite,"[5] which is desire that transfers itself to new objects, one after the next, indefinitely; an insatiable desire that always presupposes the presence of others, my fellow kind, next to me. Hegel's "unhappy consciousness"[6] is a way of noting that *humans are identical* in both their desires and hatreds, and never so close to reconciliation as when they are at war. I thus have to admit that I felt an affinity with Hegel's philosophy.

However, our analyses diverge on a fundamental point. The *desire for the other's desire* has little to do with mimetic desire, which is a *desire for what the other possesses,* whether an object, an animal, a man or woman, or even a being unto itself, its essential qualities. I did not dare to defend my theory simply and effectively because at the time and under the circumstances I thought in such concrete terms that I could not help being disappointing: I was a little ashamed of being so prosaic. I did not dare to say that humans oppose one another over *real* objects. It is the desire to acquire, much more than the desire for recognition, that quickly degenerates into what I call metaphysical desire, whereby the subject seeks to *acquire the being* of his or her model. At such times, I want "to be what the other becomes when he possesses this or that object."

How does it happen? In a much more concrete and violent manner than the "desire for recognition."[7] I do not desire the object spontaneously, but because the other next to me desires it, or because I suspect he desires it. I thus draw nearer to the object at the same time as my mediator gets closer to me. He then becomes my model, to the point that I finally completely forget the object that I initially thought I desired. Since all action is reciprocal, my rival experiences the same thing: he sees me desire an object that is near to him and he begins to desire that object again, though he had forgotten it when there was no rival. He meets me on the path to the object right when I encounter him on the same path.

I call this stage "double mediation," where each rival becomes a model-obstacle for the other. The rivals increasingly resemble one another; rivalry produces twins. One of them may win out over the other and regain his illusion of autonomy; the other will then be humiliated to the point of seeing his adversary as sacred. This attraction-repulsion is at the base of all pathologies of resentment: my worship of the model-obstacle and my metaphysical desire for his very being can lead me to murder. The model that I worship and before whom I humiliate myself, in the hope of being able to acquire his supposed power, turns back into an insufferable stranger whom I have to eliminate. *Deceit, Desire, and the Novel* thus contained the seeds of mimetic theory, according to which there was a mimetic genesis of social order in which the violence of thousands of enemy brothers threatened to cause the group to implode, but then converged onto a third party chosen at random because that individual suddenly appeared evil. The convergence of all against one is a form of monstrous imitation: as in the pathologies of resentment, the victim is at once all and nothing, loved and detested. Mimetic desire is thus at the very foundation of archaic religion.

BC: Your analysis of reciprocity would thus be much more violent than Hegel's "fight to the death,"[8] which always operates as a desire for recognition.

RG: It is obvious that, for there to be *recognition*, the master, who makes me exist simply by looking at me, must not be killed! Human consciousness is not acquired through reason, but through desire. Adversaries thus enter into conflict in order to gain recognition. The desire for recognition prevents them from killing each other. How would they be able to recognize each other if one of them died or they were both killed? In every duel, one has to be afraid of the other, recognize the other as master and gain recognition as the slave of that master. Here we can see the beginnings of the idea of empire, which was fundamental for Kojève, who inspired de Gaulle's policy after 1945. We will return to this later. In this sense, the master-slave dialectic has always seemed to me to be conciliatory. It resembles what ethologists tell us about dominance hierarchies in animal societies.

The danger in Hegel's thought comes paradoxically from the fact that it does not begin with a sufficiently radical conception of violence. This is why it is useful to read Hegel and Clausewitz together. It is immediately clear that the unity of the real and the concept lead to peace, according to Hegel, but to the trend to extremes according to Clausewitz. The latter lived in military circles; Hegel never participated in a military operation.

BC: We can feel that the concept of absolute war frightened Clausewitz, who tried to describe the gap between the concept and its reality. This goes against Hegelian dialectic, which tends toward the "concrete universal,"[9] in other words, the unity of the real and the concept. Hegel spoke of the passage from individual interest to the universal: the individual must realize himself in the universality of the State. In this respect, he gave war a special role: it brings back into the whole of the nation those who had become separated because they had been focusing on their private interest. Through war, the State reminds individuals from time to time of the need to sacrifice individual interest and merge it back into the universal. The hero appears as Spirit by denying biology. This is the foundation of law, which is based on heroic, disinterested attitudes. Hegel describes the unity of the private and the public, of the real and thought, in the "concrete universal" of a State that has to go beyond the contingencies of war. Law is the objectivized universal for which we should be ready to sacrifice our lives. It creates peoples as "ethical wholes" that are opposed to other "ethical wholes." In contrast, Clausewitz thought in terms of greater or smaller separations and gaps between real wars and the concept of war.

RG: The two thinkers were thus close but contradictory at the same time. Close because both of them were devoted to the State (Clausewitz wrote: "we regard politics as the intelligence of the personified state");[10] contradictory in the way they saw history. Whereas one described what would be achieved in the future as the unity of reality and thought, the other both feared and hoped for such unity. Perhaps this is because for Hegel such unity is at the end of the indeterminacy of history, but for Clausewitz it is at the heart of its contradictions. So we could thus say that Clausewitz destroyed the ambition to gain absolute knowledge and an abstract path to such knowledge. He reminds us of the essential violence of history, that humanity will one day be able to destroy the world. This explains the ambivalence of Napoleon as a symbol. Hegel saw him as an incarnation of the Spirit, but Clausewitz saw him as a "god of war" to whom we must respond.

Two conceptions of history

BC: It seems that, despite their differences, they both worshipped the State and rejected any form of universal ethics. While war was an ideal for Clausewitz, it was a necessity for Hegel, who considered it important to distinguish "true history" from "apparent history." True history flows from the sacrifice of individuals. Sacrificed individuals contribute to the coming of the Spirit in the form of law. For Clausewitz, by contrast, apparent history and its reciprocal engine are the only reality. We are thus dealing with two opposing manifestations of the Absolute: the catastrophic matching of war with its concept according to Clausewitz, and the abolition of time when thought grasps its "pure concept" according to Hegel. Neither leaves much room for hope.

RG: They could be considered the two greatest thinkers on war. There is thus from Jena to Berlin, and around Napoleon, the strange conjunction of two apocalypses, one warlike and the other philosophical. It is very curious, but all related to the period: Hegel and Clausewitz were not alone. Schelling and Fichte were also there . . . and they were all watching Napoleon. Look at the role Fichte played in establishing German nationalism; read his *Addresses to the German Nation*.[11] Later, we will come back to Schlegel and also to his relationship with Germaine de Staël.

In Romanticism, there is an excessive belief in individual autonomy, but it is also a necessary stage that has to be passed through in order to understand resentment, reciprocity and the law of the duel. In short, Romanticism is necessary to understand that we have entered a world of internal mediation, where there is no longer any external model to vouchsafe our conduct. We have to "cope with" violence. This explains Germaine de Staël's intuition, which was shared by many others at the time, that religion is the only recourse. Thus, in the French-German confrontation, which was filled with both hatred and fascination, there was something decisive at stake for the intelligibility of the world into which we have entered. Napoleon was an essential catalyst. We must not forget that it was against him that Germany united, which had many consequences for the history of Europe and the world.

Clausewitz was both for and against Napoleon. It is fascinating to read his work because he had a keen awareness of mimetism, yet he was situated at the source of modern individualism. His rationality is thus ambivalent. He had a very cold way of viewing war as a more intense form of trade, whereas Hegel spoke of it as self-sacrifice, and as heroic, reasoned transcendence of private interest. Hegel considered that the death of a hero contributes to the advent of the Spirit: by putting his life at stake, a hero tears himself away from his own natural and animal nature. His sacrifice makes him spiritual. This is how reason tricks conflict, which can never smother it. In contrast, Clausewitz did not see the military hero as having this spiritual nature at all. For Clausewitz, a military hero is one who manages to rise above the contingencies and the many influences to which armies are subject. In Clausewitz's dissimulation of reciprocal action and focus on an exceptional individual, there is an icy-cold theoretical Romanticism. Our passions and desires come from others; we never draw them from the depths of ourselves. It is because the adversary is hostile that I become so too, and vice versa.

Thus, for Clausewitz, military heroism is less transcendence than aggravated mimetism. For example, a counter-attack is much more effective if it is a surprise or if it includes an innovation within the codified behavior of the two armies that are spying on, studying and measuring each other. A good general cold-bloodedly dominates such situations of extreme reciprocity, but he is nonetheless not for all that autonomous. The more completely he masters his defensive strategy, the more he is controlled by violence and contributes to the escalation to extremes. Clausewitz, who was in the center of the cauldron of German nationalism just as it was beginning to simmer, seems to have withdrawn in fascinated horror from the only way reality could match the concept of absolute war: pure reciprocity.

In his work, there is attraction to but also distaste for war. Yet he even theorized this back-and-forth movement. Clausewitz thus managed to hold together totalitarian hope and political prudence. One can argue convincingly for the first chapter of his treatise as a critique of Hegelian individualism. However, the consequences of the comparison are enormous: Clausewitz glimpsed the essentially *reciprocal* engine of what Heidegger later called the technological "enframing" of the world, a scramble to keep up that has nothing to do with the Hegelian epiphany of the Spirit. Quite the contrary: the escalation to extremes makes reconciliation impossible. The identity of all humans, which Hegel thought would lead to common understanding, will in fact drive them ever further apart.

BC: You are thus playing Clausewitz off against Hegel, or rather you are using Clausewitz to chip away at the Hegelian theodicy, the way that the Spirit would be playing with human passions so as to turn them to its own ends. Why do you think that everything is tending toward the worst?

RG: Because Clausewitz was more realistic than Hegel, whose dialectic he shows to be vacuous. My point of view is thus completely rational. This is the meaning of Chapter 1 of *On War*. In that chapter, on the basis of one single intuition, Clausewitz raises himself above all Hegelianism. His view of history is more accurate, more concrete. You cannot view it from above or get an eagle-eye view of the events. I myself thought that was possible when I was writing *Things Hidden since the Foundation of the World*, in which I imagined Christianity provided the point of view from which we could judge violence. However, there is neither non-sacrificial space, nor "true history."

I reread my analysis of St. Paul's Epistle to the Hebrews, which was my last "modern" and "anti-Christian" argument. The criticism of an "historical Christianity" and argument in favor of a kind of "essential Christianity," which I thought I had grasped in a Hegelian manner, was absurd. On the contrary, we have to think of Christianity as essentially historical, and Clausewitz helps us do so. Solomon's judgment explains everything on this score: there is the sacrifice of the other, and self-sacrifice; archaic sacrifice and Christian sacrifice. However, it is all sacrifice. We are immersed in mimetism and have to find a way around the pitfalls of our desire, which is always desire for what the other possesses. I repeat, absolute knowledge is not possible. We are forced to remain at the heart of history and to act at the heart of violence because we are always gaining a better understanding of its mechanisms. Will we ever be able to elude them? I doubt it.

Hegel had no direct military experience. He therefore had no feel for the interactions that Clausewitz experienced and sought to theorize, albeit not quite successfully. However, Clausewitz's commitment reveals something essential: the escalation to extremes in which he participated as an observer and actor, in which we all participate though we do not acknowledge it. In order to understand this, we have to jump ahead of ourselves and consider the incredible impact Napoleon's actions had on the Germans. Clausewitz is fascinated by Napoleon, and this can be understood only from a mimetic perspective. In total war, in other words, the mobilization of a whole people, Clausewitz saw that war was in a new situation and that Prussia would have to do the same in order to *respond* to Napoleon. Hegel did not see this because he did not feel as much resentment as Clausewitz. Hegel did not see that what he would call the "Germanic Empire," which he supposed would succeed Greece and Rome and establish reconciliation as "objective truth and freedom,"[12] would be achieved thanks to Prussia's mimetic fury against France. Prussia's anger united Germany against France and Austria. Hegel did not want to see that the French-German reciprocity would nurture the escalation to extremes, which had nothing to do with the advent of the absolute Spirit. Clausewitz felt this, but curiously he preferred to mask his intuition by allowing his readers to think that war was still what it was in the eighteenth century and that politics could control it. When he did this, he wore his Enlightenment disguise. However, the mask slipped, as we can already guess.

BC: To paraphrase Pascal, mimetism has reasons that reason doesn't wish to see. Carl Schmitt, who had read *On War,* demonstrated that the Prussian reform, in which Clausewitz enthusiastically participated after Napoleon's fall, was designed to *respond* to the French Revolution.

RG: Indeed, Germany had to be shaken from its slumber: a few years earlier it was still worrying about the French Revolution. It thought that the Revolution was the beginning of a major movement that would rock Europe. We therefore must return to the defeat at Jena in 1806. Almost all of Prussia was invaded. Then there was Russia's defeat at Friedland in 1807, and the meeting between Napoleon and Tsar Alexander at Tilsit on the River Niemen. Thiers wrote that when Napoleon's influence was at its apogee, "the honor of being beaten by Napoleon were equivalent to a victory."[13] It seems the Tsar even said, "I have never loved anything more than that man."[14] All the art of *political* exploitation of *tactical* victories won through *strategy,* to use the Clausewitzian terminology, was in Napoleon's irresistible seduction. He almost succeeded in setting up his continental embargo against England. Napoleon was not the brutal conqueror invented by his adversaries after his fall, but indeed an artist of diplomacy.

Yet even though Napoleon called Frederick William to the bargaining table and offered to give him back some of his provinces, Prussia ended up humiliated but also fascinated. It was too military to completely detest Napoleon, and to deal with the situation, it was forced to imitate him, just as Frederick the Great had imitated Voltaire. Why have these phenomena never been given close study? Clausewitz thought over *against* Napoleon. He was thus, with others, at the origin of a movement that led to Bismarck, but especially to Ludendorff, who was the author of the Schlieffen Plan and served as Hindenburg's First *Generalquartiermeister* after 1914. Ludendorff, through his participation in the Munich Putsch of 1923, brought us straight to Hitler.

It is in this sense only, namely, a dogmatic interpretation of *On War,* that Liddell Hart was right to see in Clausewitz the potential for an apology of all-out war. In fact, his thought was much more complex, and he never advanced a thesis without suggesting another possibility, as we saw in Chapter 1 of the treatise.

Nonetheless, it is one thing to refuse to remain with a theoretical definition of war, namely, that of war as a duel, and to go on to consider practical aspects (such as calculations of probability and commanders' courage), but it is quite something else to see behind the polarity of war its "absolute, so-called mathematical"[15] factor. "Total war," whose precursors Clausewitz saw in the French Revolutionary Army and the concentration of Napoleon's forces, compelled him to consider the possibility of "absolute war" as a future response to the new type of conflict. Indeed, Clausewitz could think only in terms of a response to the event.

The primacy of defense over attack is only one way of theorizing this fundamental attitude. The theory had a long range, since after the "counter-attack" of the 1870 war, Germany prepared for the 1914 "counter-attack" and then again with the remilitarization of the Rhineland in 1936. Only the defensive conception, whether or not it was in fact accurate, was able to turn "hostile intent" into "hostile feeling" (to stick to the terms of his treatise). It alone could mobilize a whole people against an enemy that was being fabricated. Here, the concept was in a way the necessary horizon of reality, but not at all in Hegel's way of thinking, which tends to be too abstract to identify such an unglamorous law of history.

BC: Henri Bergson described his feelings when war was declared in 1914:

> Horror-struck as I was, and though I felt a war, even a victorious war, to be a catastrophe, I experienced . . . a feeling of admiration for the smoothness of the transition from the abstract to the concrete: who would have thought that so terrible an eventuality could make its entrance into reality with so little disturbance?[16]

It is as if the ease of achieving the impossible were in proportion to the difficulty in imagining it.

RG: That quotation is perfect. It shows how difficult it is for reason to imagine the worst. This is why Clausewitz is a sure antidote for all the abstraction in Hegelian dialectic. It reminds us that the more rationalist we become, in other words, the more we forget perceptible reality and history, the faster and more violently reality and history are brought back to mind. Clausewitz was a realist: he observed, with terrible lucidity, the accelerated development of history that had lost all reason and gone mad. In his treatise the conditional mood often indicates such imminence. For example, in section 23 of Chapter 1:

> When whole communities go to war—whole peoples, and especially *civilized* peoples—the reason always lies in some political situation, and the occasion is always due to some political object. War, therefore, is an act of policy. *Were it a complete, untrammeled, absolute manifestation of violence (as the pure concept would require), war would of its own independent will usurp the place of policy the moment policy had brought it into being; it would then drive policy out of office and rule by the laws of its own nature,* very much like a mine that can explode only in the manner or direction predetermined by the setting. This, in fact, is the view that has been taken of the matter whenever some discord between policy and the conduct of war has stimulated theoretical distinctions of this kind. But in reality things are different, and this view is thoroughly mistaken. In reality war, as has been shown, is not like that. Its violence is not of the kind that *explodes in a single discharge....* That, however, does not imply that the political aim is a tyrant. It must adapt itself to its chosen means, a process which can radically change it; yet the political aim remains the first consideration. Policy, then, will permeate all military operations, and, *in so far as their violent nature will admit,* it will have a continuous influence on them.[17]

This passage is crucial. In it we see the tension in Clausewitz's thought, and the real effort he makes to control his own nature and reintroduce rationality where it had already disappeared *because the principle of reciprocity had appeared* and could not be eliminated so easily. The mechanism of history is not broken, but freed by the disclosure of reciprocal action. This explains the surprising descent, once again, into the immanence of the "explosion" and the possible influence of warlike means on political ends: policy "must adapt itself to its chosen means." Next there is the famous section 24, in which war is defined as "merely the continuation of policy by other means," and section 25, in which Clausewitz categorizes the two types of war:

> The more powerful and inspiring the motives for war, the more they affect the belligerent nations and the fiercer the tensions that precede the outbreak, the closer will war approach its abstract concept, the more important will

be the destruction of the enemy, the more closely will the military aims and the political objects of war coincide, and the more military and less political will war appear to be. On the other hand, the less intense the motives, the less will the military element's natural tendency to violence coincide with political directives. As a result, war will be driven further from its natural course, the political object will be more and more at variance with the aim of ideal war, and the conflict will seem increasingly political in character.[18]

When war "seems" to become political, it is precisely when politics are no longer anything but a semblance. This leads to the conclusion in section 26:

> While policy is apparently effaced in the one kind of war and yet is strongly evident in the other, both kinds are equally political.[19]

Clearly, what he saw here was what a century later would be called "ideological wars." Leninism was nothing more than a form of military Hegelianism, to use Raymond Aron's expression, an absolute war dictated by the meaning of history and involving the extermination of "class enemies" both within and without. This is how history makes its violent return. Unable to resist, reason gives it means to proceed by justifying it. Marx and Engels did nothing but borrow from Clausewitz the apparent subordination of war to politics, but this time war was to serve the class struggle: civil war was to replace war between nations. Leninism's spin on the very definition of war helped to propagate it more widely. Civil war quickly spread through Europe and then across the world.

Ideological war is in this sense what takes us from classical inter-state war to the violence we experience today: absolutely unpredictable, truly undifferentiated violence. We are far from Hegel now. There was no "desire for recognition" between the Tutsis and Hutus, but a twin-like rivalry that went to extremes and degenerated into genocide. Take the Middle East, where the massacres of Sunnis and Shiites will only increase in the months and years to come. In this case also it cannot be said that one is seeking "recognition" from the other: rather, each one wants to exterminate the other, which is very different. There is no difference in nature between machetes and missiles, only in degree.

Clausewitz told us in his way that reason is no longer at work in history. Everywhere, politics, science and religion have used ideology to mask a duel that is becoming global. They have simply provided themes and justifications for the principle of reciprocity. The trend towards undifferentiation has been strengthened by the West's technological and military means. In a way, the trend proves that politics have been *overtaken* by technology.

Lenin and Stalin nonetheless made concrete an alliance of some of Clausewitz's theses with those of Hegelianism, which is proof that what is at stake between Clausewitz and Hegel is crucial. Lenin and Stalin tried to dictate a meaning for history, and to *make that meaning real* using strictly military means. I should say political-military means, but politics plays such a small role here. The Nazis found the experiment very interesting, and did the same thing in turn, achieving the total militarization of society that the Prussian reformers of the nineteenth century had in mind when they were studying Spain's *guérilleros*. We were thus moving, in both Eastern and Western Europe, towards two competing, profoundly mimetic conceptions of total war that would soon turn against each other once the cynical pact of 1939 was broken. They thus came to resemble each other more and more, to finally produce "absolute war."

Has Europe really recovered from the conflagration? Nothing is less certain. Now that we know how important Europe was to become in the history of the world, we have every reason to be afraid. Ernst Nolte is right to see Nazism as a response to Bolshevism, and Stalinism as a response to Hitlerism. It was much more than a repetition of the Grande Armée's defeat in 1814: it was a new form of war economy, a new kind of social contract involving the total militarization of civil life. This was the "escalation to extremes" that destroyed the heart of Europe. Ideological wars are less convincing now because we no longer really try to justify violence. They were only a stage in the emergence of a planetary principle of reciprocity. It is in the complete unpredictability of violence that we can see what I call the end of war, which is another name for the apocalypse. We are very far from the "end of history" announced by Fukuyama, the last scion of Hegelian optimism.

BC: François Furet makes Nolte's thesis more plausible by describing the 1914–18 disaster as the origin of this absolute war. According to him, the Bolsheviks did not begin it: the apocalypse in the trenches inaugurated the new era, and totalitarianism was a monstrous response to World War I.

RG: It is a way of *not wanting to see* what happened at Verdun, of wishing the apocalypse away by speeding up its course. François Furet is right, but we have to look further back in time, to Napoleon and even to Louis XIV. This is what Clausewitz said and he was right. We have to go back to France's and Prussia's hatred of the Holy Roman Empire of the German Nation. This makes for a vast field of study. I am now convinced that mimetic history needs to be written: it would help us understand what is at stake in our own time.

On this point, no one is more anti-Maurrassian and anti-positivist than I. I do not at all believe in the genius of the "forty kings who made France."[20] Maurras was very good at retelling France's history according to his own design and marshalling events into neat lines. This kind of French positivism, which still lingers today, is all the more ridiculous in that it refuses to see that France has not been among the "superpowers" leading the world since 1940. Either Europe will emerge as a whole, or its components will become pathetic specks of dust, like the Greek cities under the Roman Empire and the Italian states until Napoleon III. From this point of view, World War I was already an absurd effort to remain on the same plane as the other powers.

In short, Clausewitz's treatise constantly shows that we must not believe in the "true history" that Hegel sees growing behind the ups and downs of "apparent history," or the history that positivists describe as a national necessity or as progress. The real principle that is latent behind the alternating victories and defeats, behind the "philosophical trend," behind the "pure logic" and "nature" of war is not a ruse of reason, but the duel.

The fight to the death is thus much more than a simple desire for recognition. It is not a master-slave dialectic, but *a merciless battle between twins.* Ernst Nolte does not draw the right conclusions from his perceptions because he has not fully developed the mimetic implications of his hypothesis. Instead of trying to absolve Germany of the worst, he should have shown that the reciprocal, furious imitation between the USSR and the Third Reich caused the "absolute war" in which tens of millions of innocent people died, and in which the institution of war also died in Europe. Even in his worst periods of depression, Clausewitz would not have dared to envisage such a total degradation. While respecting all due methodological precautions inherent in such a vast enterprise, we could expand this mimetic interpretation to all of human history.

In a French newspaper I said concerning September 11 that Muslims and Westerners were twins. That was nothing new. In fact, we can wonder to what extent the excesses of the Crusades in the thirteenth century were not mimetic responses to the *Jihad,* of which we are now suffering the consequences in Europe and the Middle East. So much energy wasted to conquer an empty tomb. We need to undertake historical studies, both longitudinal and at different levels, of the conditions for the trend to extremes. This would show that it is against that baleful tendency that the institution of war was gradually established in an attempt to control what was less and less controllable. The rise in violence happens behind the actors' backs. The principle of misunderstanding contradicts the very idea of a ruse of reason.

It is thus not surprising that in the era of globalization, in other words, when wars are increasing, mimetism has gained ground since 1945 and is taking over the world. Everyone now knows that the looming conflict between the United States and China, for example, has nothing to do with a "clash of civilizations,"[21] despite what some might try to tell us. We always try to see differences where in fact there are none. In fact, the dispute is between two forms of capitalism that are becoming more and more similar, except that the Chinese, who have an ancient military culture, have been theorizing for three thousand years about how to use the adversary's strength against him. The Chinese thus feel less attraction for the Western model but imitate it more in order to triumph over it. Their policy is thus perhaps all the more dangerous in that it understands and masters mimetism. In this sense, Islamist terrorism is only a sign of a much more formidable *response* by the East to the West.

There were unmistakable signs when Hong Kong was returning to China's control, for example, those great clocks counting down the merger. The Chinese people saw the event as having absolutely extraordinary importance. The British strategy was very intelligent, and consisted in doing politics without talking about it. There was no war, but many agreements on many points, for it is well known that without the Chinese, the world's financial system would collapse. Their Achilles' heel seems to be corruption, but this did not prevent them from declaring a 10 percent increase in the gross national product in 2006, whereas prior to that they had always reduced the figures to make themselves appear less threatening to the West. When we consider that less than 10 percent of China is industrialized, we can only imagine what the future holds.

Have you heard that there have been thefts of copper all over the world? It is even being stolen for resale, as recently happened in France. This is because of the huge Chinese demand for it to fill their construction needs. I remember that at an American university last year, construction work was interrupted because "everything was going to China." Today it is copper, tomorrow it will be oil. The price increases are being caused by China, not fear of war. The Chinese will not stop; they want to beat the Americans; they want there to be more cars in China than in the United States. We always want to be better than the one we see as our model: we've heard that tune before. This is the insurmountable horizon of our history, which puts the Islamic attacks somewhat into perspective. This is why I see in Clausewitz the same mechanisms of undifferentiation that I saw in myths when trying to understand archaic religion. This is also why we have to read Clausewitz: his cold pessimism tells us, better than any other form of teaching, about the regression in progress.

An Impossible Reconciliation

BC: Your penchant for the apocalyptic puts some people off and prevents them from seeing the pertinence of the concepts you are setting up to understand the frightening future of the world. In your distrust of Hegelianism, are you not in the process of being led by Clausewitz, just as Clausewitz was led by Napoleon?

RG: It is better to put people off than to try to please everyone. Many intellectuals refuse to take the situation I describe into account. Yet is it not the reality of present-day history? I am aware that the escalation to extremes is what makes me reject Hegelianism. Clausewitz's unique intuition fascinates me to the same extent that I reject it and try to go beyond it. However, if I go beyond it, I should nonetheless integrate Clausewitz's ideas, not to justify a form of war regulated by law, as Carl Schmitt did, and even less to move too quickly to Hegelian reconciliation, the famous *Aufhebung,* which is not religious enough to my taste. Clausewitz's advantage lies paradoxically in the resentment that goads him on, in the model-obstacle who was for him the emperor and whom he constantly ran up against. We have here a concrete, formulable law. By reading Clausewitz, we know that what takes place with Napoleon is absolutely new. We can thus see that Clausewitz had a strong grip on reality, and that his theory threatens the very foundations of our complacency. The escalation to extremes is not "Clausewitzian"; it is real.

BC: Instead of contrasting Hegel and Clausewitz too systematically, could we not try to use them to think about human reconciliation, the non-conflictual aspect of human identity?

RG: This is what we will have to try to do, but without forgetting that the two thinkers contradict each another. We thus have to resort to the insurmountable law of reciprocal action, in other words, mimetism, since we now have a better understanding of the mechanisms of desire and emotions. Is reconciliation still thinkable after Auschwitz and Hiroshima? Surely not in Hegelian terms. Whence my recourse to Clausewitz and the apocalyptic. What is clear is the sameness of all people, the symmetry of myth, the leveling of all distinctions, which is the result of the fight between doubles that, in what I call the sacrificial crisis, leads to the convergence of a group onto a sacrificial victim. This primitive scenario of archaic religion gave birth to gods, rites and institutions, but today it can be nothing more than sinister play-acting, furious violence leading to thousands and even millions of deaths. Yet, with Hegel, we have seen that the spectacle of identity can lead to philosophical knowledge, and to knowledge of equality and fraternity. We thus have to try to think about identity in a different way, in terms of reverse mimetism, positive imitation. This presupposes an internal criticism of reciprocity, which always has the potential to degenerate into extreme irresolvable conflict.

It is because he believed in humanity that Hegel thought that there would be a virtually automatic reconciliation of all people. However, it was on the basis of violence as a fundamental part of history. Since it affirmed that human conflict is positive, his dialectic was a phase in the philosophical and spiritual rise of violence in the modern world. Indeed, it was by criticizing Hegelian idealism that Marx urged people to take ownership of this violence. Lenin later reproached Marx for not being violent enough. Violence thus increasingly came to be seen as indispensable to the advent of peace among humans. In his analysis of the "group-in-fusion,"[22] Sartre surpassed Lenin and almost discovered the founding murder. Clausewitz thus said aloud what post-Hegelians later discovered in an excess of violence: the escalation to extremes demystifies all reconciliation, all *Aufhebung.* The illusions based on peace-generating violence, when applied to historical reality, will illustrate the madness of the whole enterprise.

It cannot be denied, of course, that Hegel saw the terrible alternative of kill or be killed, but he thought that people would finally come to embrace one another. The reconciliation that Hegelians themselves later expelled from his work was the veritable and mysterious kernel of his genius. If we are to believe only in humanity, we have to be able to believe humans will be reconciled, even if it does not happen until the end of history. The supposed superiority of the "wise" Hegelian with respect to earlier wise men lay in the fact that Hegelian wisdom was never challenged since history was responsible for achieving reconciliation. The Hegelian could bide his time passively. So long as people were fighting around him, he could remain "above the fray." Unlike his naïve predecessors, he did not try to reconcile his adversaries. He knew the world was still plunged in darkness.

This faith in the necessary reconciliation of men is what shocks me most today. I was a victim of it, in a way, and my book *Things Hidden since the Foundation of the World*[23] expressed the confidence that universal knowledge of violence would suffice. I no longer believe that for the reasons I have just explained and which I did not see at the time. This is precisely why we have to investigate Hölderlin's silence. That great poet was the exact contemporary of Clausewitz and Hegel. His definitive retreat to Tübingen has to be understood as a rejection of the Absolute, as a radical distance taken from all the optimists who championed the rise of warmongering in Europe. Hölderlin suddenly stopped talking to his contemporaries with the invincible sadness of a Protestant, who was perhaps more vulnerable than a Catholic would have been. We have to try to take the measure of that silence, to measure up to it. These days I am looking to him for the truth that Hegel has not provided.

BC: Yet you still think that Hegel links us with the Judeo-Christian world.

RG: To the Christian world, certainly. But to the Biblical world? That is something else. Hegel had a very conventional "jealous God" approach, which is that of the Enlightenment in a way. I do not think that he fully understood the continuity between the two traditions, though it should never be forgotten. We have to affirm that modern wisdom, in so far as it aspires to non-conflicting identity, is heir to prophetic hope, the vision of universal uniformity as the imminence of harmony and peace. Enlightenment thought about equality, democracy and revolution is essentially non-Greek and Jewish in origin since it is based on the ultimate vision of identity, fraternity. We deem it messianic thought, in the sense that it is through the trials of history and through their movements that the hope of fraternity shines. It is a mistake to say that this is an imaginary "dream" or an evasion. This vision of identity is an essential product of Western history *repeating* myths, in other words, penetrating into places where difference oscillates and where distinctions are lost in conflict. This vision of a new order is based on the nothingness that separates foes, or certain categories of adversaries, the nothingness that must necessarily unite individuals. It cannot prevent them from uniting one day, even if it cannot now prevent conflict from raging.

It is because they do not understand the prophetic dimension of the loss of differences that modern forms of wisdom have reintroduced differences, conflict and obstacles to be overcome in order to finally achieve reconciliation. They hope that everything will be resolved at the end of history. In order to keep their hope in identity, in other words, reconciliation, they have multiplied the hidden differences that have to be eliminated before achieving real identity. We have seen that Hegel thought that a world state would emerge out of inter-state conflicts. Likewise, modern forms of wisdom have not wanted to give up seeing bad reciprocity as the precursor of good reciprocity. However, this alibi of the last remaining obstacle to be overcome before reconciliation, this means of postponing universal peace, has necessarily made violence grow. *More violence is always needed before reconciliation.* Auschwitz and Hiroshima have reminded us of this.

We can no longer continue thinking in this way. This unconscious apocalyptic reasoning is revealed through the escalation to extremes. We now know that suspending violence, failing to renounce it straight away, always makes it grow. Violence can never reduce violence. Yet humans continue to refuse to see the catastrophe that they are preparing by always introducing new differences and new conflicts. This misapprehension is simply part of mimetism, which is denial of our own violence.

BC: The escalation to extremes would thus be, according to you, the increasingly violent period that we have to expect before reconciliation, to the point of making reconciliation impossible.

RG: We have to think of reconciliation not as a consequence but as the reverse of the escalation to extremes. It is a real possibility, but no one wants to see it. The Kingdom is already here, but human violence will increasingly mask it. This is the paradox of our world. Apocalyptic thought is thus contrary to the wisdom that believes that peaceful identity and fraternity is accessible on the purely human level. It is also contrary to all the reactionary forms of thought that want to restore differences and see identity as only a form of destructive uniformity or leveling conformity. Apocalyptic thought recognizes the source of conflict in identity, but it also sees in it the hidden presence of the thought of "the neighbor as yourself" which can certainly not triumph, but is secretly active, secretly dominant under the sound and fury on the surface.

Peaceful identity lies at the heart of violent identity as its most secret possibility. This is the secret strength of eschatology. Hegel's thought was based on Christianity, and he understood that the voice of unity and love could rise from discord itself, from the destructive and terrible vanity of conflict. However, he did not remember that the wisest men had already failed to make that voice triumph. That failure, which Christian revelation anticipated, was overlooked by Hegel and has been ignored by modern wisdom. This misapprehension has led to the worst.

Modern forms of thought have thus been able to emerge only at specific points in history, where symmetry confronted itself, where the absence of differences appeared or the nothing separating enemy brothers urgently suggested the possibility of their union. It sufficed for humans to acknowledge that there were no essential obstacles separating them and preventing them from reconciling. Modern thinkers have tried to correct their excessive optimism. They have discovered that there are differences where we had thought they had disappeared: cultural and not natural differences, differences that can be eliminated, for example, historical, educational, social, economic, family and psychological differences. Elimination of these differences has long been seen as a condition for the new order. If the identity that is immediately noticeable around us is not a source of harmony, it is because it is superficial, false. It has to be replaced with *a more real form of identity*. This Promethean task, which requires always more violence, has contributed to the rise of totalitarianism.

Modern thought on identity has been able to discover or invent new obstacles to reconciliation. It has been able to push the epiphany of identity off to the furthest horizon, and finally eliminate it. Today, thought on identity has given up on itself. It no longer exists. In fact, Christianity has always known that this reconciliation was impossible: it is why Christ said that he brought war, not peace. Did Christianity predict its apocalyptic failure? A reasonable argument can be made that it did. This failure is simply the same thing as the end of the world. From this point of view, one could argue that the verse "when the Son of Man comes, will he find faith on earth?"[24] is still too full of hope. The Revelation has failed: in a certain manner it has not been heard.

Of course, the apocalypse cannot erase the fact that humanity has accomplished something, which is undeniably due to Christianity. The now defunct idea of reconciliation has nonetheless had successes that have shaken the world. The suspended epiphany of the identity of all men, which was the best part of Christianity, has always created new obstacles for history to overcome. If its action had been different, it would have meant that there were only differences, that history meant nothing and that there was no truth. It is the hope for identity and future reconciliation that was long the meaning of history, until that meaning became frozen in ideology and was imposed on people through the instruments of terror.

For some time I myself thought that, despite all the obstacles, the idea of identity and its intellectual obviousness could produce the epiphany by itself. It *had to* reconcile enemy brothers. I had forgotten the lessons of Greek tragedy: Eteocles and Polynices will never be reconciled. Only democratic hope can claim to put an end to the tragedy, but we now know that this is a modern platitude. Alone, man cannot triumph over himself. The possibility of paradise on Earth is always lost. God's patience is inconceivable, but it is not infinite.

This is why I think that, since it springs from Judaism, Christianity is not simply one mode of thought among others, but the original thought on identity. We have to come back to it, no matter what its detractors may say. It is the first to have seen history's convergence towards conflicting reciprocity that has to change into peaceful reciprocity in order to avoid falling into the abyss of absolute violence. It is the first to see that nothing serious or real opposes this change, which everything around us cries out for and even demands.

However, it asserts, and in this it is different from all modern thought on identity, *that an opportunity for reconciliation arose once already but was not seized.*

Unlike all other lines of thought, Christianity holds within its selfsame purview two things that we always separate with respect to reconciliation: its in-principle possibility and in-fact impossibility. When there is no longer anything separating enemy brothers and everything tells them to unite, since their very lives depend on the union, neither intellectual obviousness nor appeals to common sense, to reason or to logic are of any use. There will be no peace because war is fed precisely by the *nothing* that alone remains between the adversaries and that is nourished by their very *identity*. We have thus entered an era of unpredictable hostility, the twilight of war that makes violence our ultimate and last *Logos*.

BC: You are leaning toward the worst, though it seems that you are always hesitating and sometimes that you still believe in the Kingdom. Why do you think that the "epiphany of identity" necessarily has to take an apocalyptic turn?

RG: Because the Gospels say so and because the fact has become so obvious that it is becoming impossible not to put the cards on the table *now*. The absolute new is the Second Coming, in other words, the apocalypse. Christ's triumph will take place in a beyond of which we can describe neither the time nor place. However, the devastation will be all on our side: the apocalyptic texts speak of a war among people, not of a war of God against humans. The apocalypse has to be taken out of fundamentalist hands. The disaster is thus insignificant in relation to its certainty. It concerns *only* humanity, in a certain sense, and takes nothing from the reality of the beyond. Human violence produces the sacred, but holiness leads to the "other shore" that Christians, like Jews, vehemently believe will never be stained by human madness.

BC: The law of the escalation to extremes is thus inevitable?

RG: A close reading of Clausewitz's text will gradually show this. We have seen the timeliness of his book, and started to understand it differently than did Aron. We have to continue. We will get a better and better picture of how he was in radical opposition to Christianity, but also of how he stated a law that Hegelian reasoning and its derivations can no longer account for.

Hegel no longer has disciples today. We can no longer do what modern thought long did: *postpone*. All men are equal, not under law, but in fact. We must thus make decisive choices: there will soon be no institutions, rituals or "differences" for regulating our behavior. We have to destroy one another or love one another, and humanity, we fear, will prefer to destroy itself. The future of the world is out of our control, and yet it is in our hands: this is something to think about. The only thing that I, personally, can still do is always return to the Revelation in the New Testament. What astonishes and fascinates me is the formidable passive resistance that the message meets. Resistance is even stronger now that Hegel's star has dimmed, now that identity will soon be patent and we can no longer delay it. Thus I return to this Revelation. It tells us that reconciliation is not immanent in the course of history. Therefore Pascal, rather than Hegel, is our contemporary.

BC: So the rule of charity is the ultimate recourse?

RG: We will have to come back to the way that mimetic anthropology tries to establish that relationship, going from violent *mimesis* to peaceful *mimesis*. However, in order to think about this specific relationship, we have to reconstruct another absolutely essential relationship: that between Judaism and Christianity, between the "carnal" and the "spiritual," as Pascal said. I am especially surprised that Hegel did not see the special relationship that both unites and separates what Christians call the two Testaments. It is essential to think about. By seeing "order" and "commandment" in the Johannine *Logos*, Heidegger joined a tradition of modern thought that dated back to Hegel. Hegel turned the God of the Law into the God who crushes, the God of imperious domination. To do so is to misunderstand the Bible, and that misunderstanding is rooted in the inability of Christians themselves to see that the two Testaments are one, an inability whose roots are too often ascribed to St. Paul's teaching.

The Hegelian reading of the Bible is static and dead, and cuts the future off from texts that are essentially turned towards it. However, it cannot yet close its eyes on what the Bible is based on: the Word of equity and fraternity, and the peaceful non-difference fully revealed in the Gospels. In contrast, post-Hegelian thought takes Hegel's mistake to an extreme by symptomatically forgetting the necessarily Biblical foundations of all unmasking of violence. Violence is denounced on behalf of the "individual" against the group, in other words, on behalf of another form of violence, which is the same thing. The violence that Hegel, and also Freud, placed at the origin of the Bible tends in the thought of commentators to propagate and spread to the New Testament. Criticism's path is that of myth itself. Rationalism remythifies what it believes it is demystifying, in other words, the Bible in its entirety. The *Logos* of violence spreads its own domination over everything, and finally projects itself into the only text where violence does not triumph: the Scriptures.

BC: Was not such a path inevitable, given the similarities between the Gospels and myths, through the central role that the immolated yet divinized scapegoat plays in both?

RG: In fact, it is this similarity that has led to misinterpretation. Rationalism has fallen into the trap by continuing to use the old reflexes of mythology: to confuse Christianity with all the other religions is necessarily to make it a violent religion like the others. We will come back to this in greater detail. We need Hölderlin's help to show the essential similarity and difference between Christianity and archaic religion. When we say that the Bible is mythical, and it can appear even more mythical than the myth of Oedipus, it is because of the sovereign role that God plays in it, which appears to us as incompatible with a science of human relationships. However, the dominating God is the one that is incarnated in paternal, hierarchical difference.

Quite to the contrary, the God who arises with the consenting scapegoat is a perfectly unknown god; he is the one that is the most outside yet also the most inside common humanity. He is *the most divine and the most human*. The "royal Messiah" and consenting scapegoat, through their conjunction, realize these conditions. The incredible news, the event whose import the Western world has not yet realized, though its own history has been increasingly determined by it, is that *God is now on the side of the scapegoat victim*. He is outside of the system regulated by the play of sacred difference, the difference that modern thought has postponed with unbelievable naïveté and violence because of fear of identity. This totality can end only in death and nothingness. However, Jehovah is now outside the temple. The divine truth is no longer in the ancient city or in a chosen people: it has been expelled from the city of man, along with the scapegoat victim.

The Servant of God, and the lynching of the suffering Servant in Isaiah, is the only possible outcome of the structure because the expulsion of scapegoats is always a re-entry into the vicious circle, which has only one possible outcome: complete destruction of the world. The discovery of the role of the consenting scapegoat is a rigorous spiritual operation that must not be related to empirical data other than the Crucifixion. This is why the prophetic literature refers to a Servant outside of any specific event and any reference to a specific person or group. All attempts to *identify* the Servant with Israel as a whole seem vain. Likewise, and even though the theme of the scapegoat victim is always extremely relevant to the Prophet, the latter never says that *he* is the Servant of Yahweh.

Christ warns us in turn about the dangers of the Antichrists, in other words, those who want to be imitated. *The aspect of Christ that has to be imitated is his withdrawal.* Hölderlin made this dramatic discovery. This is why in the Bible we never find a fight to the death like that of the prophets of Thebes, for example, Tiresias and Oedipus. A fight to the death is impossible because in the Bible the point is precisely to give up claims to difference. There is thus something anonymous and impersonal in the Songs, even though the Servant sometimes speaks on his own behalf and sometimes on behalf of the community that condemned him and that later understood what it had done. An unambiguous answer is now possible to the question of what distinguishes true prophecy from false: true prophetic words are rooted in the truth of the consenting scapegoat. The consenting scapegoat does not claim to incarnate that truth; he says that truth is other and that it is more specifically there, outside of the system. However, the prophet *is not* the truth, for otherwise other "prophets" would want to seize it. The prophet bears witness to it, announces it, precedes it and in a sense follows it.

Duel and Reciprocity

"A Remarkable Trinity"

Benoît Chantre: The discovery of the duel and the escalation to extremes has enabled you to anticipate what is at stake in our discussion: our ability to delay or even prevent catastrophe. Clausewitz himself seems to have been trying to do so. After having described the law of the trend to extremes, he tried to suggest a political definition of war. This is the only way we can make sense of the ending of Chapter 1 of his treatise, which closes with a definition of war as a blend of passions, calculation, and intelligence, "a remarkable trinity."[1] This third and final definition is meant to be a synthesis and complete conception of war. However, we have the feeling that Clausewitz discovered something else along the way.

René Girard: Clausewitz was trying to persuade us that we were still in the era of classical conflicts between states. This is the result he was hoping for as he tried to hide the duel behind a rational definition of war. Thus, the ruler would "control" the strategist, who would in turn "control" public sentiment. Let's not forget that Clausewitz taught at the Military Academy, and that his unusual career, which included service in the Tsar's armies, required him to be prudent. In some ways, his attempt to rationalize resembles the way that primitive societies used to hide their violence behind myth. Ideology has replaced mythology, but the mechanisms are similar. Once he has described the trend to extremes, Clausewitz thus has difficulty convincing

us that politics can still control war. History is accelerating beyond our
control. We have to accept that its course will increasingly escape rational
management.

BC: In section 28 of Chapter 1, Book 1, Clausewitz set out the "result for
the theory" that he had described, and it is in fact a third and final definition
of war, after the "duel" and two types of war ("absolute and real war").[2] The
definition is the "remarkable trinity" that is most apt, according to him, to
shed light on the various forms that war can take, from the "trend to extremes"
to "armed observation":

> War is more than a true chameleon that slightly adapts its character-
> istics to the given case. As a total phenomenon its dominant tendencies
> always make war a remarkable trinity—composed of primordial violence,
> hatred, and enmity, which are to be regarded as a blind natural force; of
> the play of chance and probability within which the creative spirit is free to
> roam; and of its element of subordination, as an instrument of policy, which
> makes it subject to reason alone.
>
> The first of these three aspects mainly concerns the people; the second
> the commander and his army; the third the government. The passions that
> are to be kindled in war must already be inherent in the people; the scope
> which the play of courage and talent will enjoy in the realm of probability
> and chance depends on the particular character of the commander and the
> army; but the political aims are the business of government alone. . . .
>
> Our task therefore is to develop a theory that maintains a balance
> between these three tendencies, like an object suspended between three
> magnets.[3]

The "remarkable trinity" is, along with what Clausewitzians call "the
Formula" ("war is merely the continuation of policy by other means"),[4] a decisive key to his thought. It is as if war were only part of politics. Clausewitz
said that "its grammar, indeed, may be its own; but not its logic."[5] According
to him, it will always be "contained" in both senses of the term. However,
our reading of the text challenges the notion of policy having primacy over
war, and instead promotes the idea of there being only one reality to consider
here: reciprocal action. Clausewitz would like to have us believe that the
clash between two states sometimes takes on a warlike aspect, such as when
it provokes armed conflict, but sometimes a political aspect, such as when
the clash is suspended by backing down to armed observation. We, by contrast, can see that reciprocal action simultaneously provokes and suspends

the escalation to extremes, and that offense and defense are two forms of the escalation, understood as suspended polarity.

RG: To *back down* to armed observation thus means that the one who takes the initiative to back down refuses combat and admits weakness. That vulnerability in fact provokes the conflict that it was supposed to avoid, and the clash will be all the more fearsome because it had been suspended by backing down. We will analyze this phenomenon when we discuss the "strange defeat" of 1940.[6] Clausewitz implied that politics could still silence guns, but it is immediately clear that his text says something else. The manner in which a defensive strategy can delay a clash, keeping it in suspended polarity, is frightening: it is what Hitler did by reacting to the "French offensive" in the Rhineland and then invading France. At this level it was no longer a case of backing down to armed observation, but of going to extremes. The further one adversary withdraws, the more the other, owing to reciprocal action, will tend either to imitate him by also withdrawing or to attack with all the more violence since victory then appears certain.

BC: So, it is as if the duel rendered impossible the synthesis of the components of the "trinity": the people, the strategist and the head of state. The essentially mimetic nature of conflict and its basic reciprocity entail that violence grows unbeknownst to the adversaries. However, we have to keep in mind the two definitions of war as a duel and as a "remarkable trinity," and test them against the facts.

RG: It is true that here Clausewitz gives us two definitions that he intends to be complementary, but that seem contradictory, so we tend to see the second as a "correction" of the first, though the first is still there, in a sense. We thus have to understand the second based on the first. Once reciprocity has appeared, it can no longer be hidden. The ideas about reciprocal action and the trend to extremes are in fact so powerful that they go beyond military frameworks. While Clausewitz talked to us only about war, we would now like to make him speak about society. This will warp his thought in a way, but it will be done consciously. Our desire to do this comes simply from the fact that we are in a world that is more positively violent than his was, and where some of his observations on the military have become observations about the world in general. What he said about warlike reciprocity thus intersects with what mimetic theory has concluded from observing social mechanisms. The clash between two armies is consistent with the logic of human relations that has been described using a comparative approach in anthropology. The logic of reciprocity entails that adversaries increasingly resemble each other: the escalation to extremes is thus an implacable law. Every action entails a reaction, every criminal act leads to revenge, and vengeance is all the worse when its execution has been delayed.

However, human relations are not like the relations between that fireplace and this armchair. In order to understand reciprocity, we have to go from the simultaneity of objects in space to the succession of events in time. We thus go from the first to the second definition of war: a duel is an immediate confrontation between two armies, a combat, a fight to the death; the "remarkable trinity" is control of the duel by the government, and thus the power to suspend the conflict in order *to render it more decisive.* Clausewitz was not a Chinese strategist: he did not want to win without firing a shot. He wants to fight and asserts the primacy of defense. He wants a glorious victory. As we have guessed, he is too mimetic, too full of resentment, to try to avoid a confrontation. *He wants the trend to extremes* much more than he wants aggressive war, which Liddell Hart accused him of wanting, because for Clausewitz the duel is the real description of war. There is thus in Clausewitz's thought a single form of reciprocal action that sometimes accelerates the duel, which leads to combat, and sometimes suspends it, to prepare the way for more decisive combat. You have to be able to attack immediately, "Chinese style," to avoid war. This possibility presented itself to Albert Sarraut in 1936 and to Charles de Gaulle in 1940, as we will see. However, the opportunity was not seized and we need to see why. Personally, I think that the acceleration to extremes makes the preventive attitude utopian. The "remarkable trinity" thus does not place the duel under the control of politics: it sets it in time.

"Reciprocal action" is therefore always functioning, even when combat has not yet occurred: the two adversaries, the attacker and the defender, will become more and more similar as they observe each other, and their "hostile feeling" will grow. If they both withdraw, it will be only to attack each other more fiercely later; if one withdraws, that withdrawal could be a sign for the other to attack. One thing is thus sure: there will be a clash, and it will occur when the lack of differentiation between the two adversaries reaches a point of no return. Reciprocity and the loss of differences are one and the same thing. In *Violence and the Sacred* I suggest that only an exterior point of view that is both inside and outside the community can perceive this resemblance when each, from the inside, thinks there are increasing differences. In primitive societies, the exterior point of view, which is one with the religious point of view, is what in the "sacrificial crisis" produces the convergence of all enemy brothers against a third party considered responsible for the disorder. When rituals, the "brakes" applied to reciprocity, disintegrate, we leave the sequence of peaceful exchange and enter into violent, undifferentiated simultaneity, in other words, we enter into what is proper to the sacrificial realm. What Clausewitz called "reciprocal action," without necessarily seeing the anthropological consequences, is synonymous with the ability that humans have to increasingly imitate one another while at the same time completely misapprehending the fact that they are doing so. Duel, reciprocal action and the escalation to extremes thus end up as equivalent. They correspond precisely to what I call undifferentiation.

War and Exchange

BC: Should we therefore conclude that Clausewitz's concept of reciprocal action (*Wechselwirkung*), which covers *exchange* between people, market trade and bellicose relations, implies an apperception of the duel as the hidden structure of all social phenomena?

RG: I think so. It is the only theoretical intuition that can perceive undifferentiation, which can be described in many ways: simultaneity in action, the trend to extremes at the heart of the alternation of victories and defeats, the reciprocity at the heart of every kind of exchange. Clausewitz's theory of war thus allowed him to think of the duel as a concrete abstraction, an idea that could be made real. The duel is the simultaneity, the face-to-face that remains only potential when military action is suspended or "discontinuous," but that passes into action when military action is "continuous" and tends to extremes. The use of *Wechselwirkung* and its two meanings, "reciprocal action" and "exchange," shows why Clausewitz established an equivalence between war and monetary exchange, and why he saw no real difference between the two activities. In this respect, his thought is a formidable precursor of Marx's: trade would not be a metaphor for war, but would concern *the same reality*.

We are far from Montesquieu, for whom trade is what makes it possible to resolve armed conflict. Clausewitz criticized the French Revolution for its exalted aspect and its disdain for private activity. By contrast, he thought that the Prussians were less interested in trade than in war, but that the two activities were the same. Note that Montesquieu's pacifying vision of trade is still very common among economists today, who often have no idea that money's purpose is to neutralize risk of war. From this point of view, it is not by chance that the European aristocracy went into business once heroes and warriors went out of style. France fell behind England very quickly: Louis

XIV still had imperial goals in Europe when England was already conquering the world much more efficiently. Trade is a formidable form of war, especially since it results in fewer dead. It was for strictly economic reasons that French aristocrats were poor in 1789, and also that England and Germany finally beat Napoleon.

BC: Let's try to get a better understanding of the idea that war and trade are the same thing by looking at the well-known discussion in anthropology of the back-and-forth between the gift and counter-gift. A fundamental presupposition of that form of exchange is suspended reciprocity, for if the gift and counter-gift succeed each other immediately, they can be compared, and then the principle of reciprocity reappears and, with it, war.

RG: Indeed, the gift I receive is never equal to the one I have given: it is worth either more or less, depending on the case. However, no one will notice if the counter-gift does not come right away. If, on the other hand, it comes too soon, it can lead to retaliation owing to what was initially only a misunderstanding, a poor interpretation. One of the individuals will provide an excessive reaction to the presumed hostility of the other, thereby very quickly transforming "good reciprocity" into "bad reciprocity," and concord into discord. Sometimes people even kill each other to get rid of bad reciprocity. This is why the rules of exchange are so complex: their purpose is to dissimulate reciprocity, the "supreme law"[7] of the duel, which will always reappear.

In this respect, money is a crucial discovery: it is a neutral means of exchanging. You bake a baguette, I buy it right away for what we consider to be the market price, and we are no longer bound up with each other. The business is finished. I do not have to give you a counter-gift and we both go home happy. However, Clausewitz is not Montesquieu, as I mentioned before: he understood that even monetary exchanges do not manage to hide the duel. That is not their purpose. Diplomacy may be designed to replace war, but *monetary exchanges are also war*:

> The decision by arms is for all major and minor operations in war what cash payment is in commerce. Regardless how complex the relationship between the two parties, regardless how rarely settlements actually occur, they can never be entirely absent.[8]

Through a commercial metaphor used to define military engagement, Clausewitz sees that there is a sacrificial and warlike dimension to money, and that a "decisive battle" and a "cash payment" are equivalent, though "settlement" is less frequent in war *stricto sensu* and more frequent in trade.

In a way, trade is constant low-intensity war, while war is more or less controlled by politics and most often intermittent. When it becomes continuous, we escalate towards extremes. Trade thus has all the features of war: if smooth settlement of exchanges degenerates into furious competition, a trade war can become a real war. When one nation does not manage to win a contest, it quickly tends to blame its failure on unfair competition. Protectionism is a sign that competition can degenerate into military conflict. Clausewitz was obviously thinking about Napoleon's growing hatred of England: it was for commercial stakes, which was the form the war took with England, that he drenched Europe in blood. In their ferocity, the Napoleonic Wars revealed the violence inherent to commercial competition. Those wars were to trade what the principle of reciprocity is to exchange. Therefore, can trade control war, as many optimistic free marketers think? Perhaps, up to a certain point, so long as we remain within a reasonable form of capitalism.

BC: We therefore have to consider money's *tendency toward neutrality* as an essential discovery in the history of human relations: up to a certain point, money makes it possible to avoid the counter-gift, in other words, to avoid comparison and the return of reciprocity.[9]

RG: But at the same time it does not solve all the problems. The mechanism can jam. Money fetichization is one way it can seize up, by freezing what is meant to circulate among people and is intended to facilitate their inter-relations. What symbolizes the link among people and prevents them from "coming to blows" also has a sacred origin: money replaces the victim on whose head people used to find reconciliation. Lucien Goldmann, who helped me greatly at the beginning of my career, liked to compare the market economy to the world of desire in novels. He was very sensitive to the degeneration of exchange from "qualitative" to "quantitative," in which relations between people and things, and among people themselves were "replaced by a mediatized and degraded relation: the relation with purely quantitative exchange values."[10] However, this presupposes that the exchange was initially "qualitative." I do not share this point of view. We have to say instead that exchange has always been "quantitative," and that this feature has been aggravated by capitalist practices. We exchange goods so as not to exchange blows, but trading goods always contains a memory of trading blows. Exchange, whether commercial or bellicose, is an institution, in other words, a form of protection, a simple means. If the institution is seen as an end, we fall back into violent reciprocity. Our emotional and spiritual lives have the same structure as our economic life. The Fathers of the Church were not so far from Marx when they made money the inferior symbol of the Holy Spirit and spiritual life.

If the monetary flow is stopped and relations interrupted, then there is capitalization. Trade can transform very quickly into war, and today, since traditional war is no longer available as "cash payment," trade can become the trend to extremes. From this point of view, we can reasonably fear a major clash between China and the United States in coming decades. The Chinese are much better at trade and diplomacy than at the arms race. Commercial relations have nothing to do with moral relations: they involve reciprocity regulated by money, which is quite different. It can always degenerate into conflict. Of course, justice can sometimes take over for money, but justice itself can be a fragile institution, and may not be able to control what money has been unable to ward off. Here, we have to make distinctions, refine this intuition by means of a comparison with other types of rituals, and especially bring economists in to work on the issue. Let us suppose for the purposes of our discussion that trade is an institution designed to control violence and that moral relations are of another order since they presuppose forgiveness, in other words, a total gift.

This is why a present is always poisoned (the German word *Gift* means "poison" but also "present") because it does not presuppose monetary neutrality. It brings two people into play, and there is always the potential that they will come to blows. In a way, a gift is always an object that we try to dispose of by exchanging it for something that our neighbor also wants to get rid of. Here we are touching on the ambivalence of the sacred. What makes our life intolerable is expelled, less to poison the life of the other than to make our own tolerable. We get rid of what poisons us like a "hot potato" that is tossed from hand to hand. This is the primitive law of exchange, and it is highly regulated. It is easier to live with the wives of others than with one's own.

As soon as the rhythm of exchange accelerates, reciprocity appears as what it is: consistent with the law of the duel. This is why in primitive societies two parties involved in an exchange suspend "cash payment" for as long as they can. This happens in the most commonplace trades: it is never good to agree too quickly on the purchase of a cow or a house. This is also why justice is slow, and "drags along" in both divorce and the most odious criminal cases. The slowness, which does not seem justified on the surface, is entirely reasonable from an anthropological point of view: it serves as a brake on reprisals, it is a crucial "friction" that slows down relations, thereby preventing them from degenerating into reciprocity. Exchanges must not be seen for what they are, in other words, reciprocal. This is the law that has to be complied with in order to live together. Life is livable only if reciprocity does not appear. Many anthropologists have trouble seeing this, in particular, Lévi-Strauss. They compete with one another to describe the complexity of the differences and social rules, without seeing that the rules are only there to prevent the return of reciprocity.

Clausewitz showed us that reciprocity creates a framework for exchange, and that the laws of war secretly govern all human relations. This awareness is very revealing of crumbling military and commercial institutions that are increasingly impotent to hide the duel. This is why he often began his discussions with the mention of "reciprocal action." By the way, you are aware that the word "reciprocal" is impossible: we do not know what it means. Some definitions give it a cosmic turn: it would refer to the action of the moon on the tide. This has always intrigued me. What if our little everyday wars were in line with natural laws? If they were, then it would suffice for them to go uncontrolled long enough for there to be worldwide consequences. The effects of reciprocity would tend to spread contagiously. It is thus because Clausewitz spoke about reciprocal action right away that Chapter 1 of *On War* is complete. When it returns to long developments on strategy, Clausewitz's book loses the powerful tension that we find in the beginning, which, as we have seen, had implications for the next two centuries. Raymond Aron could not conceive of what we have just described, the imminence of the duel behind contingent history, because that was a threat to his rationalism. However, the timeliness of Clausewitz's treatise unfortunately no longer has anything to do with the Cold War. The "ray of light"[11] provided by the "remarkable trinity" shines differently today. The virtue of great texts is that they survive different interpretations, and always have new things to tell us. We have not finished being surprised.

THE LOGIC OF PROHIBITIONS

BC: Does this mean that you think that Raymond Aron's rationalism was shared by the anthropologists of his time?

RG: Of course. In his writings, the rationalist prejudices of recent anthropology are very clear. It refuses to understand the logic of religion. We mentioned above some of the analyses in *Violence and the Sacred*. I would like to go back to that book, which is the key to my work. We are not going off topic, even though it will require us to travel back in time thousands of years. Recent anthropology has stopped understanding archaic prohibitions because it does not see that they were directed against violence. Instead, anthropologists have leapt into the arms of psychoanalysis to say: prohibitions are the results of the complexes of legislators who are afraid of sex. However, when we look at prohibitions, we see that they are never directed against sexuality in itself, but against the mimetic rivalries of which sexuality is only the object or provides the opportunity. This is very different.

We can thus conclude from this that hominization began when such internal rivalries became strong enough to break animal dominance networks and unleashed contagious vengeance. Humanity was able to *be born and survive at the same time* only because religious prohibitions emerged early enough to counter the danger of self-destruction. But how did the prohibitions emerge? Foundation myths (or myths of origin) are the only things that explain this. In general, they usually begin with a story about a huge crisis symbolized in some way: in the myth of Oedipus it is a plague epidemic, in others it is a drought or flood, or even a cannibal monster that was devouring a city's youth. Behind these themes there is a breakdown of social ties, what Hobbes called the "war of all against all."

What happened? As soon as the agitation "undifferentiated" all members of the society, imitation became stronger than ever, but functioned differently and had different effects. When the group became a crowd, imitation itself tended to reunite it, substitutions occurred, and the violence converged onto increasingly fewer adversaries until it focused on only one. People then discovered the cause of the trouble and they finally rushed as a single body to lynch its now universal enemy. The same mimetic energy that caused growing disorder so long as there were enough rivals to oppose one another finally brought the whole community together against the scapegoat, and thereby caused peace to return.

The result was so sudden and unexpected that the reconciled people saw it as a supernatural gift, and the only one who could have filled the role of the gift giver was the victim of the unanimous lynching: the scapegoat chosen unconsciously by the mimetism of the lynchers. The scapegoat thus re-united the group. This is why many victims are described as "foreign visitors." Primitive communities were probably very isolated from one another, and a visit by a stranger probably caused great curiosity mixed with fear. A single unexpected action by the stranger could cause unpredictable panic and turn the visitor into a new god. Every lynching resulting from a mimetic crisis thus gave birth to a new god. Every time a conflict later erupted in the community, the past crisis would be remembered and all contact with the individuals involved would be prohibited. If violence returned, it would be interpreted as caused by the god's anger. Only the god's prestige thus permitted the appearance of permanent prohibitions that were gradually turned into a system that was more or less consistent and sustainable.

Religious prohibitions surely checked huge escalations of violence. However, the fear they inspire fades, and when that happens their ability to prevent transgressions also fades. Yet the purpose of prohibitions and ritual sacrifices was to calm the god's anger, in other words, to keep violence out of the group. I think that the two great institutions of archaic religion, namely prohibitions and sacrifice, have played an essential role in the passage from pre-human to human societies, precisely by preventing hominids from destroying themselves. Archaic systems must also have been reborn from their ashes from time to time owing to their inability to eliminate violent reciprocity once and for all. We know this thanks to the penetrating intuitions of Greek and Indian religions.

By contrast, what could not be predicted was that two religions radically different from the others would one day put an end to the eternal return of religions. The Biblical and Christian tradition was the first to upset the supremacy of the crowd, to see violent unanimity from the other side, and to pinpoint the principle of reciprocity. Christ, the last prophet, then places humanity before a terrible alternative: either continue to refuse to see that the duel is the underlying structure of all human activities, or escape from that hidden logic by means of a better one, that of love, of positive reciprocity. In this respect, it is striking to see how closely negative and positive reciprocity resemble each other: almost the same form of undifferentiation is involved in both cases, but what is at stake is the salvation of the world. This is the real paradox that we have to try to understand, for from now on it will not be the scapegoat who is judged guilty, but humanity itself, by history. We are thus entering into an eschatological perspective, which is the only one that can shed light on our situation today, and much more light than Clausewitz's "remarkable trinity."

BC: Small archaic societies were always in danger. You have often said that Christianity freed us from our sacrificial crutches, but at the same time it made us responsible for our destiny. Were not the "crutches" that we lost the only way to meet the danger? In other words, is not one of the consequences of Christian revelation that we no longer *believe* in catastrophe,[12] even though it is scientifically predictable?

RG: Quite right. In a way, our progressism has come from Christianity but betrays it. More precisely, it could only have issued from a watering down of the apocalyptic feeling. I am convinced that it is because Christians have gradually lost the sense of eschatology that they have ceased to influence the course of events. It was probably beginning with Hiroshima that the idea of the apocalypse completely disappeared from the Christian mind: Western Christians, French Catholics in particular, stopped talking about the apocalypse just when the abstract became real, when reality began to match the concept.

You mentioned Bergson's profound comment on the way the abstract so easily becomes concrete. I think that it has become possible to see catastrophe as banal because of our very rationalism, for example, that of Raymond Aron, who saw "total war" as only a concept. I have been wondering about this refusal to take reality into account for over 40 years. It resembles Lévi-Strauss's basic disinterest in rites and sacrifices, and his desire to study only myths and what he called "the savage mind." These constructions are beautiful, but very fragile. As soon as I feel that a myth is hiding something, that there is a skeleton in the closet, my ears prick up and I am on the alert.

In this respect, I would go so far as to say that rationalism, the refusal to see the imminence of catastrophe (which is something archaic societies saw very clearly indeed), is our way of continuing to fend off reality. As Péguy said, we are "the coarsest and most superficial of mythologists."[13] This is why Hegelian dialectic does not work for me: I find it too rationalist and not tragic enough. It flies through conflict without ruffling its feathers. Like Clausewitz, I smack into the law of the duel, and I stop there.

THE END OF RULES

BC: Many people criticize you for that, and say you focus too much on violence.

RG: They do not want to see what is going on around us. We therefore have to complete what Clausewitz only glimpsed before he sought refuge behind a differentiated conception of conflict, which presupposes an inter-state framework that no longer functions in conflicts today. "Cash payment" and hand-to-hand fighting are things of the past, or at least they are not the same as they were. We have entered the era of technological war, "surgical strikes" and "zero deaths," which are the new forms of the duel. We could reverse the proposition and say that asymmetrical wars are built on a new conception of security, and that it is out of the refusal to see casualties that we have rejected the "cash payment" and "decisive action" that Clausewitz saw as the ultimate truth of war. It is not that I am sorry to see this conception go, but at least it did not entail closing our eyes. A striking example of the blindness is the quagmire in Iraq that the Americans will be able to escape only in a catastrophic manner, with the resulting stream of dead bodies and unending succession of murders. The loss of the rules of war leaves us facing the terrible alternative between attacking and defending, aggression and response to aggression, which are one and the same thing. Clausewitz was well aware that the adversarial principle would be increasingly powerless to control growing hostility. The primacy of victory, raised to the status of a rule, becomes overarching, and in the background there is deep disdain for the adversary, who finally has to be *slaughtered*. This attitude authorizes us to flout all the rules of honor.

When Clausewitz spoke of "exterminating the enemy," he was prophetic without realizing it. Of course he always insists on the idea that victory lies in defeating the opposing army or even in overthrowing the enemy state, but the ideological wars that he predicted, in which politics tries to keep up with war, proved to be terrible crusades that resulted in the massacre of entire populations. Carl Schmitt saw this when he spoke of a "theologization"[14] of war in which the enemy becomes an Evil that has to be eradicated. His efforts to establish a legal framework for war were directly related to this observation. In order to prevent violence from spreading madly, there have to be legal limits. Carl Schmitt thus thought that the legal construction of designated enemies would represent progress. This is the thesis of a certain right-wing politics. It leads to a theory of a "state of exception" that many are calling for today, given the growing threats. This is the strength but also the limitation of this line of thought. It is true that it points out the danger of pacifism: to outlaw war is paradoxically to allow it to spread everywhere. Pacifism fans the fires of warmongering. However, Carl Schmitt's legal voluntarism has proven vain because the aftermath of World War II has shown that the escalation to extremes has been relentless. His cause is lost. Indeed, such voluntarism is in contradiction with Schmitt's commitment to Nazism, and was thus a rear-guard position.

BC: Yet he nonetheless had a strong intuition that modern war is situated between two catastrophes: on one side religious wars, and on the other the era of technology of total destruction.[15] He thus considered it urgent to structure the conflict and to rethink the laws of war at a time when the institution was at risk of disappearing. We cannot deny that Schmitt tried to analyze the duel. In *The Theory of the Partisan*,[16] he showed that the partisan is the link between the warrior and the terrorist, between an adversarial relation and hostility. As strange as it may seem, Schmitt was against those who praise war. He seems to have wanted to resist a course of events that he hoped was not inevitable.

RG: Schmitt is in fact persuasive in his genealogy of terrorism. Through his analysis of how Napoleon got bogged down in Spain, he saw clearly that the partisan was the first "to wage irregular war against the first regular army."[17] War began to be waged by partisans at exactly the same time as Napoleon was imposing changes on the armies of earlier times. The French Revolution was thus such a huge event that some of its consequences are still being played out in the escalation to extremes, of which Clausewitz was one of the first great military analysts. Thus, terrorism would have its roots in the Revolutionary Wars, of which Napoleon's "regular" army was the ultimate transformation. "Irregular" war was a contemporary of "regular" war, and they strengthen each other mutually so as to finally become equivalent. In this respect, the Russian partisans' response to the Grande Armée's invasion came in the wake of the Spanish partisans' response, but with greater violence. Perhaps we have had to wait for the symbolic catastrophe of September 11 and the Americans' "response" in Iraq for the equivalence of "regular" and "irregular" wars to finally become clear. This is the real structure of reciprocity, which is all the more terrible when the response is postponed. We are witnessing a fundamental breakdown in the law of exchange.

We have to think in Clausewitzian terms about what the introduction of terrorism means today. In the end, it is an escalation of total war in the sense of Hitler and Stalin. It means a war in which there is no longer a legitimate army, but only Russian partisans ready to do anything. The Germans have never had a resistance like that of the Russians, which attacked Hitler's armies from behind. Carl Schmitt is thus an essential link in the description of the terrorist as beyond the partisan. If we compare the roles of partisans in the two world wars, we can see a geometrical increase in weaponry and all the other aspects described by Schmitt. He was thus a lucid analyst of the "victory of the civilian over the soldier," and of the shift from conventional war to "real" war. His description of the partisan ensures the passage from war to terrorism. A "theory of the partisan" thus became in his mind a theory of modern war. However, he believed that this intermediary status could be governed legally. He thought that the partisan was the symbol of a new legal-political framework that put an end to classical law and urgently called for a new legal definition of "friend" and "enemy."

He believed that we needed to make sure the collapse of nation-states *would not be accompanied by* the end of codified war, or else the apocalypse would be hastened.

In this, Schmitt misunderstood the conditions of modern war. He did not see what was at stake in nuclear deterrence, for example. Everything that worked on that principle has, since 1945, operated like a kind of agreement between mafia families rather than like something ruled by law. In other words, nothing has been legalized; nothing has gone through the United Nations. In order for deterrence to work, there had to be no meddling, so it was a kind of mafia system. Schmitt saw this major problem with respect to the *end of wars,* and he tried to resolve it as a jurist. This is exactly like the doctor who believes too much in medicine. War cannot be treated like an epidemic. Of course, Schmitt was right to think that the fact of not *choosing* between war and peace leads to incurable growth in potential violence, yet he nonetheless underestimated the role of unbridled technology. He did not see that democratic, suicidal terrorism would prevent any *containment* of war. Suicide attacks are from this point of view a monstrous inversion of primitive sacrifices: instead of killing victims to save others, terrorists kill themselves to kill others. It is more than ever a world turned upside down.

The next step will consist in acquiring dirty bombs containing nuclear waste. It even seems that American technicians are working for terrorists without knowing it, and now building pocket-sized atomic bombs. We have indeed entered into an era of ubiquitous, unpredictable hostility in which the adversaries despise and seek to annihilate each other. Bush and Bin Laden, the Palestinians and the Israelis, the Russians and the Chechnyans, the Indians and the Pakistanis: the conflicts are all the same. The fact that we speak of "rogue states" proves how far we have left behind the codification of inter-state war. Under the guise of maintaining international security, the Bush administration has done as it pleased in Afghanistan, as the Russians did in Chechnya. In return, there are Islamist attacks everywhere.

The ignominy of Guantanamo, the inhumane American camp for presumed terrorists who are suspected of having ties with Al Qaeda, demonstrates the contempt for the laws of war. Classical war, which included respect for the rights of prisoners, no longer exists. It remained to some extent in the conflicts of the twentieth century, when war still resembled a kind of contract. The fact that it persisted even at the heart of the clashes in the last century shows that the laws of war date from very long ago, from feudal times and a very old aristocracy. It was made into a system in the sixteenth and seventeenth centuries. In this respect, Carl Schmitt was an heir of Grotius and Pufendorf. The loss of the law of war is a clear sign that the West is getting entangled in its contradictions.

BC: For Schmitt, the absolute threat was thus less the end of *the* world than the end of *a* world governed by the laws of war. In a way, we could thus say that there are fewer wars today than before. We could even say that there are no wars at all, since the institution is dead and has been replaced by unpredictable outbreaks of violence. You emphasize the apocalyptic aspect of this situation, but could we not instead see these outbreaks as the repercussions of violence?

RG: That kind of reasoning is possible. The twilight of war could result in the worst, as it could in the best. There is no destiny involved because humans are entirely able to renounce their violence. Ancient India had a capacity for renunciation that the West does not imagine. There is an implacable Hindu view on this precisely because that culture does not fear to acknowledge that human activity essentially comes under the category of war. The *Iliad* is nothing next to the *Mahābhārata*. This is not a question of believing in catastrophe at all cost or of comparing the number of dead today with that of yesterday in order to bring the seriousness of our time into perspective. We have to understand that the *unpredictability of violence* is what is new: political rationality, the latest form of ancient rituals, has failed. We have entered a world of pure reciprocity, the one of which Clausewitz glimpsed the warlike face, but which could also show the opposite countenance.

The fact that we no longer confront a clearly demarcated enemy makes it no less improbable that a battle will result in positive reciprocity and a world order as Napoleon was seeking, though he was not devoid of cynicism. We are not in the "war of all against all," but in a time of all or nothing. Thus, Schmitt provides a profound rereading of an aspect of Clausewitz that we cannot reject. It involves seeing strategy as a means of serving politics. However, it is a little like the idea of establishing a social contract when everyone is fighting. The social contract is obviously false because it is when it is needed that it cannot be made. Schmitt's failure, his apology for the "sovereign decision" that decides between war and peace, proves once again the reality of what Clausewitz *also* glimpsed: that war has acquired an autonomy that politics will be able to control less and less, unless it goes one up and becomes totalitarian. Wars became "ideological" and "total," but now they are entering their twilight. How can we go back? I fear that political science will be of no help here.

We continue to think about the acceleration of contemporary conflicts as if they followed the same rules of logic as they did in the past. People still use the rationalist reading of Clausewitz, with its refusal to see the imminence of the duel. Today we are heading toward a form of war so radical that it is impossible to talk about it without making it sound hyper-tragic or hyper-comical, so unlimited that it can no longer be taken seriously. Bush is a caricature of the warmongering violence of which Americans are capable outside of the framework of any political reason, and Bin Laden and his imitators respond in an equally "sovereign" manner. I have to admit that I feel powerless to describe the new form of conflict, of which even Schmitt probably did not see the radical nature. Who are the new kamikazes who will soon have miniaturized nuclear weapons in their hands, and who, in compliance with the principle of pure reciprocity, will use them without any rules, reviving ancient divisions and inventing new ones? It is clear that "total war" involving all citizen-soldiers in the defense of the threatened nation, which Clausewitz and later military theorists who had read his work (including what Carl Schmitt himself called partisan war) said leads straight to terrorism, to this barbarian escalation, is unrelated to war because it escapes all ritualization.

Of course, terrorist attacks may be particularly cruel, but they are limited. Yet should we conclude from this that the trend to extremes is petering out? I do not think so. It is very clear that firepower has taken the place of politics. Heidegger is very perceptive when he describes the "enframing" of the world by technology as a necessity beyond human control.[18] There is a perfect example of the powerlessness of politics: the Cuban missile crisis. The Russians did not back down for political reasons, only for technological reasons, because they knew that they would lose an atomic war. That is all there was to it.

I knew someone who was close to the Kennedy administration. He told me that the crisis was terrible. Those close to Kennedy were not warmongers like those close to Bush, and for them the situation was horribly frightening. The Cold War really culminated in the Cuban missile crisis; after that the USSR declined. This is therefore a case in which technological threat was just as important as the effectiveness of war, and in fact replaced the latter. However, seeing technology as the destiny of Western metaphysics is too abstract a definition of what we are experiencing. Hegel and especially Clausewitz have made it possible for us to gain a more concrete vision of the engine of history. We have seen the master-slave dialectic radicalized by the escalation to extremes. We have thus placed ourselves back at the heart of violence.

A Return to the Simple Life?

BC: While the Hegelian *Aufhebung*, which is supposed to go beyond the necessary contradiction and the reconciliation of all humanity, seems to overlook
the truth about violence as it is revealed in Napoleon's actions, Clausewitz
insists on the reality of the duel, the fight to the death. It is as if we had to go
through it…

RG:… in order to think about the Kingdom. Yes, this would be the
paradox, but our analysis needs more clear-cut oppositions. We have to read
and reread Clausewitz to see that reconciliation is never permanent. There is
always the risk of the escalation to extremes.

BC: This is one of the paradoxes revealed in Clausewitz's correspondence
with his wife, Maria von Brühl. Let's read a passage, quoted by Raymond
Aron, that some of Clausewitz's biographers have tried to see as a private
confession and expression of religious sentiments shared with his wife. It was
written in 1807, when Clausewitz was a prisoner in France after the defeat
at Jena. (It was a comfortable exile because he had time to visit the Louvre
and write often and at length to the one he loved.) The passage concerns his
reluctance to blame providence or destiny:

> I realize that we, discerning nothing, or at least little of the totality of its
> plan, have no right to incriminate it. Yet it is clearly because our heart will
> never turn aside from the generations we see carrying faithfully the burden
> of life over the centuries, to find peace in faith, that our reason itself cannot
> completely detach itself from this earth and turn towards heaven. Moreover,
> it falls neither to our heart nor our reason to do it. Our view of the world
> must not be distracted by religion; it is a heavenly power which allies with
> all that is noble here below, and I, for my part, have never been spurred to
> some good deed and without feeling the desire, even the hope, of carrying
> out a great one. This, in my view, justifies my inability to take my eyes off
> the earth and secular history, and reconciles the feelings of my heart with
> the conclusions of my feeble mind.[19]

RG: I did not remember that letter, but I find it very interesting.
Raymond Aron was right to quote it: Clausewitz's confessions are rare. We
can see clearly in this passage how difficult he found it to get over the duel,
to switch to a different order, as Pascal might have said. No matter how powerful its injunctions are, religion must not distract the soldier from revenge,
but rather serve revenge. We can sense that the "good deed" encouraged by

heaven could have been only Prussia's return to dominance. Clausewitz's "religious feeling" tied him ever more tightly to what he called "secular history." Action always takes precedence over speculation. In his thought, there is a theory of war, but not a philosophy of war. Conceptualizing the duel should entail trying to control it, but Clausewitz sought to serve it. This is what I see in this letter, in which he is supposed to be talking about his "religious feelings." Thus he could not have helped us explain what is beyond the duel and that I call "good transcendence," though he told us a lot about bad transcendence. Clausewitz's god is the "god of war." We will therefore have to integrate Clausewitz's thought into an implacable dialectic, and move on to a new type of rationality. Aron will no longer be able to guide or contradict us.

BC: What about Levinas' thought? His great work, *Totality and Infinity*,[20] was published in 1961, the same year as *Deceit, Desire, and the Novel*.

RG: Why not? I remember meeting him in the 1970s. He clearly wanted to discuss ideas with me, but I was intimidated and declined, as I often do. It will thus be your job to bring him in at the right time. *A priori*, it is a good idea: we will need his critique of Hegel. I have read less of his work than that of other contemporary philosophers, such as Sartre and Heidegger. It will be interesting to try to understand what distinguishes him from both Hegel and a certain type of phenomenology.

BC: We will need him especially to deal with the duel and to escape reciprocity, which is what we are trying to do right now, and to think about the relationship with the Other, which is an essentially *irreversible* relationship.

RG: However, we will also have to rescue Levinas from the apology of difference to which his thought has so quickly been reduced. I will always bet on *identity against difference*. Do not forget that I am remaining on a strictly anthropological level, *on which every action calls for a response*. The "relation to the Other" is all very well, but I see it as a front for a whole theory of humanitarianism that I reject, as you know. Humanitarianism is just a dried up form of humanism. Of course I think that in Levinas' work there is a strong theory of the discontinuous and changes of orders or levels, but I want to think about the continuous. This is why we have to leave behind the difference between war and peace, and try to understand the mysterious kinship between violence and reconciliation, negative and positive undifferentiation, the mimetic crisis and what Christians enigmatically call the "mystical body." It is impossible to go from one to the other except through a transformation internal to mimetism. The worst is not necessarily a sure thing, but we have to keep in mind the other possibility: that of the destruction of the whole world, since humanity now has the means to do so.

BC: It seems that to understand this movement, this internal change, we have to examine the duel and try to describe it, which is what Clausewitz does his best to avoid. To think about the duel would be to think about *violence and reconciliation at the same time,* and thereby go from one form of reciprocity to the other, from one *identity* to the other.

RG: In descriptions of extreme duels, of which there are many in medieval literature, you always find a hint of a kind of love, passion. This is the contradiction that is so difficult to describe. It is said that analyzing mimetic mechanisms is obsessive, but no one admits that the obstinacy comes from the fact that people *do not want to read,* except through the prisms of infinitely more opaque systems. Apologetics, especially when apocalyptic, has no purpose other than to open the eyes of those who do not want to see, and what we do not want to see is precisely that *reconciliation is the flip side of violence,* the possibility that violence does not want to see. People do not want to be told that they are not autonomous, that others are acting through them. Indeed, they want to hear it less and less, and are therefore more and more violent. Christ caused a scandal because he said this and revealed to humanity that *the Kingdom is approaching at the same time that humanity's madness is growing.* Michel Serres once told me that I was not far from what Bergson called the "law of twofold frenzy," and that I should go in that direction. I have never taken the time to explore that intuition.

BC: We have only to reread the text. It is at the end of *Two Sources of Morality and Religion.* In it, Bergson developed two complementary laws for thinking about history: the "law of dichotomy" and the "law of twofold frenzy." [21] These are the two paths taken by a single tendency, and each is taken to its extreme. We can quote a few passages from the last part of Bergson's book, which are consistent with what you have just said:

> It is difficult not to wonder whether the simple tendency would not have done better to grow without dividing in two. . . . There would have been, then, no risk of stumbling into absurdity; there would have been an insurance against disaster. Yes, but this would not have given the maximum of creation, in quantity and quality. It is necessary to keep on to the bitter end in one direction, to find out what it will yield: when we can go no further, we turn back, with all we have acquired, to set off in the direction from which we had turned aside. Doubtless, looking from the outside at these comings and goings, we see only the antagonism of the two

tendencies, the futile attempt of the one to thwart the other, the ultimate defeat of the second and the revenge of the first: man loves the dramatic: he is strongly inclined to pick out from a whole more or less extended period of history those characteristics which make of it a struggle between two parties, two societies or two principles, each of them in turn coming off victorious. But the struggle is here only the superficial aspect of an advance. . . . that signifies oscillation and progress, progress by oscillation. And we should expect, after the ever-increasing complexity of life, a return to simplicity. . . . But the simplification and complication of life do indeed follow from a "dichotomy," are indeed apt to develop into "double frenzy," in fact have all that is required to alternate periodically. . . . The truth is that it is generally for the sake of our luxuries that we want our comforts, because the comforts we lack look to us like luxuries, *and because we want to imitate and equal those people who can afford them.* In the beginning was vanity. . . . But that true, complete, active mysticism *aspires to radiate,* by virtue of the charity which is its essence, is none the less certain.[22]

RG: Bergson was indeed talking about the crux of what we are trying to explore. First, because he went beyond the master-slave dialectic, and indeed the passage you quoted could be seen as containing a criticism of that dialectic. Next, because he glimpsed the duality of the two principles and the two types of mimetism that they entail: mimetism of luxury and contagion of charity. However, he refused to think of that dualism as a conflict or duel. In contrast, I agree with Pascal that truth is essentially at war with violence. Christ brought war, much more than a "return to the simple life." When Bergson mentioned the overall peaceful back-and-forth of these two trends, each of which goes to its extreme before passing the baton to the other, I felt like I was hearing a form of Hegelianism. To say that "the struggle is here only the superficial aspect of an advance" is, as we know, to return to the Hegelian dialectic, which is false in that it relativizes the duel and does not see that it always implies a risk of the escalation to extremes. To "thwart" the progress of the escalation to extremes is perhaps a "futile attempt," but not in the way that Bergson says. On the contrary, it is vain in the sense that there may no longer be any way to resist that course of events. This is exactly what I was saying earlier, when I doubted that the escalation to extremes could come to an end some day. Reality is thus very different, and much more tragic. I am not saying that we should give up trying to resist, but I would have preferred it if Bergson had thought of a "return to simplicity" as an essential opposition to the escalation to extremes. He did not. The rejection of the crisis, even by a consistent empiricist, is once again a form of idealism.

Yet Bergson has a much less abstract conception of religion than Hegel. He touches on things that I think are essential, but the absence of the tragic bothers me. Bergson did not go so far as to think of the advent of the worst, but of a "frenzied" situation that, once finished, would naturally lead to another one. History would "oscillate" like a pendulum. This is not eschatological enough for my taste. The rationality that he promoted still contains a means of being protected against catastrophe. So it is not surprising that when war was declared in 1914, the abstract became concrete without his realizing it. I guess that Bergson was not sufficiently forewarned.

Péguy was quite different in that he *felt catastrophe coming*. You have persuaded me that he was not as much of a warmonger as I thought. Indeed, he could not have been a warmonger and defended Dreyfus as he did, unless he was the right kind of a warmonger: one who "fights for the truth." Perhaps fighting to defend a scapegoat gave him this taste for reality. I do not think that Bergson got involved in the Dreyfus affair. Yet there was a great deal of barbarity in that typically Clausewitzian situation, in which the high command replaced politics with impunity, and the army dictated to the government. The Dreyfusards resisted. They did not believe that the conviction was a sure thing, that it was part of a necessary chain of events that had to pursue its own course to the end, and that the Captain would be rehabilitated in time. Since I am apocalyptic, I reject any belief in providentialism. We have to fight to the end, even when we think it is "vain."

Coming back to mimetic theory, I would say that it tries, in a way, to describe the worst. No offense to Bergson, but I am like the rest of humanity and I like drama. In this respect, I find Clausewitz powerfully dramatic. He delved into the foundations of modern history in a much more concrete manner than Hegel. He had mud on his boots, of course, but he touched on things that are much more interesting than what we find in *The Phenomenology of Mind*. Note that I am not trying to oppose Bergson's spiritualist optimism with a form of apocalyptic pessimism. I am trying to remain as close to reality as possible, and am only observing that, more than 70 years after *Two Sources of Morality and Religion,* we have not returned to the "simple life" that Bergson predicted. The "taste for luxury" has grown and now it is leading the whole planet into its frenzy. The simple life is a long way from returning. Thus, I see in the "law of twofold frenzy" a new way of postponing, when in fact we should see our catastrophe as imminent. Only consciousness of imminence can turn our mimetic behavior into responsible action. This takes nothing away from the power of Bergson's concepts, from the brilliant opposition of the "static" and "dynamic," of "morals of pressure" and "morals of aspiration." Such ideas signal the introduction into philosophy of anthropological data, and I can only approve. Yet, in contradiction to Bergson's serenity, I think that the worst is beginning to happen, and so I am trying to describe it as closely as possible. Clausewitz helps me in this—up to a certain point, as we will see.

CHAPTER 4

The Duel and the Sacred

<hr/>

THE TWO AGES OF WAR

Benoît Chantre: Our discussion about Clausewitz sheds new light on another precept in the Gospels: "Love your enemies." Once we have acknowledged that the Kingdom program has not been realized, this precept no longer means "make your enemies into friends," which becomes the implicit rule of pacifism, but "respect rules of honor if you have to fight." This is quite different. We can therefore see the distinction between a principle of adversariality and one of hostility. Hostility seeks to triumph over the opponent. By contrast, adversariality presupposes an honorable fight. Clearly, Clausewitz leans towards the former, and is drawn to the duel understood as a fight to the death. This is precisely why Charles Péguy, whom you have quoted, tried to define a different conception of the duel in the years before World War I, by playing Corneille off against Clausewitz. He writes that, in the Corneillian duel, it is not the victory that counts, but the fight. In a way, we have to know how to restrain war in order to consider reconciliation.

In July 1914, just before leaving for the front, Péguy wrote in his *Note on Descartes and Cartesian Philosophy* concerning "chivalry's system of thought, notably that of French chivalry":

War is often spoken of as an immense duel, a duel between peoples, and conversely a duel is often spoken of as a war that has so to speak been reduced and schematized, a war between individuals. War is spoken of as a large-scale duel, and duel as a small-scale war. This is full of confusion. Many significant historical obscurities would perhaps be cleared up and many difficulties resolved if we would only distinguish between two types of war that may have nothing in common. I would not even say that the old struggle for survival is divided into two types, one for honor and the other for power. . . . There is a species of war that is a struggle for honor, and a completely different species that is a fight for domination. The former originates in the duel. It is the duel. The latter is not and does not have the same origin. It is even everything that is most foreign to the duel, to codification, and to honor. However, it is not at all foreign to heroism.[1]

This passage is relevant because Péguy came to the same conclusions as we do, first when he distinguished two opposing notions of war, and second because he defined two forms of heroism: one oriented towards the "grandiose" nature of the escalation to extremes, and another that tries to control that outbreak of violence and to neutralize war. The former fails to describe the duel; the latter conceives of it in a radical way. The critique of Clausewitz is obvious here: there is nothing less "Prussian" than the primacy of battle over victory. It is impossible to go from violence to reconciliation without passing through this intermediary stage. Yet a question remains that Péguy was unable to answer: can we fight without hatred in the context of modern war?

René Girard: History has unfortunately proven since Péguy's time that we can plan genocides quite calmly. From the massacre of the Armenians, to the horrors of the Shoah and Cambodia, and the crimes in Rwanda, whole peoples have been coldly murdered, sometimes even with bureaucratic zeal. "Hostile intention" proves even more effective when it does not need "hostile feeling": in this, Clausewitz's warrior patriotism was different from totalitarian coldness, a veritable pathology of national interest.[2] However, he is unconsciously headed in that direction since he did not want to see the terrible consequences of the law of the duel, which is a mimetic law that leads to escalation.

Clausewitz hides behind praise for the warrior's strength because he is afraid of the duel; he wanted to preserve appearances at any cost and so tried save political rationality by giving it the leading role. The difference between the two forms of heroism is thus essential because it explains two periods of war: the age of adversariality and the age of hostility. Understood as an escalation to extremes, all codes of war implode in the duel, leading to the era in which we live today, that of unpredictable worldwide violence. I think that Péguy's comments are superb and that you have brought them up at the right time, but I fear that they do not at all describe the conflict that was emerging in 1912.

Péguy was describing an undeniable form of heroism, and you have identified the stakes involved. If we stayed on the intellectual plane, Péguy would certainly win, for he really thought about the duel, which, despite appearances, Clausewitz did not do. Moreover, he thought about it in a more convincing way than Carl Schmitt did, for he looked at it on the moral level and not just from the legal point of view. The quote you have provided shows that he conceived his own, different idea of the duel: clearly, he has Clausewitz in his sights. He even says that Clausewitz contradicts himself. Yet it seems that Péguy has forgotten that Clausewitz was first a prime witness, the observer of a new context for violence. He described the reality of a historical trend with much more acuity, I believe. Bergson and Péguy are profound metaphysicians, who dare to think of an alternative, something beyond war, a good transcendence. Clausewitz, by contrast, describes what I call "bad transcendence." We thus have to investigate that "god of war" he saw rising behind the person of Napoleon.

BC: The two ages of war could provide a means of sketching out a paradoxical law that is both similar to and different from Bergson's "double frenzy." On one hand, we would have the escalation to extremes, and on the other a return to origins, a "tracing back" of history as Péguy said, towards what you call the founding murder. The two movements would be linked: the closer we get to the end, the further back we go. The more history tends towards the worst, the less we will be able to hide the need for a clear discussion of archaic religion.

RG: Exactly. It is now time for that discussion. This is why mimetic theory does nothing but analyze archaic religion. It does so from the prophetic tradition and Christian revelation. In St. Paul's terms, only a "second Adam" can stand up to the first. It is now clear that the further we progress in history, the further we regress back to that Alpha point. Historical Christianity and what we are obliged to call its "failure" are nothing but the accelerated bridging of the beginning and end of time. So it is no longer simply reciprocity that we have to study, but the sacred to which it leads, a sacred that has been deprived of value owing to Jewish and Christian actions, but that has become all the more formidable for that reason. This corrupted sacred is one with violence, in other words, one with the founding murder. Remember what Pascal said:

> The knot of our condition takes its twists and turns in this abyss, so that man is more unintelligible without this mystery than this mystery is unintelligible to man.[3]

The Passion reveals mechanisms of victimization: it is coiled up in the "twists and turns" of original sin and reveals them to the light of day. Christ thus imposes a terrible alternative: either follow him by renouncing violence, or accelerate the end of time. In both cases, he places us face to face with original sin and forces us to look into the "abyss." What does this mean if not that Christianity has archaic religion as its only horizon? This is the apocalyptic truth that no one wants to see. As you suggest, Péguy feels that such "tracing back" goes against the tide of history. He has a heroic intuition of this because he is seeking to slow down this irresistible trend. However, history has shown that heroism cannot restrain the escalation to extremes. Pascal saw it all immediately. Yet the brilliance of the *Pensées* fails to describe history and its formidable capacity for regression. It is up to us to draw out the apocalyptic conclusions of what Pascal glimpsed: *the truth of the original sin appears only in relation to the growing resentment to which it gives rise.* Nonetheless, we cannot deny that Pascal is close to this truth at the end of the twelfth Provincial Letter:

> It is a strange and tedious war when violence attempts to vanquish truth. All the efforts of violence cannot weaken truth, and only serve to give it fresh vigor. All the lights of truth cannot arrest violence, and only serve to exasperate it.[4]

Here, Pascal was clearly describing a manifestation of truth that would be contemporary with the escalation to extremes. Note that he no longer said "war," but "violence." This is already apocalyptic thought.

A WARLIKE RELIGION

BC: The *reciprocal* intensification of violence and truth gives us a better understanding of the "law of twofold frenzy." We have perhaps arrived at the moment of a possible inversion of the first trend, to the "end of time" that would make violence coincide with its truth. Pascal suggests that this could reconcile humans, but could also be at the expense of the whole world.

RG: This would be the result of the true escalation to extremes that Clausewitz only glimpsed. Here we find a much more essential reciprocity, a ruthless fight between violence and truth. Truth is in a defensive position, in the Clausewitzian sense. It is thus the one that wants war. Violence reacts to truth, and it is thus the one that wants peace. Yet it knows very well that it will never have peace again because its mechanisms have been revealed. This is the true and only duel that runs through all of human history, to the point that we cannot say which opponent will win. Only an act of faith enables Pascal to say that "violence has only a certain course to run, limited by the appointment of Heaven."[5] But will truth triumph in this world? Nothing could be less certain.

In this sense Clausewitz is a good antidote to progressivism. *Completing* what he only glimpsed means rediscovering what is most profound in Christianity. Aside from his Dreyfusard commitment, what is important about Péguy is that he tried to think about the duel otherwise than as a fight to the death. Indeed, thinking about it as a fight to the death is precisely to not think about it. The inability to think about violent reciprocity is specifically what intrigues me about Clausewitz. Clearly, it involves a form of religious regression and a kind of return of the archaic that we have to study. As we have seen, Clausewitz closes the door as soon as he opens it. In a way, the opening in Book 1 dominates the whole book, but at the same time we have stopped on the threshold and not entered its implications.

What does he tell us? The war he described was Napoleonic war, which is *grosso modo* the one a commander would prefer if he wants victory. However, something much worse is contained in the reality of reciprocal action. We can thus suggest that, on one hand, Clausewitz is a man of the Enlightenment and that, on the other hand, at the level of his deep thought, he is not. I tend to think that the reason why he could not finish his book, and was constantly rewriting it until his death is because of that: he could not bridge the gap between his rationalist side and the intuition that he did not completely describe, but that haunts him. If you describe the intuition in too much detail, you might go too far. Or perhaps it cannot be thought about directly and is *for that very reason* interesting. This is the mystery in his book, and perhaps also its hidden profundity.

We looked at a letter by Clausewitz to Maria von Brühl in which he mentions his "religious feeling," and we have seen how hard he had to work to get away from the duel. It is not a question of age. I do not agree with Aron that there is a difference between a romantic Clausewitz and the mature writer. He was much too mimetic and patriotic. That kind of passion is difficult to abandon. I also see that, like Péguy, you are thinking of *Polyeucte* by Corneille and the transformation of the hero into a saint. I admire that kind of inspiration. Yet is it our world? I fear not. In fact, I do not like heroism very much. Thus I would not look to it for the passage from violence to reconciliation, but in a choice offered to humanity once and for all: it is less a passage than an alternative. The overturning of idols and what Claudel spitefully called Polyeucte's "imbecilic rodomontades" also scare me a little. It is like Clausewitz upside down: still too violent for me.

It is not Enlightenment reason but *religious rationality* that I would like to call upon to understand the oscillation that is always possible between one form of undifferentiation and the other. These intuitions have been around throughout Christianity, but they were not eschatological enough for me. Only religious rationality can enable us to understand what I have grasped through study of the forms of archaic religion, namely, that a victim who has been made into a devil is thereafter made a god. This transmutation is in no way rational, in the sense of Enlightenment rationality, but it is not superstition either. The same logic prevails in what we are trying to think about now. It forces us to change how we reason.

Naturally, I doubt that Clausewitz felt the call of the Kingdom of God or a need to transcend his hatred of Napoleon. I am even not far from thinking that *it was that hatred that makes him write,* makes him theorize. Let him keep it. Without it, he would not have the mysterious intuitions that run under the surface of the text. It is a little like what we see in Dostoevsky and Proust. These are the kinds of ideas that interest me, the ones that are never completely formulated because the individual is caught in an escalation to extremes in which he participates, as if there were always revenge to be had on someone or something. We cannot escape mimetism; we always participate in it in some way, and those who acknowledge it interest me more than those who try to dissimulate it.

I became aware of this obvious point only gradually. I long tried to think of Christianity as in a higher position, but I have had to give up on that. I am now persuaded that *we have to think from inside mimetism.* Thus, Clausewitz should be read attentively. He was filled with something over which he had no control and that he forces us to think about. So, I am lying in wait. It is very interesting that he hesitated, as if he thought a prohibition applied to him with respect to the duel. We should not say that at the end of his life he had finished only the first chapter of his treatise and that all the rest would have been rewritten if he had lived longer. It should be pointed out that Chapter 1 is more profound and more mysterious because it is the only one that speaks of human relations in general. The others, in contrast, are more limited, and more closely resemble what one might imagine before reading *On War.*

Since he presupposed that Clausewitz had rational control, Aron's thoughts on this point are completely unrealistic. That kind of abstraction and detachment from reality is completely unheard of. It smacks of a bottled-up politician or an intellectual who thinks like a politician, which is the same thing. Imagine for a minute what would have happened in the Cuba crisis if Khrushchev had had a little too much to drink. When you think about what power is and all the chance circumstances that lead up to major decisions! Pascal again: "Cleopatra's nose, had it been shorter."⁶ One such happenstance too many, and war breaks out. How could it be possible to contest the madness of war? This is what Aron called the *break* between Chapter 1 and the rest of the treatise. He also could not envisage a match between real war and the concept of war: he thought that there was an unbridgeable divide there also. Aron wants to be an optimist because he wants to remain on the political plane and, being closed to religious conceptions, his thought had limitations. Thus, I would not define Clausewitz as a kind of schizophrenic, but as a deep thinker who rapidly abandons his first, most brilliant, intuition, yet allowed it to color his whole book. We will have to content ourselves with that, and return to completing Clausewitz.

BC: The essential issue is thus heroism.

RG: It is true that Clausewitz seems to have quickly dropped his initial line of thought, and then to have concentrated on a typology of the "warrior genius." We should spend some time looking at this paradox. Why did Clausewitz, who glimpsed the principles of reciprocal action and the escalation to extremes, in other words, the apocalyptic course of history, prohibit himself from taking that brilliant line of thought to its logical conclusion; why did he instead fall back on a form of individual heroism? It would be a kind of renunciation if the duel were not always implicitly there. What is not made explicit, but is often the real engine of a theory, is what Nietzsche called *ressentiment.* I take this intuition a little further by saying that resentment, according to its mimetic definition, produces *misapprehension,* in other words, the sacred.

We thus have to try to see how much Clausewitz's resentment of France, incarnated in the fascinating personage of Napoleon (the "god of war"), produced a depreciated sacred that functioned all the more effectively because it was not conscious. Clausewitz would like his "remarkable trinity" to be a more complete concept of the phenomenon of war and able to subsume all forms of war. He does not say what kind of commander or what type of government we would be dealing with in this trinity. Later, we learn that it is Frederick II, in other words, Frederick the Great, Voltaire's friend, who was both head of state and war leader. However, the example of Napoleon was always in the background, undermining that model. Clausewitz tries to convince us that he was still speaking of Frederick the Great, but holes appear everywhere in his pretence.

BC: The "remarkable trinity" is a complex definition that is designed to provide a way out of the duel. Are you suggesting that its very name shows that it is impossible to analyze?

RG: Indeed, why speak of a "trinity?" The choice of religious vocabulary should have caught the eye of his commentators, especially Raymond Aron. This is proof, if any were needed, that warrior heroism is related to violent religion. Around the same time, Joseph de Maistre wrote, "War is thus divine,"[7] expressing a much deeper premonition about the supernatural character of the escalation to extremes. With Clausewitz we are therefore at the crucial point in the establishment of a warrior ideology, a sort of mythology gone off its hinges. This heroic aspect escaped me at first because I was concentrating on the mimetic features that we have identified. But now we can see that what Clausewitz called "military genius," the topic of Chapter 3 of Book 1, seems to perform a threefold synthesis of emotions, calculation and wisdom, and incarnates a kind of resistance to the mimetic principle that eliminates everything. The genius is a *temporary* brake on the principle of undifferentiation.

BC: This resistance to the mimetic principle is temporary because it takes place in the framework of the polarity as we have defined it, in other words, with a view to a definitive victory: at some point, the mimetic principle will be resolved as it always is, since there will be no combatants left.

RG: The point is always to win, to come out on top, even if that requires experiencing all the ups and downs and interactions of real war. To my mind, resistance to the mimetic principle means that the military genius is independent and does not easily yield to surrounding influences. Clausewitz says that he must not be "phlegmatic," "sensitive" or "easily inflamed,"[8] but "wise." The military hero belongs to the class of

> those who do not react to minor matters, who will be moved only very gradually, not suddenly, but whose emotions attain great strength and dura-bility. These are the men whose passions are strong, deep, and concealed.[9]

Here, we can of course see the commonplaces of the anthropology of the time. Kant is probably there again. However, what is important is to see that understanding situations, the "coup d'oeil"[10] and "tact" in the midst of "endless minor obstacles,"[11] is all in service to the duel, the decisive battle that is the only one that counts. This explains the *continuity* that can be felt in this absolutely determined character. Clausewitz wants to fight; everything converges on hand-to-hand combat. He is drawn more to Napoleon than to Frederick the Great, and he cannot help himself: the "god of war" underlies the text. In order to make the right decision, in other words, the most triumphant, the military genius, who incarnates the synthesis of passion, calculation, determination and political reason, must nonetheless battle chance and necessity, and the harshest aspects of real life.

Look at the incredible conclusion of Book 1, in which Clausewitz wrote about "friction." We should almost quote both pages; they are so modern with respect to the attention to concrete, practical detail. Previous treatises never focused on such facts. In the seventeenth century, no one spoke of the misery of war, which provided the obsessive theme of Jacques Calot's engravings. This taste for the concrete is clearly linked to the advent of democracy, but also to the involvement of the general populace in the military:

> We have identified danger, physical exertion, intelligence, and friction as the elements that coalesce to form the atmosphere of war, and turn it into a medium that impedes activity. In their restrictive effects they can be grouped into a single concept of general friction. Is there any lubricant that will reduce this abrasion? Only one, and a commander and his army will not always have it readily available: combat experience. Habit hardens the body for great exertions, strengthens the heart in great peril, and fortifies judgment against first impressions. Habit breeds that priceless quality, calm, which, passing from hussar to rifleman up to the general himself, will lighten the commander's task.[12]

Use of mechanical imagery to describe a group of humans, poorly greased, poorly oiled, was rare at the time. Note also the concern to know the source of the lubricant: this is even more striking. When we look at the "friction," we see that Clausewitz is concerned with integrating all extremes of human life into his theory, including the nastiest things, lice, and diseases. We find him obsessed with waterlogged terrain, marching under extreme conditions. In the end, he is telling us that a war can be lost because of such "details," for insignificant reasons. To be a great military genius is to fight against such chance conditions, to deal with all sorts of ordeals at once. I did not notice this aspect at first. Chapter 1 of Book 1 is completely mimetic in its conception, but Chapter 8 seems not to be at all. There is a clear contrast. At the end of Book 1, we have the rise of the hero, a gradual way out of mimetism, since it concerns a unique, rare individual: the great commander. Clausewitz is probably thinking of Napoleon and the shoeless soldiers in the Italian campaign. The emperor's glory and genius were such that the troops forgot all that. This is certainly a mystique of war.

BC: Yet Clausewitz thought it was important to note that the hero's "rise" above all the contingent circumstances is not guaranteed:

> The ardor of his spirit must rekindle the flame of purpose in all others; his inward fire must revive their hope. Only to the extent that he can do this will he retain his hold on his men and keep control. Once that hold is lost, once his own courage can no longer revive the courage of his men, the mass will drag him down to the brutish world where danger is shirked and shame is unknown. Such are the burdens in battle that the commander's courage and strength of will must overcome if he hopes to achieve outstanding success.[13]

This passage proves the point to which military heroism makes it possible to "achieve outstanding success," in other words, for Clausewitz, wars of overthrow. The alternative is clear: either "outstanding success" or the vilest animality. What distinguishes humans from animals is their ability to conduct "great" military operations. How could this not be frightening.

RG: Indeed, here we see the beginnings of a kind of military superman, but we should not be unfair to Clausewitz or judge him too quickly, and retrospectively, for what happened later. His views were always paradoxical and full of tension. That is why he speaks of a "military genius" rather than a hero, which perhaps has too many theatrical connotations. A military genius is one who *knows how to respond,* and who is thus immersed in mimetism, but at the same time able to channel the unpredictable, contagious currents that result in panic or obedience. A military genius is not alone; he is always in the midst of others, in the world of the reciprocity of war. This makes Clausewitz deeper and more disturbing, in fact, more "modern," than Nietzsche.

PRUSSIAN RESENTMENT

BC: This military superhumanity that you highlight is that of Prussia, which at the time could view itself only in terms of its conflict with France. Elsewhere,

Clausewitz describes the French as an essentially military people. That his view of history would be so far behind the times is striking. Could it be that Frederick II's admiration of Voltaire's country was *turning* into envious hatred?

RG: Let us pause for a moment on the issue of Clausewitz's lack of clear thinking, and look at it using quotations gleaned by Raymond Aron. That blindness is the only thing that can help us to understand the source of the heroic model, which is one with what has to be called a religion of war. Here, a psychological inquiry could be decisive, as it is every time resentment is at issue.

Clausewitz died on November 16, 1831, just after he was appointed Chief of Staff by Gneisenau, who was responsible for suppressing the Polish insurrections in the east. Clausewitz, who has been head of the Military Academy since 1818, thought that he would finally be able to apply his theories. He thus feverishly continues making campaign plans against France, which he feared would re-militarize again after the 1830 July Revolution. It is understandable that this frightened him because, if taken seriously, the destruction of Prussia would have really been the destruction of *the* anti-French force. Clausewitz was well aware that the Austrian Empire was declining. It was not yet the world Musil describes in *The Man without Qualities,* but almost. For him, Prussia was thus the last rampart against French hegemony. France's return would be the end of the world.

Clausewitz died quickly, in only a few hours. Was it really due to cholera? "According to the statement of the doctor, his death was due more to the state of his nerves, shaken by a deep pain in his soul, than to the illness."[14]

His wife's description, appended to the last letters Clausewitz sent to her and in which he mentioned his "melancholy," seems to corroborate the doctor's observations:

> At least his last moments were peaceful without suffering, though yet there was something anguished in the expression and the sound of his last gasps. It was as if he had decided to reject the burden of life which had become too heavy for him. Soon his features were peaceful and composed. Yet an hour later, when I saw him for the last time, his countenance was again tormented, marked by a terrible suffering.[15]

Here I think that we have a very intimate picture of Clausewitz's resentment, exacerbated in the last months of his life by his dread of the French Revolution and his contempt for Poland. Yet Clausewitz was at the heart of the army that would soon be the most powerful in the world. He is thus the victim of a cliché. I am thinking of course of the way Tolstoy portrayed it in *War and Peace*. The characters in Dostoevsky's novels are also similar. Clausewitz regretted that the Congress of Vienna had not reduced France's territory and had only removed its conquests. He had an almost pathological fear that France would again disturb the balance in Europe, *once again lay claim to an empire* through a new revolution. The imperial issue is crucial. All those countries were clashing furiously to achieve supremacy in Europe. This explains not only France's and Prussia's hatred of Austria, a relic of the Holy Roman Empire, but also Clausewitz's formation of a certain picture of France when he criticized the Congress of Vienna's moderation in 1815:

> But what is the result of this moderation? It is that France, though defeated and disarmed, will never cease to have at her disposal the means which guarantee her *autonomy and independence.*[16]

His obsession with the French threat and his fear that France, which he both admired and hated, would one day regain its "autonomy" and "independence" are perfectly consistent with what I call underground psychology in my books. The subject demands autonomy only because he thinks that the model he has chosen is autonomous or could become so. This kind of clinging to a false difference, when the emergence of the duel announces a rise in undifferentiation, is consistent with Clausewitz's concomitant attempt to rewrite his treatise in a less warlike and apparently more political manner.

In fact, Clausewitz would have liked to reduce France in size, just as pieces of Poland were parceled out after each new conflict. It seems obvious that the same violence tormented him in his last moments. The "military genius" ideal sprang from that envious passion, but it is a model that Clausewitz does not fully comprehend, just as the "remarkable trinity" does not keep the duel in check, but strengthens its import. What is tragic in his work lies entirely in the resentment that is stronger than all attempts at rationalization. Clausewitz, like all Prussians of his day, sees France as the most military nation in Europe. He knows that Frederick II imitated France, wrote poems in French and was entirely fascinated by Paris, even and especially from a military point of view. However, he also knows that France, like any model that is venerated to excess, looks down on Prussia.

Voltaire's example is essential to understanding Prussian resentment. Who remembers that Voltaire ran off to Paris with Frederick the Great's poems in order to make him a laughingstock in Europe? The King soon realized it, and sent his men after the writer. When they finally stopped him in the Prussian provinces of Rhineland, the whole party was searched. In the end, the King's verses were found and Voltaire was allowed to leave for Europe, but without the poems. Frederick II was no fool. In fact, Voltaire first quarreled with Maupertuis, the President of the Austrian Academy at Potsdam. It was a terrible altercation between intellectuals, in which Voltaire forced Frederick II to take his side so that his whole system of "French culture" would not be destroyed. Then Voltaire takes off with the King's poems in his pocket. Clausewitz certainly knew about this. He also must have heard about the description of Westphalia in *Candide*. It was terribly cruel especially when you recall it was the French victory that had impoverished Westphalia after the Thirty Years' War. In *Candide,* at the house of Cunégonde's father, there are a few geese, but pork is served every day, which is why Westphalia is the best of all possible worlds. This is all tragic because the French-German hatred, which found an outlet for a time in Austria, finally exhausted Europe and brought it where it is today. Who speaks German in France? Who speaks French in Germany? Undifferentiation has been replaced by indifference.

It is clear that one of the basic mistakes of French politics was to play the Prussian card against Vienna at certain decisive points, in other words, always against the Empire because it was the old enemy and France also wanted to be imperial. An old French reflex: when things are going badly, declare war on Austria. The Austrians boasted of a sort of ontological superiority over France: they *were* the Empire. The Seven Years' War followed, and it was catastrophic. That conflict, in which France remained allied with Prussia for such a long time and which fostered Frederick II's rise as much as possible, was real madness. In order to have an army and be able to meet the challenge, Frederick II had to make a huge effort. For him, it meant playing with the big boys. He spent phenomenal amounts of money to have an army equivalent to that of the Austrians and French. Indeed, Napoleon did not destroy that colossal army: the French Campaign is striking proof of that. It was still to some extent "gentlemen's war," and it was less the army that had to be vanquished than the general.

Yet it was because Frederick had almost succeeded that the battles of Jena and Auerstedt were such terrible shocks. Voltaire's irony proves that in France people did not really believe in Prussia. Its ambitions were not taken seriously, and this was a big mistake. However, it was threatened in a way that the Empire could not be, for the Prussians were, at bottom, a nation that had been formed very recently. This is crucial to understanding Clausewitz and the effort he made to continue building a Prussian ideal while at the same time hiding as best he could, in other words, poorly, the mimetic principle that drove his thinking. German unity was built around Prussia, but first it had to beat Austria at Sadowa in 1866. France strengthened Prussia's militarism. Both Bismarck and Napoleon made Austria lick their boots, and the German Empire was proclaimed in the Hall of Mirrors at Versailles. The mimetic circle was closed.

BC: This detour was necessary to understand Clausewitz's singular role in the emergence of Prussia and then of Germany as great military powers. France, the former model, became an obstacle with Napoleon, the "monster" who synthesized in his own person the Ancien Régime and the Revolution. For Clausewitz and the Prussian officers, Prussia's *military* identity was redefined in opposition to Napoleon, and the same soon happened with that of Germany as a whole under Bismarck and Wilhelm II.

RG: Everything was ready for a new national identity to emerge. The stage was set for the humiliation of the Treaty of Versailles in 1918, and then Germany's *response* to France, which would annihilate Europe. It is understandable that Péguy wanted to play *Polyeucte* against *On War*. It was a lucid reading of the theoretical presuppositions of many Germans, and also of a certain type of military culture (for we have to admit that Clemenceau, a sincere Dreyfusard, was not Ludendorff). However, that combat was nonetheless behind the times, *given the facts*. When Péguy talks about the duel, he speaks as a philosopher and writer. He would have liked to be able to resist "modern" war, which was tending, as at the time of the Dreyfus Affair, toward total contempt for politics. Yet he was also caught in the French-German "knot," in its "twists and turns": Corneillian adversariality would not be worth much in the face of German hostility. Finally, death prevented Péguy from seeing the confrontation between two equally brutal enemies at Verdun. The escalation to extremes smashes all codes and destroys all military rituals. There is then mimetic contamination of one "warlike race" by the other. This is undeniable.

BC: The "remarkable trinity" is the most complete concept of war in Clausewitz's work and entails the control of the people by the commander and the commander by the government, such that it becomes crystallized in the "military genius." Do you think that the trinity increases rather than controls violence?

RG: That is not what Clausewitz says, but it is what his theory entails. He thus succeeds and fails at the same time. On one hand, he suggested an almost perfect conception of all the forms of war at the time, but, on the other hand, the concept was a fortuitous combination that was unable to *make sense of or encompass* the duel. The expressions "military genius," "strength of character" and "military leader" were consistent with the new conditions of war, in which violence alone had become autonomous. Clausewitz's terminology was intended to be realistic and grandiose, the complete opposite of Corneillian heroism, which can always turn into sainthood. This means that it was no longer possible to get around the duel and use Christian morality to combat that more modern, and thus more sinister, force. Clausewitz's letter to Maria von Brühl shows this clearly. It becomes even more unthinkable after Verdun.

However, I appreciate the fact that you have pointed this out. It is true that there will always be heroic figures and that Péguy's commitment will remain a model. There are other examples from the French Resistance. Clausewitz's definition of military genius was understood "in the French style" by generations of professors and students at the Military Academy: Joffre and Foch were nothing like Ludendorff. Corneille still inspired them. General de Gaulle always saw himself like that, and his son said he was capable of great passion but could at the same time control it completely. There is unquestionably a military culture specific to France, and it was incarnated one last time in de Gaulle's actions before the defeat in Indochina and deadlock in Algeria. At that point, the Cold War completely changed the balance of power and we were gradually led into increasingly asymmetrical conflicts and "surgical" wars, which are the mimetic doubles of the terrorist carnage we experience today. It seems that military culture is dead in the West, though not in the East. Note how the elimination of compulsory military service has gone unnoticed among us.

The Military Genius and the Superman

BC: Could we not simply say that history is no longer being written in terms of battles, as was seen by the historians of the Annales School?

RG: Yes if you like, but because at the time we could still speak of "battles" and violence still produced meaning. That stopped long ago, and its sterility is now obvious: this is the law of the escalation to extremes. People have literally unleashed violence, and Clausewitz was present at a decisive point when the shackles were broken. He saw violence rising under the increasingly meaningless surface of events. The "military genius" is alone at the end of Book 1: he is floating on the surface of the swamp. However, there is a good reason why Clausewitz did not call him a "hero." All of this is much more common-place and at the same time much more archaic. This is the paradox. Moments of enthusiasm never erase the memory of periods of friction. What he wrote about becoming accustomed to war is quite striking. Everyone benefits from it and it is an experience that is useful at all levels, for even the smallest commands can be difficult. Liddell Hart must have been struck by Clausewitz's praise for the *totality* of war.

> In war the experienced soldier reacts rather in the same way as the human eye does in the dark: the pupil expands to admit what little light there is, discerning objects by degrees, and finally seeing them distinctly. By contrast, the novice is plunged into deepest night.[17]

War is a terrible darkness, but once one has become used to it, it becomes indispensable. Clausewitz has a dark and shadowy side that is quite surprising. However, he did not glorify war; instead he intellectualized it to the maximum. His text is as far as it could be from Jünger's *Storm of Steel,* for example. Yet war is a human experience that affects everyone, from the simple soldier to the commander. It is an exceptional experience in that it is an incomparable human ordeal. For Clausewitz, there was nothing greater, and so his point of view was aristocratic. It seems to me that an aristocrat is essentially a war leader.

BC: He who is not afraid of confronting the enemy face to face?

RG: Or of leading others after him. What is rather significant in Clausewitz's thought is his insistence on the fact that everything is decided in battle. The result is not known until the end, through tactics. This is the "remarkable trinity" that we must constantly consider: politics and the governor, strategy and the commander, and the people. In the end, "the Imperial Guard entered the furnace,"[18] and Hugo chooses all or nothing, complete victory or total defeat. Once again, only the duel, in other words, literally, hand-to-hand combat, is decisive. After successive skirmishes, the truth of war lies in the "decisive battle." Everything tends toward the duel. Clausewitz did not in any way promote wars of maneuver or tactics of deception. He even criticized most of his predecessors for favoring an extremely watered down version of war. He thus disprized what Liddell Hart called the "indirect approach," for example, undermining the adversary's morale.

Liddell Hart, who had seen a century more of military escalation, had good reasons for saying that combat should be avoided. The primacy of tactics over politics no longer makes any sense today. For Liddell Hart, a battle was at best the consequence of a very good maneuver, but for Clausewitz, the exact opposite was true. For him, peace is to war what strategy is to tactics, and what a firefight is to hand-to-hand combat. The "decision" becomes clearer each time, as if you were adjusting the focus on a camera. In a way, in relation to strategy, politics is nothing but talk. However, strategy is in turn only discourse in relationship to tactics. Within tactics, fighting with firearms is always less decisive than hand-to-hand combat. We are thus nearing the heart of violence, which is murder. There is a truth about violence, and that truth is unveiled in the primacy of combat. It cannot be denied that there is something very important in this. It is the absolute of rivalry.

Faced with such realism about violence, we have to admit that honorable combat is only an intellectual point of view, even when it is meant in its noble, Pascalian sense. While I am struck by the acuity of some of Clausewitz's observations, I immediately reject the consequences. Nothing should be expected of violence, unless, like Pascal, we see it as *resistance to truth*. This is the Christian position. What you have called "the reciprocal intensification of violence and truth" is a definition that competes with the trend to extremes, and the only one we can use in opposition to Clausewitz. The apocalyptic truth is precisely what Clausewitz rejects, after having glimpsed it. He sees no difference between violence and truth. In this, he is the most anti-Pascalian thinker there could be.

What does he tell us but that the "strange and tedious war"[19] is inevitably lost? For him, the truth of war is that violence is truth. Moreover, war is the truth of politics, and within war, tactics are the truth of strategy. In other words, we are always going towards the duel. Everything becomes clear, and converges on this central point, this unique intuition. All this is terrible. It is brilliant because it is absolutely opposed to Christian love. It really is "violence and the sacred." I never imagined that one day I would read analyses that would be so consistent with my own. I would even say that they make them absolute because Christianity made them relative. Clausewitz could have seen war as a game, even an extraordinarily dangerous one. Instead, he saw it as an absolute. He never came out and said it so baldly, but he constantly suggested it.

For example, look at the end of the last chapter of Book 1. Clausewitz speaks of those "experienced officers" that a "state that has been at peace for many years" has every interest in consulting by drawing them away from their "theaters of war" so that they can pass their expertise on to soldiers who are inexperienced or who have been softened by peace.[20] What does that mean other than that such officers inoculated against the mêlée of battle are able to model an effective relation to war, in other words, proper access to something sacred because they are still in contact with it, still have one foot in the holy of holies? "However few such officers may be in proportion to an army, their influence can be very real."[21] They are inoculated with the *sacred*. For Clausewitz, becoming accustomed to war is an initiation experience. War is the only field in which craft and mysticism are completely united at the most crucial points.

We have to understand "combat-readiness"[22] in the strong sense of a process in which the initiate comes into proper contact with the truths of war and violence. At the same time, in the military, physical training is closely intertwined with moral training. Clausewitz sees these two things as completely connected. Bad experiences are thus part of becoming accustomed to battle, and the worst are often the most important: this is a rule of initiation. He describes first coming under fire[23] in an impressive manner; we can hear the projectiles crashing around us. Then he tells us that half an hour later it is all over, there is no more hesitation, we have crossed the line, we have survived the ordeal. Clausewitz may not have found war beautiful, but he still had a passion for it, a feeling that violence is really the sacred, even though it may be an inferior form of the sacred. I wonder whether he does not regress further into the archaic, in a more extraordinary manner, than anyone else.

BC: From his point of view, only animals flee battle, and humans become human only in war.

RG: What would such an intuition mean except that it is war that makes the man? History constantly shows this. Clausewitz clearly glimpsed this fundamental aspect of violence. Just as comparison of archaic societies leads to the conclusion that humanity springs from sacrifice, Clausewitz observes that man returns to sacrifice, in a way, but for reasons he considers essential. He is not thinking about Christianity at all. The military superman is finally nothing more than an attempt to regenerate, to *correct* humanity to prevent it from falling back into the "brutish world."[24]

BC: In this sense, we cannot deny that Clausewitz anticipates what would happen in the future. Totalitarianism soon emerged as a powerful form of nihilism, an impulse to take decadence to the furthest extreme so that, out of that dissolution, a superior form of humanity would emerge.

RG: Indeed, by resorting to force, humanity would obtain an identity that was *more real*. Note that in the nineteenth century all of Germany became caught up in that feeling. Nietzsche himself, whose genius was incomparable, felt this. In aphorism 125 of *The Gay Science,* he believes that new gods will appear. Listen to the man with the lantern who "seeks God"; he expresses this perfectly:

> What were we doing when we unchained this earth from its sun? Whither is it moving now? Whither are we moving? Away from all suns? Are we not plunging continually? Backward, sideward, forward, in all directions? Is there still any up or down? ... What festivals of atonement, what sacred games shall we have to invent? *Is not the greatness of this deed too great for us?* Must we ourselves not become gods simply to appear worthy of it? There has never been a greater deed, and whoever is born after us—for the sake of this deed he will belong to a higher history than all history hitherto![25]

The "greatness" of the deed that is "too great for us" obviously reminds us of Clausewitz's trend to extremes. We have to be gods to be worthy of the "divine" decomposition. Nietzsche was party to our modern situation when he wrote this aphorism. Though it was 50 years after Clausewitz, he takes his cue from him when he describes the virility and courage of the superman. However, what was strictly military in Clausewitz's case took on metaphysical aspects in Nietzsche's, who clearly had powerful intuitions about archaic religion. This is proof, if such were needed, that this intuition keeps pace with the escalation to extremes. Nietzsche sees the mechanism of the founding murder where Clausewitz only has the feeling that humiliated Prussia could be reborn. Moreover, Nietzsche sees that there is something in Christianity that is radically opposed to this hope for rebirth. Initially, he was thinking about the death of the Christian God, but along the way *that death becomes a murder* owing to the true, hidden Passion of Christ that produces a veritable return of the repressed:

> God is dead. God remains dead. And we have killed him. How shall we comfort ourselves, the murderers of all murderers? What was holiest and mightiest of all that the world has yet owned has bled to death under our knives: who will wipe this blood off us?[26]

The first death of God does not lead to the restoration of the sacred and ritual order, but to a decomposition of meaning so radical and irremediable that an abyss opens beneath the feet of modern man. In the aphorism, we have the impression that the abyss finally closes when the second announcement begins, this time on the order of the superman and Zarathustra: "What festivals of atonement, what sacred games shall we have to invent? *Is not the*

greatness of this deed too great for us? Must we ourselves not become gods simply to appear worthy of it?" The aphorism affirms the eternal return, but it
reveals the engine of that return: the collective murder of arbitrary victims.
It goes too far in the revelation and destroys its own foundations. Owing to
the very fact that it bases the eternal return on collective murder, its true
foundation, violence, which should remain hidden in order to be a foundation, is undermined and secretly sabotaged by the very thing that it believes
it is triumphing over: Christianity. Nietzsche's entire tragedy is *to have seen
but to have not wished to understand* the undermining performed by the Bible.
Violence no longer has any meaning. Yet Nietzsche tried to reinvest it with
meaning by betting on Dionysus. In this there is a terrible tragedy, a desire for
the Absolute from which Nietzsche was not able to extricate himself.

We have discussed the underground passion that motivated Clausewitz.
However, he did not sink into despair *because there was the army,* that aristocratic model, that outlet that Nietzsche was lacking. Nietzsche was totally
involved in what was supposed to be the creation of values, a re-invented
aristocracy—which was in reality the abyss of a will to power. Clausewitz
is much cooler. Without really thinking about it consciously, he glimpsed
the corrupted sacred that remains in violence and war, and he made that
sacred into something transcendent, *an ideal to be achieved.* What he seemed
to secretly desire was everything that frightens the tiny archaic societies and
that they try to ward off through prohibitions. However, such societies are
very fragile; they are not powerfully armed nations. This is why any form of
encouragement of heroism seems to be either behind the times or dangerous. In the latter case, what is in question is less heroism than the "military
genius" or "god of war," in other words, something both very new and very
primitive.

THE ENEMY FACING ME

BC: Levinas was not far from what we are trying to describe. In *Totality and
Infinity,* he wrote that war is a means of escaping the totality that enslaves
parts to the whole, individuals to the group, existences to essence. He went so
far as to write that "war is produced as the pure experience of pure being."[27]
He thus took to their extremes the Hegelian analyses of war as renunciation
of selfish interests. However, a fight to the death is no longer a sacrifice of
individual interests to the general good. It is the first stage of an exit from the
state-legal totality, which is to be accomplished fully in the relationship to the

Other. Levinas therefore gave love the eminent role that is its due. War is no longer man's essence. Man escapes that reductionist essence in his relationship to the Other, who is already the *living* enemy facing him:

> Only beings capable of war can rise to peace. ... In war, beings refuse to belong to a totality, refuse community, refuse law. ... They affirm themselves as transcending the totality, each identifying itself not by its place in the whole, but by its *self.*[28]

It is as if we had to go through the ordeal of the real to escape Hegel and his divinization of the state. It is in the confrontation with otherness that the individual acquires self-consciousness. The self has no meaning except in the relationship, *even when the relationship takes the form of a duel.* Can we not say, following Levinas, that only experience of war can allow us to think about reconciliation?

RG: It would literally be a trial by fire. You are reacting to what we have just found in Clausewitz, which frightens us. What I understand from your quote is that once again humanity is born from war. Indeed, you have introduced Levinas at precisely the right time to help us conceptualize the duel. From this perspective, heroism would be the test for freedom. We are not so far from Clausewitzian "initiation." Levinas was not a warmonger and he clearly did not believe in regeneration through war, but there is a criticism of pacifism in his position. He *finished Hegel,* just as we are trying finish Clausewitz. He took a trend in philosophy to its logical conclusion, just as we are doing with a trend in anthropology. Beyond war, Levinas thought about a relationship to the Other that would be purified of all reciprocity. Beyond undifferentiation and its implacable structure, we are trying to imagine the Kingdom. Levinas' text is frightening if we read it as an apology for war. Yet it is instructive if we read it as an exploration of transcendence in the etymological sense of the term, in other words, an *escape* from totality. Levinas attacked the state and totalitarianism. Hegelianism was clearly in his sights.

BC: Levinas concluded that all ontology is warlike in the sense that it sacrifices the individual to the city, the part to the whole. We therefore have to get away from the ontology whose essence is revealed by war. Ethical relations, the original relationships that envelope the duel itself, are what makes it possible to escape from totality.

RG: I am rather in agreement with this approach. Through Hegel, Levinas went beyond an entire philosophical tradition. However, I think that my theory is both close to and yet different from what I understand by this. I wrote that in the history of Western thought, Plato represents less

a forgetting of being than a deliberate dissimulation of the violence that
he saw at work in imitation. Imitation frightened him, and he had a very
clear understanding of its relationship with religion, in other words, with
violence. He would have liked to perpetuate repression of that knowledge.
For example, look at the fate he reserved for poets, those dangerous imitators. However, refusing to see imitation also means depriving oneself of the
only means of escaping the primacy of the whole over the individual. With
Aristotle it is already too late in a way: *mimesis* had already become peaceful,
and would remain so until Gabriel Tarde. Which is to say that the falsehood
has simply grown. It is in this sense that we can say that ontology is warlike:
it wants peace, not war; order, not disorder; myth, not revelation of the
violent origins of myth.

Revelation of the falsehood specific to totality requires the duel and thus
reciprocal action. There is violence in the revelation. It is proportional to
how much we do not want to see mimetism and the play of false differences.
Clausewitz is one stage in the late, apocalyptic emergence of awareness of
this. That a philosopher like Levinas should be interested in violence as a
"pure experience" can therefore only spark my interest. By taking Hegelian
thought to a more radical level, he revealed its weaknesses. This brings about
a troubling yet healthy return of what Hegelianism had repressed. According
to what you have said, Levinas saw the duel, like love, as an escape from
totality that we absolutely need. However, it is in the sense that it *explodes*
totality.

BC: Indeed, this contains a deep eschatology: turning towards the Other
also means destroying totality *through the duel*. Did Christ say anything different when he said he brought war and peace?

RG: No. He let the cat out of the bag by revealing the essence of totality. He thus placed totality in a frenzy because its secret was revealed to the
light of day. This would be the ordeal of war: the revelation of the essentially
violent nature of all ontology. However, what Levinas did not seem to see is
the mimetic nature of rivalry, which is at the heart of violence. Yet the "pure
experience of pure being" is perhaps a necessity. In that respect, we cannot
refuse to think about war, or to engage in it if circumstances require. Thus,
if I understand what you have said, it is a way of expelling Corneillian honor
and heroism.

BC: When Levinas wrote that the process of escaping totality also has to
be thought of as a passage from the sacred to the saintly, from reciprocity to
relationships (in other words, religion), he was at the crux of our discussion
of the transformation of heroism into saintliness.

RG: So long as there is no return into Hegelian error. There is no possible passage to reconciliation. That Promethean hope has been cast away forever. Our apocalyptic rationality forces us to be somewhat brutal. With Christ, a Model of sainthood became a part of human history once and for all, and superseded the model of the hero. Trying to reconstruct a heroic model can lead only to the worst, as we see with Clausewitz.

However, the passage by Levinas gives us a glimpse of something. A theory about the Other puts totality into a panic because it reveals its warlike essence. By affirming that the duel is already the relationship to the Other, it shows that the relationship sits at the heart of violent reciprocity. In the same way, we could say that it is because he has survived the duel with Tiresias that Sophocles' Oedipus goes with Antigone towards the sainthood of *Oedipus at Colonus*. Oedipus says nothing; he is dazed. Instead, he lets the people around him speak. The sacrificial victim has put a wrench in to the works of the sacrificial mechanism. Though expelled from the city, he is not banished to the outer darkness. This was the time of Greek cosmopolitanism, which freed the city. This is the price of sainthood.

Levinas was perhaps touching on the mysterious similarity between violence and reconciliation that we were speaking of earlier. However, this is on the condition of pointing out that love does violence to totality, and shatters the Powers and Principalities. In my mind, totality is actually myth, but also the regulated system of exchange, everything that hides reciprocity. "Escaping totality" thus means two things for me: either regressing into the chaos of undifferentiated violence or taking a leap into the harmonious community of "others as others." It means that each must stop being a simple link in a chain, a part of a whole, a soldier in an army. We can feel that Levinas was trying to go beyond the Same, beyond the ontology that makes individuals interchangeable, to find the Other. Going beyond the Same would require first a theory of the duel. In a way, I can also love the person whom I am fighting. The law of war codified the special relationship between adversaries. The consideration due to prisoners was for a long time tangible proof of this, though we know that time has now passed.

BC: You are saying that the truth about combat, and the truth about violence is undifferentiation. In order to identify a real difference, or to make identity itself a difference, we thus have to pass through undifferentiation. This puts us on dangerous footing. Péguy wrote that, faced with the "hatred that binds us together more deeply than love ... we need an immense dialectic to only begin to recognize ourselves in it."[29]

RG: At that point, Péguy must have thought he was on to something absolutely essential. I am linked with the other through mimetism, the growing resemblance between us which finally engulfs us. We are in the Same, to use Levinas' vocabulary. War is indeed the law of being.

BC: It is because adversaries do not want to see their growing resemblance that they embark on a escalation to extremes. They will fight to the death so as not to see that they are similar, and thus they will achieve the peace of the graveyard. However, if they recognize that they are similar, if they *identify themselves* with each other, the veil of the Same will fall and reveal the Other, the vulnerability of his face. I can lower my guard before the otherness of the person I am facing. Confrontation is not inevitable.

RG: What you are calling *identification* would be resistance to imitation, a rediscovered distance. You are being very optimistic. Lowering your guard before the sudden epiphany of the face of the other supposes that you can resist the irresistible attraction of the "same" that the "other" incarnated only a few instants before. It supposes that we both become "others" at the same time. This process is possible, but *it is not under our control*. We are immersed in mimetism. Some are lucky enough to have had good models and to have been educated in the possibility of taking distance. Others have had the bad luck to have had poor models. We do not have the power to decide; the models make the decisions for us. One can be destroyed by one's model: imitation is always what makes us fail in identification. It is as if there was fatalism in our violent proximity to the other.

The event you are suggesting is thus rare, and presupposes an education based on solid, transcendent models, what I call external mediation. We should keep in mind that it also corresponds to a period of war that is now obsolete. Given the increase in undifferentiation at the planetary level and our entrance into an era of internal mediation, I have reasons to doubt that this paradigm can be generalized. The escalation to extremes is an irreversible law. It is because we are irresistibly drawn to one another that we can no longer go from war to reconciliation. Of course, brotherhood would consist in acknowledging that we are all similar. If we were not so mimetic, we could even do without violence. However, the problem is once again that mimetism defines humans. We have to have the courage to look squarely at this aspect of reality.

As we have seen, Clausewitz was not interested in peace: he was a war theorist. The attacker wants peace and the defender wants war, so the latter will win. What is interesting about this notion is that it goes beyond the well-defined area in which Clausewitz thought it applied. What Clausewitz glimpsed is the reality of the trend to extremes and not its mere possibility. This is fundamental. This is why we should not spend too much time on the duel: it is fascinating but will result in nothing but violence. We have to at all costs avoid thinking of war as a *passage* towards reconciliation. In our critique of Hegel and his dialectic, we saw that such a passage was impossible. Postponing reconciliation always causes violence to increase. Levinas does not say that such a passage is possible. He says that outside of totality, there is war *and* love. We are faced with this alternative more than ever.

Escaping totality means disturbing its mechanism. Totality that is no longer closed on itself, that no longer has its secret hidden, transforms into pure violence. War is the first stage in the fury, but then there is something beyond war, we know that now. Is it tangible on this Earth? I doubt it because we have rejected the only Model that we have been given to follow. At least we can say that holiness prefigures that hereafter.

BC: Thus, you go so far as to think that unleashing of violence goes hand in hand with revelation of the divine nature of the Other?

RG: In effect, that is the paradox that interests me.

BC: Thus, it would be the essentially religious nature of reconciliation that would unmask violence? Thinking about the religious dimension of love, as Levinas does, would be to *finish* the world, in both senses of the word. From this point of view, Nietzsche would be right: the Biblical and evangelical tradition would be the worst thing that could happen to humanity.

RG: Yes, because it suggests that humanity can become divine by renouncing violence. This paradox corresponds to reality, but Nietzsche was wrong to reject it. Christianity invites us to imitate a God who is perfectly good. It teaches us that if we do not do so, we will expose ourselves to the worst. There is no solution to mimetism aside from a good model. Yet the Greeks never suggested we imitate the gods. They always say that Dionysus should be kept at a distance and that one should never go close to him. Christ alone is approachable from this point of view. The Greeks had no model of transcendence to imitate. That was their problem, and it is *the* problem of archaic religions. For them, absolute violence is good only in cathartic memory, in sacrificial repetition. However, in a world where the founding murder has disappeared, we have no choice but to imitate Christ, imitate him to the letter, do everything he says to do. The Passion reveals both mimetism and the only way to remedy it. Seeking to imitate Dionysus, to become a "Dionysiac philosopher," as Nietzsche tried to become, is to adopt a Christian attitude in order to do the exact opposite of what Christianity invites us to do.

People would probably have preferred to remain children, as Saint Paul suggests, even though they would have been losing out. They would not have been able to become adults. We thus have to view optimism with suspicion. The gravity of our time requires it. We are not *necessarily* moving towards reconciliation, but the idea that humanity has no salvation other than reconciliation is indeed the opposite of the escalation to extremes. This is why Pascal says that truth fails to calm violence and can only "irritate" it. The truth that irritates violence dates back to the founding murder that no one wants to see. It points it out and nullifies it.

Levinas did not write an apology of war. He says that it is an experience that we cannot get away from. Of course, heroism may be another path, but it is unpredictable. No one can talk about it until it has happened. Heroic models, understood as models that can be imitated, are now null. This is why totalitarian regimes have always tried to construct them. The latest, and most difficult to understand, is indeed the terrorist model. We are now beyond tests of strength, beyond the point at which you rightly hope that we will pause to make the distinctions we have made. War is absolutely not justifiable: it is not something that we necessarily have to undergo. Its intensification, in contrast, reveals that a truth is in the process of emerging.

BC: Are you suggesting that the heroic approach can be nothing but a plan to dominate?

RG: That's right. The heroic approach appears with the failure of Revelation in the background. It presupposes imitation of the other, a desire to appropriate the other's strength and to dominate him. The confrontation necessarily results in an escalation because the other appropriates the desire for appropriation. Intelligent imitation, which is self-conscious, is something else entirely. Think about the conversion of Saint Paul. He keeps repeating, "Stop imitating one another and making war; imitate Christ, who will link you with the Father." Christ restores the distance with the sacred, whereas reciprocity brings us closer to one another to produce the corrupt sacred, which is violence. In primitive societies, violence is one with the god's *proximity*. Gods no longer appear today because violence no longer has an outlet; it is deprived of scapegoats (those divinized victims) and is bound to escalate. Hölderlin was the only one at the time of Hegel and Clausewitz to have understood the danger of proximity among humans. Indeed, the Greeks had a name for the god who mixed with men, the god of reciprocity, of mimetic doubles and contagious madness: Dionysus. That is the name the Greeks gave to the fear they felt when the god was too close.

The Apocalyptic Turn

BC: So, what is the violence that was awakened when Christ revealed to humanity the workings of human relations and the danger of reciprocity?

RG: It is less Dionysus than "Satan falling like lightning," Satan deprived of his false transcendence.[30] Satan is not an obscure god. It is the name of a decomposing structure, the very one that Saint Paul called "Powers and Principalities." From this perspective, if we agree to follow Christianity, violence is laid bare, unleashed, and its sterility revealed in the eyes of all. Christ replaced Dionysus, which is something that Nietzsche did not want to see. Violence now founds nothing; only resentment is constantly growing, in other words, mimetically, faced with the revelation of its own truth.

Saint Paul shows this in his Epistle to the Colossians, when he writes that Christ "disarmed the rulers and authorities and made a public example of them, triumphing over them in it."[31] Christ exasperated mimetic rivalries. He agreed to be their victim in order to reveal mimetic rivalries to the eyes of all. He caused them to appear everywhere: in the society, in families. There is no totality that does not run the risk of being affected by the doubling that used to be contained by sacrifice. The linear time that Christ forced us to adopt makes the eternal return of the gods impossible, and thus also any reconciliation on the head of innocent victims. Deprived of sacrifice, we are faced with an inescapable alternative: either we acknowledge the truth of Christianity, or we contribute to the escalation to extremes by rejecting Revelation. No man is a prophet in his own land because no land wants to hear the truth about its own violence. It will always try to hide it in order to have peace, but the best way to have peace is to make war. This is why Christ suffered the fate of prophets. He came close to humans by throwing their violence into a panic, by showing it naked to all. In a way, he was doomed to failure. The Holy Spirit, however, is continuing his work. It is the Holy Spirit that teaches us that historical Christianity has failed and that the apocalyptic texts will now speak to us more than they ever have before.

Greek tragedy is a decisive stage on the path to this discovery because it challenges the mythological solution. There were many doubles in Greece, and duels always occurred. There was neither the singular nor the plural, but always a crisis. There are Eteocles and Polynices, *Seven Against Thebes*, the famous chorus, which is also double. I always see the duel as the end of misleading differentiation. Rivalry between twins always precedes a murder that re-establishes the unity, the false peace that every society needs. *Totality* of the city, *duality* of enemy brothers, *unity* of the victim: this is how the victim-based polarization works. The city controls its own violence by concentrating it on a third party.

This is why the apocalyptic process consists in turning all human foundations on their heads: the unity of the consenting emissary-victim, the duality of war, the imminent explosion of totality. It is no longer men who create gods, but God who has come to take the place of the victim. The prophets and psalms prepared this fundamental interpretation of the coming of God, who is simply one with the cross. *Here, the victim is divine before becoming sacred.* The divine precedes the sacred. It re-establishes the rights of God. The God, the Other who enters, then upsets the "whited sepulchers." He destroys the whole system. This is why Saint Paul said that the Powers and Principalities had also been hung on the cross, exposed to the eyes of all. They will never recover.

BC: We are, in fact, at a point when the duel can no longer be an institution, when the mechanism of war has been destabilized for good.

RG: Yes, in order to leave the way open to the possible explosion of totality. Not only can the duel no longer be an institution, but it is what all institutions have tried to dissimulate in order not to disappear. We can even say that institutions are held together only by resistance to the emergence of the duel. In Clausewitz's day, war was still an institution. It was codified and controlled by politics, or at least he pretended to believe it was. It still hid the principle of reciprocity to some extent.

This is why Clausewitz sees the escalation of the duel, the confrontation between two nations that go from hostile *intent* to hostile *feeling,* but refuses to take his thought about this trend to its logical conclusion: the pathology of national interest to which it leads. Indeed, the emergence of the duel presupposes the disappearance of differences, the end of all the institutions whose only purpose is to control violence. Clausewitz's military voluntarism, which is implied in his definition of "military genius," played a role in what came to be called "Prussianism" and later "Pangermanism." His refusal or inability to take his thought on the dynamics of the duel to its logical conclusion was symptomatic of both a conceptual defeat and a regression of European history towards a corrupt form of the sacred, in other words, the destruction of everything. However, the destruction concerns *only* the world. Satan has no power over God.

We should take a closer look at Clausewitz's proximity to the "god of war," who bore the name of Napoleon at the time. We now know that the emergence of reciprocity leads to the escalation to extremes. That process overwhelms individuals and nations; we cannot do anything about it. Something panics; the secret underlying the Powers and Principalities is disclosed and the edifices crumble. To acknowledge this truth is to complete what Clausewitz was unable, or did not want, to finish: it is to say that *the escalation to extremes is the appearance that truth now takes when it shows itself to humanity.* Since each of us is responsible for the escalation, we naturally do not want to recognize this reality. The truth about violence has been stated once and for all. Christ revealed the truth that the prophets announced, namely, that of the violent foundation of all cultures. The refusal to listen to this essential truth exposes us to the return of an archaic world that will no longer have the face of Dionysus, as Nietzsche hoped. It will be a world of total destruction. Dionysiac chaos was a chaos that founded something. The one threatening us is radical. We need courage to admit it, as we do to resist giving into the fascination of violence.

BC: Remaining alert and trying to turn back the course of events would thus be taking care not to renew the escalation? Could this precautionary principle be extended to all areas: political, military, technological and environmental?

RG: But it might be too late. Historical Christianity has failed, and with it modern society. Christ's denunciation of sacrificial mechanisms constantly exacerbates violence. This is simply to say, once again, that the Other's coming is in the process of destroying totality. I think that this is the price of eschatology. It is because the Model of holiness appeared once in the history of humanity that so many heroisms are trying to suppress it. Heroism is a value that is too corrupted for us to trust: in a way, scoundrels have always been infiltrating it, especially since Napoleon.

This is why we should not waste time on the duel, but see it as a clear sign of what is coming to fulfillment. The reason that people fight more and more is that there is a truth approaching against which their violence reacts. The Christ is the Other who is coming and who, in his very vulnerability, arouses panic in the system. In small archaic societies, the Other was the stranger who brings disorder, and who always ends up as the scapegoat. In the Christian world, it is Christ, the Son of God, who represents all the innocent victims and whose return is heralded by the very effects of the escalation to extremes. What will he declare? That we have gone crazy, that the adulthood of humanity, which he announced through the cross, is a failure.

No one wants to see or understand that Christ's "return," in the implacable logic of the apocalypse, is simply the same thing as the end of the world. Contrary to what Hegel wanted to believe, humans are not only *not* embracing one another, but have become able to destroy the world. I think we have to be very clear on this point, for continuing to "think war" on the level of heroism will quickly lead us, like Clausewitz, to return to the supposed sacredness of violence, and the belief that it is fertile. There is nothing it can establish now. To believe there *could* be is to accelerate the trend to extremes. Sin consists in thinking that something good could come from violence. We all think this *because we are all mimetic,* and we stick to our beloved duel.

To convert is to take distance from that corrupted sacred, but it does not mean escaping from mimetism. We have just understood that the process supposes a passage from imitation to identification, the re-establishment of distance within mimetism itself. This is all very easy to say, I will grant you that. Especially since violent reciprocity will always win.

BC: Levinas chose to begin by situating himself in a relationship. He says little about reciprocity. We therefore have to think about relationships within reciprocity. This would be more concrete, and perhaps less idealistic.

RG: In fact, we always have one foot in each camp.

BC: This is the position that enables you to expose the traps of reciprocity. I understand that Clausewitz helps us to think about an acceleration of history that we can fear will lead to the worst, but your assessment of this process seems too global. I do not want to give up so soon on the possibility that we could resist this course of events.

RG: You are right to insist that our resistance has prevented the world from exploding for a long time. How much longer will it be able to do so? This is the question we have to ask, and you are making me point out one of my weaknesses. I tend to believe that the Christian perspective will allow me to go far beyond these things and to look at them from a distance. My attitude towards Clausewitz has perhaps been too mischievous. It is my romantic side, which is repressed in a way, but always crops up. I come to Clausewitz through Chopin, feeling uninvolved, finally. Indeed, I should say that in a way all that is obsolete, no longer true.

My big excuse is eschatology. Is eschatology compatible, as you would like it to be, with heroic resistance to the course of events? Yes, in so far as it can produce examples that can be imitated, but they will always remain "invisible to eyes of flesh," as Pascal says. No man is a prophet in his own land. Since we have spoken of Corneille, why was there no eschatology in the Christianity of the seventeenth century? There was a little in Bossuet's writings, but not much. It is very interesting to wonder about the various contexts that Christianity has had. In the Middle Ages, it had apocalyptic periods in which Christians realized they were in the process of completely failing.

However, Christianity has always been too young for eschatology. Perhaps it is ready now, for what is threatening us has become tangible.

In a way, Clausewitz *made war on eschatology,* and this is why I can correct him, catch him red-handed acting like a dilettante. I have the impression I can tell him: "You just wait, you'll see!" He remained a servant of politics; he admitted it himself. He was a classical aristocrat, but also a man of the Enlightenment because he had perhaps understood more about the French Revolution than he says. The rationalism in which he was steeped makes him forget, or fail to recognize, that religion is nothing like an ethereal sphere, as he seems to suggest. Clausewitz is all the more upsetting because he formulates the apocalypse without realizing it. He therefore never says it outright. In some ways, he reminds me of Chateaubriand, who was also secretly more of a rationalist than a romantic. Clausewitz was a super Chateaubriand because he found a topic with a real future. God knows that it even has a terrible future. I see this as more on the level of a discovery, almost a literary goldmine, which is all the more exciting because it is never really made explicit.

The escalation to extremes resulting from reciprocal action is such a major discovery that it extends to surprising areas. It tends to become a universal law. We are thus dealing with a forceful writer, who is all the more powerful because he refuses to take his intuition to its logical conclusion. We thus have to complete what he has given us to read. In this respect, Levinas's sentence is impressive: "war is produced as the pure experience of pure being,"[32] the only possible escape from totality. Perhaps we have no choice. Perhaps we have to go through this.

BC: When Levinas thinks about the Other coming towards us, he leaps into eschatology. If the course of time were literally reversed, what conclusions could we draw?

RG: That it is urgent to take the prophetic tradition into account, including its implacable logic, which escapes our narrow rationalism. If the Other is approaching, and if a radically different thought about the Other is becoming possible, perhaps it is because time is approaching its fulfillment.

BC: The discussion about the duel was thus necessary, even by default. Carl Schmitt's great mistake, though his reading of Clausewitz was very profound, was perhaps to have believed in the fecundity of violence, whether it is founding or instituted, war or law.

RG: But Schmitt is interesting to study for this very reason. We have seen that his legal construction of the enemy was obsolete with respect to what was emerging behind the general principle of hostility. It was impossible to redefine law based on violence when widespread destruction of all foundations was already underway. Clausewitz was announcing the end of Europe. We see him predicting Hitler, Stalin and all the rest, which is now nothing, the American non-thought in the West. Today we are truly facing nothingness. On the political level, on the literary level, on every level. You will see; it is happening little by little. Corneillian heroism is from a time when people thought war could still establish law. It was in this spirit that we have often talked about Marc Bloch, the perfect example of the Resistance.

BC: "La vraie saison des juges," republished in the 1990 French edition of *Strange Defeat,* is a remarkable text. In it, a few weeks before he was shot by the Germans, Bloch said that justice is not vengeance, but that it has to be severe when it acts in truth. His own death can be seen as an example.

RG: But are we still in a world where force can yield to law? This is precisely what I doubt. Law itself is finished. It is failing everywhere, and even excellent jurists, whom I know well, no longer believe in it. They see that it is collapsing, crumbling. Pascal already no longer believed in it. All of my intuitions are really anthropological in the sense that I see law as springing from sacrifice in a manner that is very concrete and not philosophical at all. I see this emergence of law in my readings in anthropology, in monographs on archaic tribes, where its arrival was felt. I see it emerge in Leviticus, in the verse on capital punishment, which concerns nothing other than stoning to death. This is the birth of law. Violence *produced* law, which is still, like sacrifice, a lesser form of violence. This may be the only thing that human society is capable of. Yet one day this dike will also break.

CHAPTER 5

Hölderlin's Sorrow

THE TWO CIRCLES OF THE GOSPELS

Benoît Chantre: When we dig a little deeper into the phenomenon of war as Clausewitz described it, we find that politics is part of violence, not violence part of politics. The institution of war did not elude violence, but tried to slow its escalation. We have seen that this institution no longer exists. Yet should we not keep trying to maintain this resistance?

René Girard: Of course, but individual resistance to the escalation to extremes is essentially vain. The only way it might work is if it were collective, if all people stood "hand in hand," as the song goes. We have to give up this happy automatic escape, which underlies every form of humanism. However, we also still have to keep in mind the possibility of positive imitation because we have seen that imitation is central in the genesis of violence. Nonetheless, the great tragedy of our era of "internal mediation" is that positive models have become invisible. Recognizing imitation and its ambivalence seems to be the only way of feeling that it is still possible to go from reciprocity to relationship, from negative contagion to a form of positive contagion. This is what the imitation of Christ means.

However, this transition is not a given, and it is even less conceivable: it is on the level of a specific conversion, of an event. It cannot be denied that the Gospels contain a formidable intuition about mimetism: Christ invites us to work from within mimetism. However, the Spirit takes us where it will. We thus have to reason more and more at a global level, leave behind strictly individual perspectives, and consider things "in big chunks." From this point of view, the apocalyptic narratives are crucial. They are the only ones that force us to take a radically different point of view. Why have they been concealed to such an extent? The question has never really been asked. They were very present in the first period of Christianity. In the Middle Ages they were read from the point of view of the Last Judgment in a way that was much more naïve than in the time of Saint Paul, but they were still known. Look at the tympanums in cathedrals.

We have to maintain the force of the Scriptures because the apocalyptic texts have gradually been forgotten, just when their relevance is more and more obvious. This is incredible. The joyful welcome of the Kingdom, which the texts describe, has been smothered by a double trend: catastrophic darkening on one hand, and indefinite postponement of the Second Coming on the other. The constant, slow distance in relation to the Gospels casts a shadow on what was supposed to be luminous, and delays it. The anti-Christianity that we see today thus reveals this in a striking way as the next step in a process that began with the Revelation. The "time of the Gentiles"[1] that Luke describes suggests the Judgment has been delayed, and this has gradually imposed a new perspective on the Gospels. It has injected an insidious, growing doubt about the validity of the apocalyptic texts. The "time of the Gentiles" is nonetheless an extraordinary period, that of a civilization that is incommensurable with others and that has given humanity power that it had never had before. Thus, if we exaggerate a little, we can say that that time has gradually confiscated the Revelation and used it to its own ends, to make atomic bombs.

This is why I draw attention to these texts in order to advocate a more passionate reading of the Scriptures. I think that there is no complete text without the apocalypse to conclude it: "when the Son of Man comes, will he find faith on earth?"[2] The evangelists insist on this question. This is where the apocalyptic question arises, less perhaps in the apocalypse of John, to which everyone rushes when eschatology is at issue, than in the texts of the three other evangelists, Mark, Matthew and Luke, who always precede it with the story of the Passion. The Synoptic Gospels have a fundamental structure in which human history is inserted into that of God. The second circle of history (and its catastrophic end) is *contained in the first circle,* which finishes with the Passion. Luke very enigmatically implied that after Jerusalem falls there will be a "time of the Gentiles":

For there will be great distress on the earth and wrath against this people;
they will fall by the edge of the sword and be taken away as captives among
all nations; and Jerusalem will be trampled on by the Gentiles, until the
times of the Gentiles are fulfilled.[3]

All the exegetes want to see this as an allusion to the destruction of the
Temple by Titus in A.D. 70, and they conclude from this that Luke's text is later
than the three others. These theories are completely uninteresting because the
fall of Jerusalem does not mean only A.D. 70, but also 587 B.C. The evangelists
were continuing the Jewish prophetic tradition, which was attentive to "signs
of the times." Here too human history is caught within that of God. The fall of
Jerusalem is thus primarily an *apocalyptic theme:* Christ is not a soothsayer but a
prophet. One of the wonders of the texts is that they make it impossible to know
whether or not they are speaking of Titus. However, historians mix everything
up without even realizing that the mixture is part of what they are talking
about, and that what they are talking about could not care less about them.

There is no doubt that the apocalyptic passages refer to a real event that
will follow the Passion, but in the Gospels they were placed before it. The
"time of the Gentiles" is thus, like the seventy years of servitude to the King
of Babylon in Jeremiah, *an indefinite time between two apocalypses,* two revela-
tions. If we put the statements back into an evangelical perspective, this can
only mean that *the time of the Gentiles, in other words, the time when Gentiles will
refuse to hear the word of God, is a limited time.* Between Christ's Passion and his
Second Coming, the Last Judgment, if you prefer, there will be this indefinite
time which is ours, a time of increasingly uncontrolled violence, of refusal to
hear, of growing blindness. This is the meaning of Luke's writings, and this
shows their relevance. In this respect, Pascal says at the end of the twelfth
Provincial Letter that "violence has only a certain course to run, limited by
the appointment of Heaven."[4]

Clearly, this is the idea that Hegel tried to recuperate when he imagined a
true history beyond apparent history: a theodicy of the Spirit beyond historical contingencies, a "ruse of reason" in which Napoleon himself was to play
a role and which was also to use Napoleon mercilessly. Hegel saw modern
escalation as increasingly rational, when of course the opposite is true. Hegel's
was a very powerful enterprise, which was only natural since it was based
on the best of the Christian tradition, but, as I have said, it degenerated very
quickly. Therefore we must not leave history, but try to understand it in a
more realistic manner as acceleration towards the worst, which must have an
apocalyptic meaning.

Reality is not rational, but religious. This is what the Gospels tell us. This is at the heart of history's contradictions, in the interactions that people weave with one another, in their relations, which are always threatened by reciprocity. This awareness is needed more than ever now that institutions no longer help us and we each have to make the transformation by ourselves. In this, we have returned to Paul's conversion, to the voice asking, "why do you persecute me?" Paul's radicalism is very appropriate for our time. He was less the hero who "rose" to holiness than the persecutor who turned himself back and falls to the ground.

BC: Does the "time of the Gentiles" in Luke refer to the time when institutions will resist the rise of the principle of reciprocity?

RG: Precisely, and in a way, that time is in the process of coming to an end. This is why Luke tries to maintain a separation between the destruction of Jerusalem and the end of the world, which will come after the "time of the Gentiles." There are no such historical clues in Mark and Matthew, which indicates that they were both written prior to the year 71. However, what is essential is that Luke went deeper and in greater detail into the apocalyptic tradition. Note in passing that the exegetes never reflect upon this kind of thing. What does Luke tell us? That Gentiles are new, and that they have to be given the time to experience Christ. Paul said the same thing in the Epistle to the Romans: the Jews failed everything despite the prophets, and the Christians have to be careful not to do the same thing. What is the Holocaust if not that terrifying failure?

Christians have to assume their responsibility for that horror. They had been warned 2000 years ago and they have proven incapable of avoiding the worst. It would of course be absurd to deny, out of repentance for this, the Jews' *share* of responsibility for Christ's Crucifixion, but no comparison is possible between the death of one they considered a troublemaker and the millions of victims of the Holocaust. John Paul II's request for forgiveness at Yad Vashem is sublime, and has to be seen as a sign of the times: that of a reconciliation that is more necessary than ever between Jews and Christians, who carry the same message, who are the vessels of the same eschatological truth.

BC: Could you go back to your view of this structure of the Gospels?

RG: There is an initial circle, which is Christ's life and ends with the Passion. There is a second circle, which is human history and ends with the apocalypse. The second circle is contained in the first. Human history, undermined by a destructive principle, an escalation to extremes that now threatens the whole world, becomes a prelude to the Passion. What could be suggested by this structure if not Christ's return at the end of history? Paul had a premonition that the Jews would be reintegrated in the return, that they would end up understanding that Christianity was not a conspiracy against them. The classical interpretation of this reconciliation is as a sign of universal reconciliation.

Luke places the "time of the Gentiles" between the Passion and the Last Judgment. He thus makes a clear distinction between the two. This involves deep reflection on the meaning of the Gospels and of history from the evangelical point of view. There is nothing nihilistic about the apocalyptic spirit: it can *make sense of* the trend toward the worst only from within the framework of very profound hope. However, that hope cannot do without eschatology. Identifying the dangerous emergence of the principle of reciprocity and showing it at work in history should be the rule of all apologetics. Mimetic theory is essentially Christian. I would even go so far as to say that it tries to take Christianity to its ultimate meaning, to complete it in a way, because it takes violence seriously.

At the San Francisco Seminary, there was a Catholic exegete who was very well considered by historians, even atheist historians: Raymond E. Brown. He placed a lot of emphasis, and with reason, on the fact that John was writing without having read the Synoptics. This seems essential because it allows us to appreciate the symmetry of the intuitions and the insignificance of the small differences, of dates and various inconsistencies, of everything that is so delicious to the great-grandchildren of Renan. There is thus a *reason* for the apocalypse. Luke may have taken Mark and Matthew deeper, while John may have been writing without having read them, but he said the same things. How do the texts shed light on the system of relations among humans? This is the crucial question. In order to comprehend their importance, we have to see the texts' anthropological and theological dimensions, and understand that the apocalypse is the point when the two dimensions meet.

Therefore it is much more interesting to say that Luke saw the efficiency of violence when it is performed by a group, that he understood that bad violence reconciles enemies. This is a brilliant intuition. After the Passion, it is written: "That same day Herod and Pilate became friends with each other; before this they had been enemies."[5] People once again imagine that this is a historical clue, but in fact the meaning of this verse can be only anthropological. From this point of view, historicism is only a double of archaic reconciliation. This is all we have to show in order to refute the idea that the Gospels are anti-Semitic. Why do you think there was a small crowd that asked that Jesus be put to death? Bad violence reconciles enemies. It reconciled Pilate and Herod. They participated in the Crucifixion together, and then they were reconciled. Bad violence was unanimous against Christ; they were part of it. We find this only in Luke.

This is an obvious revelation of the founding murder, which is a mechanism that no longer works after the Passion, or rather, it runs on empty because its workings have been exposed to the light of day by the Crucifixion. The "times of the Gentiles" are the times of gradual disintegration of sacrifice's effectiveness. In the First Epistle to the Thessalonians, the most ancient text of the New Testament, which experts consider to date from less than 20 years after the Crucifixion, Paul tries to soothe the faithful, who were disappointed by what they saw as the regrettable delay of the Second Coming. He told them not to be impatient, *to both believe and not believe* in the Powers and Principalities. There is no point in getting impatient, and especially one must not rebel because the system will collapse on its own. Satan will be increasingly divided against himself: this is the mimetic law of the trend to extremes. Mimetism is contagious and will *attack nature itself.* We are thus in the process of seeing that, far from making them obsolete forever, the confusion between nature and culture in the apocalyptic texts, which used to be seen as naïve, is becoming unexpectedly relevant, with the ultramodern theme of the contamination of nature by human hands.

Look at Matthew 24, which is similar to Mark 13 and Luke 17, and also located right before the Passion. It tells us that we are at "the beginning of the birth pangs":

Beware that no one leads you astray. For many will come in my name, saying, "I am the Messiah!" and they will lead many astray. And you will hear of wars and rumors of wars; see that you are not alarmed; for this must take place, but the end is not yet. For nation will rise against nation, and kingdom against kingdom, and there will be famines and earthquakes in various places: all this is but the beginning of the birth pangs.

Then they will hand you over to be tortured and will put you to death, and you will be hated by all nations because of my name. Then many will fall away, and they will betray one another and hate one another. And many false prophets will arise and lead many astray. And because of the increase of lawlessness, the love of many will grow cold. But anyone who endures to the end will be saved.

And this good news of the kingdom will be proclaimed throughout the world, as a testimony to all the nations; and then the end will come.

A text like this is powerfully concrete and relevant. As we read it, we enter the heart of reality. What is Christ announcing in this passage from Matthew? That the escalation to extremes (note the mimetic doubles: "nation will rise against nation, and kingdom against kingdom") will make "the love of many...grow cold." Thus, Providence cannot be tied to secular history, as Clausewitz wrote to his wife. Pascal was right: there is a reciprocal intensification of violence and truth, and it now appears before our eyes, or at least before the eyes of a small number, those whose love has not grown cold.

The "time of Gentiles" can be defined as a slow withdrawal of the religious in all its forms, a loss of all guides and markers, a questioning without answers, even an ordeal, especially for the elect, who find no comfort anywhere. This is to such an extreme that Mark (13:19–20) wrote:

> In those days there will be suffering, such as has not been from the beginning of the creation that God created until now, no, and never will be. And if the Lord had not cut short those days, no one would be saved; but for the sake of the elect, whom he chose, he has cut short those days.

The interminable descent, the corruption that constantly reduces the number of Christians, is dangerous for the elect. However, that small number has to hang on right until the end, despite the false prophets. You can see how the mimetic perspective is fundamental. The false prophets are the ones who claim to "have god," to speak in his name and are therefore to be imitated. It is impossible not to think of the mimetic struggle between Oedipus and Tiresias in Sophocles' *Oedipus the King*. At the time of the Greeks, violent reciprocity indicates the imminence of the god, in other words, the violent sacred. What each is trying to snatch away from the other was the divinity that he claimed to have, and the more they fight, the nearer that divinity approaches, until it is tangible in the destruction threatening the group. Everyone is a false prophet at the end of the sacrificial crisis; in other words, everyone is possessed, inhabited by the god. The fascination specific to the sacred is one and the same as the contagion of violence. The clash between Tiresias and Oedipus is a fine symbol of mythological duels, that Greek way of always sparring with chaos, as if it were necessary to negotiate with it.

What does Matthew's text tell us if not that such struggles will return, but in more terrible form. He went even further: conflicts among nations will go hand in hand with "famines and earthquakes," which clearly means that the fighting will have cosmic consequences. It will no longer be the plague in Thebes, but ecological catastrophes on a planetary scale. Suddenly there is a justification for diminishing distinctions between the natural and the artificial. How is it possible to still refuse to hear these texts? Paradoxically, what strikes me is not only the growing consistency of war with its concept, but of the evangelical text with the period that we have entered: the time of violence's growing sterility. This truth will become, *has become* striking. We are perhaps at the end of the historical circle following the destruction of the Temple, the "time of the Gentiles" that was supposed to last until the end. We have to think about all of this as something that is happening very slowly, and of which we can only suggest the shape. However, it will become clearer.

BC: The end of the world and the advent of the Kingdom?

RG: Yes, that will become clear to a small minority of course, but we have finally completed an era of thought that may be the era of violence itself. The "end of history" or "end of time" may not be the end of the world, even though Christ warned us that there will be famines and earthquakes, but the end of the world in which Powers and Principalities dominate. Naturally, we cannot know whether the end of that domination will coincide with the end of time.

BC: What you are saying is that violence no longer has the capacity to produce law?

RG: That's right.

BC: That it is incapable of producing truth, of producing reason?

RG: Yes, it's finished. It is impotent. Thus, this is real anarchy. We need only a simple example. The people who experimented the most with this reality in the twentieth century were the communists because they very quickly had to resort to violence, and saw and experienced its powerlessness. They were able to defend themselves against German aggression only because of old Tsarist Russia, which was still there. The portrait of General Kutusov was in Stalin's office. They were terribly aware of this since they made all sorts of concessions. Their own violence was sterile, and they finally reincorporated "Holy Russia," in other words, a Christianity which they suddenly found less distant than they had thought.

However, they did not beat the Germans with communism. I think that the point when they became aware of their total failure was when they were going to win because they had used one of Peter the Great's plans, and this was also when they saw that communism did not exist, that it could not have historical reality. In the end, people like Gorbachev were educated by people who had understood this. Look at how he is fighting for the environment now. He has lost all confidence in politics. He did not at all share in Stalin's money-grubbing side. Indeed, that aspect was so rooted in Old Russia that Stalin did not realize it and thought he was a communist.

The Germans were also unable to build anything on violence. The advantage that we have in France today is that nationalism is very weak, so even though we are in a complete fog, we may perhaps finally become aware of all of violence's failures. I think that we are finally *living in the moment of truth*. We have a rendezvous with reality. It is perfectly conceivable that something new will come of this. Violence's barrenness may perhaps be a sign that conflicts will diminish, that there will be a kind of returning undertow.

BC: When do you think violence became unable to establish anything?

RG: It has been less and less of a foundation as history has accelerated and politics has lost importance. Perhaps we could say that, in the Western world, it was able to found things until the time of Roosevelt. The American intervention at the end of World War II was probably the last act of the Napoleonic drama, which was part of the overall European tragedy, in which mimetic hatred had been growing for centuries. In this respect, it was symptomatic that the Holy Roman Empire played the role of scapegoat for three centuries: this was Europe's only *political possibility,* and it was in reference to and against that Carolingian relic that Europeans killed one another. The dismemberment of the Austro-Hungarian Empire by the Treaty of Versailles shows this powerful resentment. The American landing later highlights the end of European leadership. The very term "American intervention" is interesting in this respect. It proves that we have gone from an era of codified war to an era of *security,* where we think we can "resolve" conflicts just as we cure sickness, with increasingly sophisticated tools. We are far from the worship of the state that is so dear to Clausewitz and Hegel.

BC: But very close to an apocalyptic theme. As I am listening to you, I am thinking about the end of the First Epistle to the Thessalonians (5:1–5), which is strangely consistent with what you have just said:

> Now concerning the times and the seasons, brothers and sisters, you do not need to have anything written to you. For you yourselves know very well that the day of the Lord will come like a thief in the night. When they say, "There is peace and security," then sudden destruction will come upon them, as labor pains come upon a pregnant woman, and there will be no escape!

RG. It is very troubling, and this passage clearly has profound anthropological meaning. It explains why Christ says in the Gospels that he has not come bearing peace. He is aware that he is putting an end to the effort to dissimulate the mechanisms of violence. He does not present himself as a warrior. On the contrary, he claimed membership in the Jewish prophetic tradition, which aims to *demonetize* violence. It is thus *because Christ deprives them of scapegoats* that the Powers and Principalities will be destroyed. People will escalate violence in reaction to the Revelation because they will be increasingly unable to find an outlet for their mimetic struggles.

God, through his Son, subjected himself to human violence. He made violence come out *against himself* in order to reveal it to the light of day. This is the paradoxical reason that the God in the Bible and Gospels appears more violent than the gods of the Antiquity, when in fact He is precisely the opposite. The Greeks hid their scapegoats, which is very different. The Psalms reveal that violent people are not the ones who talk about violence, but that it is the peaceful people who make it speak. The Judeo-Christian revelation exposes what myths always tend to silence. Those who speak of "peace and security" are now their heirs: despite everything, they continue believing in myths and do not want to see their own violence.

The great paradox in all this is that Christianity provokes the escalation to extremes by revealing to humans their own violence. It prevents people from blaming the gods for their violence and places them before their responsibility. Saint Paul was in no way a revolutionary in the modern sense of the term. He tells the Thessalonians that they have to be patient, in other words, to obey the Powers and Principalities that will be destroyed *anyway*. The destruction will happen one day because of the growing imperium of violence; deprived of a sacrificial outlet, it is unable to establish the reign of order except by escalating. It will require more and more victims to create an ever more precarious order. This is the terrifying future of the world for which Christians carry the responsibility. Christ will have tried to bring humanity into adulthood, but humanity will have refused. I am using the future perfect on purpose because there is a deep failure in all this.

This is why eschatology is simply the obverse of scientific reality when we look at things from a Darwinian perspective. It is because humanity was incomplete, because it was resorting to the falsehood of sacrifice, that Christ came to complete its "hominization." The completion is a coming. Thus, we should take Christ literally when he tells us that he is bringing war: he has come to destroy the old world. However, because of humans themselves, the destruction will take time. Of course, 2,000 years is a short time compared with millions of years: the time preceding the Return, otherwise known as "perdition," will come upon humanity "as labor pains come upon a pregnant woman." The apocalypse thus comes before the Passion. The Gospels had to bring up the possible end of humanity so that Pontius Pilate, ignoring the depth of his statement, could say to the crowd *"Ecce Homo,"* "Here is the man,"[6] the one who will die because he is innocent.

The relevance of the apocalyptic texts is therefore absolutely striking when we finally accept their meaning. They say paradoxically that Christ will only return when there is no hope that evangelical revelation will be able to eliminate violence, once humanity realizes that it has failed. Christians say that Christ will return to transform the failure into eternal life. Nonetheless, we should not underestimate the insertion of the Spirit into history, nor exceptional individuals, nor the opening of groups to the universal. The Spirit has been incorporated, but the process has failed. The positivity of history should not be eliminated, but shifted. The rationality that mimetic theory seeks to promote is based entirely on the shift. Saying that chaos is near is not incompatible with hope, quite to the contrary. However, hope has to be seen in relation to an alternative that leaves only the choice between total destruction and realization of the Kingdom.

BC: Here, you return to a *reason* for the apocalypse that is indispensable to a clear understanding of your faith. Your approach is all the more original because it is anchored in a Darwinian point of view, and sees the apocalypse as the "completion" of hominization. These analyses don't upset anyone as long as we're talking about archaic religion, but they become unsettling as they bear more on our own time. Claiming that "the time is nigh" means rejecting the distance from religion that Western thought has been taking for three centuries. By making the apocalyptic texts coincide with the modern era, are you not trapped into letting the metaphor lead your argument?

RG: I'd like to reverse your reasoning by saying that it is because we have wanted to distance ourselves from religion that it is now returning with such force and in a retrograde, violent form. The rationalism that you mention was thus not real distancing, but a dike that is in the process of giving way. In this, it will perhaps have been our last mythology. We "believed" in reason, as people used to believe in the gods. Auguste Comte's formidable naïveté is a clear symptom of this. Such positivism is essential for understanding our delay in deciphering the signs of the times.

Positivists believe in reason in order to close their eyes to the catastrophes that are imminent today. Yet reason cannot do everything. Human relations, and the irrational aspects that they involve, will have unexpected consequences: we are more tied to the future of the world than ever before. We have seen Raymond Aron's failure to "contain" Clausewitz. In contrast, Emmanuel Levinas made us take a step towards eschatology. We now have to go further and say two things: *one can enter into relations with the divine only from a distance and through a mediator: Jesus Christ.* This contains the whole paradox that we have to deal with. It contains the new rationality that mimetic theory seeks to promote. It proclaims itself to be apocalyptic reasoning because it takes the divine seriously. In order to escape negative imitation, the reciprocity that brought people closer to the sacred, we have to accept the idea that only positive imitation will place us at the correct distance from the divine.

The imitation of Christ provides *the proximity that places us at a distance.* It is not the Father whom we should imitate, but his Son, who has withdrawn with his Father. His absence is the very ordeal that we have to go through. This is when, and only when, the religious should no longer be frightening, and the escalation to extremes could turn into its opposite. Such a reversal is nothing more than the advent of the Kingdom. What form will that advent take? We cannot imagine it. We will be able to do so only if we abandon all our old rationalist reflexes. Therefore, once again, everything depends on the meaning we give to religion.

The one that mimetic theory seeks to construct is relevant because it is anchored in a tradition and is also not incompatible with the advances of the "human sciences." Durkheim glimpsed this, but it was precisely his rationalism that prevented him from seeing the difference between Christianity and archaic religion. Only Christians can face the truth of the original sin because they alone assert so strongly that everything began with the founding murder, that sacrifice made humanity. Of course, the Christian religion has some features of archaic religion, but that is because the Passion is modeled on the "folds" and "lines" of the founding murder, and reveals to us all its workings: what was misapprehension has become revelation.

"Near is / And Difficult to Grasp, the God"

BC: Could it be the thought about this difference and this resemblance that is at the heart of apocalyptic reason?

RG: Exactly. Proof that it is possible to link eschatology with the modern period, and that I am not falling into the "metaphor trap," is provided in Hölderlin's work. His writings have haunted me for a long time, though I have rarely had the occasion to dwell on them. They suddenly come to mind because they are at the heart of the French-German junction. It is through Hölderlin, and no one else, that we can understand what was happening at Jena in 1806.

This was a decisive date. It was when Hegel saw "the world-spirit on horseback" from his window, and Clausewitz drew nearer to the "god of war." At the same time, Hölderlin was sinking into what was soon to be called his "madness." These three events occur in the same year, and only the long train of thought on which we have embarked can bring them into perspective. Hölderlin withdrew for 40 years into a tower owned by a carpenter in Tübingen. He had visitors, and people spoke with him, but his host said that he spent entire days reciting his works and even prostrated in total silence. Hölderlin stopped believing in the Absolute, which was not the case of his friends from earlier times: Fichte, Hegel and Schiller. However, he never gave signs of excessive madness. We have to rise to the nobility of this silence.

Hölderlin is much less haunted by Greece than we have been led to believe. I see him instead as frightened by the return to paganism that infused the classicism of his time. He is thus torn between two opposites: the absence of the divine and its fatal nearness. This marked two of his major works: *Hyperion: Or the Hermit in Greece* (1797–99) and *The Death of Empedocles* (1798–1800). Hölderlin's soul oscillates between nostalgia and dread, between questioning a heaven that is now empty and leaping into a volcano. By contrast, all of his friends are so troubled by the absence of gods whose return they desired so ardently. Yet the gods are dead for very specific reasons, which are clearly related to destabilization of the sacrificial mechanism. We have seen that the acceleration of history makes these reasons tangible. The absence of the gods and the presence of the absolute are related themes: the first leads to the second. If heaven is empty, how can we people it? As we have seen, Nietzsche asks that question in aphorism 125 of *The Gay Science*. Hölderlin's contemporaries looked to Greece to fill in the vacuum. Hölderlin also let himself fall into that trap for a while, but his withdrawal and immense sadness reveal greater lucidity.

BC: How would you define his apocalyptic thought?

RG: Let's go straight to the beginning of one of Hölderlin's greatest poems, appropriately named "Patmos." Its lines have been commented upon many times, especially since Heidegger saw in it the "enframing" of the world by technology. They announce the return of Christ much more than they do that of Dionysius:

> Near is
> And difficult to grasp, the God.
> But where danger threatens
> That which saves from it also grows.[7]

The *presence* of the divine grows as the divine withdraws: it is the withdrawal that saves, not the promiscuity. Hölderlin immediately understood that divine promiscuity can be only catastrophic. God's withdrawal is thus the passage *in Jesus Christ* from reciprocity to relationship, from proximity to distance. This is the poet's basic intuition, which he discovered just when he began his own withdrawal. A god that one can appropriate is a god that destroys. However, the Greeks never sought to imitate gods. It was not until Christianity that the mimetic perspective imposed itself as the only possible form of redemption, given the revealed madness of humanity.

Hölderlin thus felt that the Incarnation was the only means available to humanity to face God's very salubrious silence: Christ questioned that silence on the cross, and then he himself imitated his Father's withdrawal by joining him on the morning of his Resurrection. Christ saves humanity by "breaking his solar scepter."[8] He withdraws at the very point when he could dominate. We in turn are thus required to experience *the peril of the absence of God,* the modern experience par excellence, because it is the time of sacrificial temptation, the possible regression to extremes, but it is also a redemptive experience. To imitate Christ is to refuse to impose oneself as a model and to always efface oneself before others. To imitate Christ is to do everything to avoid being imitated.

It was thus God's silence that can be heard in that of the poet. The death of the gods, which so frightens Nietzsche, is simply the same thing as an essential withdrawal in which Christ asks us to see the new face of the divine. Mimetic theory has allowed us to conclude that the purpose of the Incarnation was to finish all religions, whose sacrificial crutches had become ineffective. Thus, mimetic theory also examines the withdrawal of the gods, but sheds light on it from an anthropological standpoint. It is because he is "difficult to grasp" that this god "saves" from "where danger threatens," in other words, from the time of the corrupted sacred. What does Christ feel on the cross if not that silence? What in turn do the disciples feel on the road to Emmaus but the withdrawal of the Son who had gone to join his Father? The more God's silence grows, the more dangerous violence becomes, as the vacuum is filled by purely human means though now devoid of the sacrificial mechanism. And, by the same token, the more holiness emerges as a distance from the divine.

I do not interpret these verses like Heidegger, who by dint of dissimulating his Catholicism gives the possibly false impression that he recommended a return to paganism. In 1962, his enigmatic statement to fascinated journalists from *Spiegel*[9] that "only a god can save us," led to the supposition of an improbable return of the Greek religion. There was something of Dionysius in this, in other words, a nostalgic choice of Hellenism over Christianity. Heidegger is following the German *Aufklärung* tradition. By contrast, Hölderlin put up greater resistance to the ambivalent swerve towards the pagan that was shared by Enlightenment thinkers at his time. He thought that the great classical tendency towards Hellenism would be compatible with Christianity if there were not so much ill feeling toward Christ.

Most people who quote Hölderlin follow in Heidegger's footsteps, in other words, they obscure the fact that Hölderlin was deeply Christian, or rather *became more and more so as he withdrew from the world.* To speak of Hölderlin's "madness" in relation to his withdrawal, which lasted nearly 40 years, is to misunderstand the poet's ordeal. In his interior exile there was a form of mystical quietism, which was anything but a desire to become a god or to live forever. What the poet understood when he was on the point of leaving the mimetic giddiness of worldly existence, the ups and downs of which he experienced with terrible intensity, as his fascination with Goethe and Schiller proves, is that *salvation lies in imitating Christ,* in other words, in imitating the "withdrawal relationship" that links him with his Father. The relationship sanctifies while reciprocity sacralizes by creating ties that are too strong. Hölderlin was in a better position than anyone else to understand this, for he had suffered so much from the models that he had adopted. Christ is the only one who immediately places us at the right distance. He is simultaneously "near and difficult to grasp." His presence is not proximity. Christ teaches us to look at the other by identifying ourselves with Him, which prevents us from oscillating between too great proximity to and too great distance from the other whom we imitate. If we were to identify with the other, we would be imitating him in an intelligent manner.

Imitating Christ thus means thwarting all rivalry, taking distance from the divine by giving it the Father's face: we are brothers "in" Christ. In this, Christ *completed* what the pagan gods had only sketched. As he sank into the withdrawal of his Father, Christ invited each of us to model our will on that of his Father. To listen to the Father's silence is to abandon oneself to his withdrawal, to conform to it. Becoming a "son of God" means imitating this withdrawal, experiencing it with Christ. God is thus not immediately accessible, but mediately: through his Son and the story of Salvation, which as we have seen takes on the paradoxical appearance of an escalation to extremes.

We can now get a better understanding of the exact meaning of the two lines by Hölderlin: "But where danger threatens / That which saves from it also grows." They explain why Hölderlin's silence and sadness occurred at the same time as Prussia's return to the scene of German history. Hölderlin's withdrawal occurred at the very point when there was a frightening acceleration of history in Germany. In this, the poet was infinitely more lucid than his friend Hegel. It is as if he felt the terrifying future and saw that humanity would be unable to hear the truth. This is why I see in his distancing not only an apocalyptic attitude, but also a form of rediscovered innocence and, I dare say, holiness. It is perhaps the only form of resistance that can be made to the heroism that nations can offer.

BC: You have never before expressed yourself so clearly with respect to Hölderlin. Does this reading date back to the beginning of your work?

RG: At least to 1967, the year of publication of the *Pléiade* edition of his works that I have been rereading constantly, especially since we have been working together on Clausewitz. I recently visited the places where Hölderlin lived: the *Stift* where he met Hegel and also the tower of the carpenter Zimmer. I was very moved. For me, discovering Hölderlin was a turning point. I read him during the most hyperactive period of my life I have known, at the end of the 1960s, when I alternated between elation and depression in the face of what I was trying to construct.

Hölderlin is a complex writer, but prodigious from the mimetic point of view. He was a manic-depressive of incredible intensity. Everything he said about the oscillation of his relations with those close to him is impressive. From his adolescence on he suffered the agony of "bipolarity," the melancholic shift from one extreme to the other. He himself told Suzette Gontard that the oscillation was related to "insatiable ambition." He had to be Schelling or nothing: this was the cruel alternative facing him, for he felt in his bones that the world had become completely unstable. In a world where we are each judged by our friends and loved ones, serene models no longer have any meaning. Meditation has been interiorized: the models are there, within reach. They invade me for an instant and I think I can dominate them, but then they escape and it is they who dominate me. I am always too far from or too close to them. This is the implacable law of mimetism. Reread *Hyperion*: this is the phenomenon that is repeated on almost every page:

> There is a forgetting of all existence, a hush of our being, in which we feel as if we had found everything.
>
> There is a hush, a forgetting of all existence, in which we feel as if we had lost everything, a night of the soul, in which no glimmer of any star nor even the fire from a rotting log gives us light.[10]

Thanks to Hölderlin, that great beggar for other people's affection, I understood that Nietzsche's madness was related to Wagner's apotheosis. To me, *Ecce Homo* says only one thing: "I am the author of *Zarathustra,* and I have thus become the model for the master of Bayreuth." This is why Nietzsche was profoundly shaken in Nice when he read Dostoevsky's *Notes from the Underground,* a book on bipolarity if there ever was one. However, while Dostoevsky resisted, Nietzsche succumbed to the unbearable tension that he wanted to maintain between Dionysius and "the Crucified." By contrast, Hölderlin saw his final withdrawal as the only means of ceasing to oscillate between self-glorification and self-repudiation, the only means of overcoming that torture. He finds Christ in a more heroic and saintly manner than through becoming a clergyman, as his mother had wished when he was a student. He passes through the hell of bipolarity, the never-ending come-and-go of mimetic desire that makes us feel like we are everything when the "god is near," and like nothing when the god moves away. Christ escapes, and allows us to escape, this alternation of the pendulum; he never becomes a rival for Hölderlin. The poet's great silence consisted therefore in a mysterious relationship to the absence of God, an imitation of his withdrawal. Hölderlin identifies himself with Christ in many of his poems. Is the Passion anything but an affirmation that Heaven is empty, that the gods are no longer there, that they have become "difficult to grasp?" It used to be enough to fight, to enter into violent reciprocity, in order to make them appear. The Christian *rupture* henceforth prohibits this. The worst thing one can now do is believe in violence.

Whatever its origins, Nietzsche's madness certainly derives from the constant, increasingly accelerated switching from "the Crucified" to Dionysius and from archaic religion to Christianity. Nietzsche did not want to see that Christ has taken Dionysius's place once and for all; that he had both appropriated and transformed the Greek heritage. Nietzsche thus allows himself to be swallowed up in violence's fight to the death with truth. In fact, he feels that combat more strongly than anyone else. However, his madness puts a terrible end to the *Aufklärung.* One must not choose Hellenic religion over Christianity, but hold both at the same time, and accept the idea that Christianity could have transformed the Greek view on the world. This is one of Hölderlin's most powerful intuitions, and one of the means of also escaping from obsession with the two worlds. We are indebted to the great eschatological thinker Franz Rosenzweig for publishing in 1917, in other words, at the height of the French-German conflict, a precious document entitled "The Oldest Systematic Program of German Idealism." It was written by Hegel, but surely conceived by Schelling and Hölderlin:

We so often hear that the great multitude should have a sensual religion. Not only the great multitude, but even philosophy needs it. *Monotheism of reason and the heart, polytheism of the imagination and art, that is what we need!* First I will speak about an idea here, which as far as I know, has never occurred to anyone's mind—we must have a new mythology; this mythology must, however, stand in the service of ideas, it must become a mythology of *reason.*[11]

In the minds of the three friends, responsibility for the new mythology would be incumbent on the *poet.* At one time, Schelling thought he was this poet, who would "plant Christianity's idealistic gods into nature itself, just as the Greeks placed their realistic gods into history."[12] The plan faded, and in the end only Hölderlin continued it, but in work that was broken and fragmented, and finally contradicted every didactic aspect that Hegel and Schelling had wanted to include. It takes the form of a central intuition based on the observation that there is absolute similarity but also absolute difference between the Christian and the archaic. In a way, one might say that the Greek gods were victims of bipolarity, of the duel, and that peace is never achieved. To bet on Dionysius is to believe in the fertility of violence, while today we can see it as essentially destructive. The "monotheism of reason and the heart," which in fact means Catholicism, is the only way to rediscover a degree of stability in an equilibrium that has become essentially unstable, *a situation that is a result of the Revelation.* Everything is adrift, extremely fragile. In order not to see these powerful intuitions at the origin of Hölderlin's withdrawal, psychoanalysts have of course looked towards sexuality. Yet if there was one thing that worked in his life, it was sexual relations. Everything else was broken. Proof that his sexuality was normal is that Suzette Gontard, far from having had enough of him, often was the one to seek him out during their affair. Of course, in the letters in which he portrayed his great idol as a divinity, Hölderlin frightened Goethe. However, you should not believe that there was anything there that could have been resolved by Freud or Heidegger.

BC: According to you, how did Hölderlin experience the tension between Christ and Dionysius, Christian religion and archaic religion?

RG: We need only look at his poems and listen to how they show the effort he made to escape the oscillation. Hölderlin also hesitates between Greece and Christianity. "Patmos" reveals the difficulty he has in distinguishing between Christ and Dionysius: evoking the "mystery of the vine" to speak of the Eucharist is clearly syncretistic. By contrast, poems like "The Only

One" are less ambiguous. It is persistently bad faith to deny that in these cases
Hölderlin chooses Christ, even though he is strongly tempted to follow his
friends and though the ambiguity of his position is never completely eliminated. When we reread the first version of the poem, we see that the poet's
faith results from a terrible struggle:

> [I] . . .
> Have looked upon much that is lovely
> And sung the image of God
> As here among human kind
> It lives, and yet, and yet,
> You ancient gods and all
> You valiant sons of the gods,
> One other I look for whom
> Within your ranks I love,
> Where hidden from the alien guest, from me,
> You keep the last of your kind,
> The treasured gem of the house.
> My Master and Lord!
> O you, my teacher!
> Why did you keep
> Away? And when
> I asked among the ancients,
> The heroes and
> The gods, then why were you
> Not there? And now my soul
> Is full of sadness as though
> You Heavenly yourselves excitedly cried
> That if I serve one I
> Must lack the other.
> And yet I know, it is my
> Own fault! For too greatly,
> O Christ, I'm attached to you,
> Although Heracles' brother,
> And boldly I confess,
> You are the brother also of Evius
> Who to his chariot harnessed
> The tigers and right down
> As far as the Indus

> Commanding joyful service,
> First planted the vineyard and tamed
> The fierceness and rage of the peoples.
> And yet a shame forbids me
> To associate with you
> The worldly men. [. . .][13]

Here the movement of Hölderlin's soul is clear. He is going from one god to the next, studying the abyss of divine withdrawal, regretting not being his friends' equal, yet choosing Christ hidden behind the other gods. Here, Hölderlin demonstrated his only "weakness": an irrepressible love for Christianity. Dionysius who "tamed / The fierceness and rage of the peoples," can clearly be felt here. How can we fail to see Euripides' *The Bacchantes* and its god, who has some "share in the war-god's sphere. For when an army stands armed in its ranks, terror can make it scatter before it touches a spear."[14] Hölderlin had read that. If we cite passages from the third version and its alternate readings from the manuscripts of "The Only One," the poet's choice becomes clearer still:

> It would shame me
> To liken you
> To the worldly ones;
> And I know well
> The Father who made you
> Is the same as you.
> Christ stands alone
> Under the visible Heaven and stars,
> Visibly assigned by God's will
> To the sins of the world
> To the misunderstanding of the Knowledge,
> when unceasing daily cares overwhelm the human,
> and the spirit of the stars above Him.[15]
> . . .
> . . . But the strife
> I am drawn to is this: necessity
> makes the sons of God carry
> The signs in themselves.
> The Thunderer has provided in another way.
> But Christ gives himself up.

Hercules is like the princes.
Bacchus is the spirit of the community.
But Christ is the end.
The presence
Which the heavenly beings lack, which
They cannot give to others,
Christ gives.[16]

Remaining in God's withdrawal: this is Christ's superiority. "The presence / Which the heavenly beings lack, which / They cannot give to others, / Christ gives." He is thus the One who raises up the divine hidden in all religions, who frees holiness from the sacred. The other gods are now nothing more than puppets whose consent or freedom is not their own. Hölderlin said that the Father intervened on behalf of his Son in a manner that cannot be applied to other gods. When he argues this, the poet is no longer under the influence of his friends. He is seeking less a synthesis than a kind of compossibility between the archaic and the Christian. He is well aware that *both a difference and a similarity have to be taken into account,* and that the Greek religion cannot be used as a weapon against Christianity. Christianity has changed the Greek religion forever.

There is thus something fundamental at play between the two forms of divine proximity, which are both similar and contrary. There is an essential difference between divine promiscuity and God's presence. It is very dangerous to ignore the distinction. What saves is the understanding that there is only one good distance: the imitation of Christ in order to avoid the imitation of men. This is because Dionysius no longer exists. The great "strife" that "draws" Hölderlin has to take place between the archaic and the Christian, but this does not mean that one will destroy the other. It is not a war. The latter raises up the former. Nietzsche clearly feels these things, but in another way and more than 50 years later. He wanted to keep opposing Dionysius to the "Crucified." The reality that Hölderlin felt is deeper and more mysterious: Christ has replaced Dionysius, and thereby exposed himself to fiercer violence from the very thing he has demystified.

This brings us back to the decisive lines that begin "Patmos," in which the identification with the Apostle John—he whose "attentive" eyes "Saw the face of the God exactly"[17]—is complete. The two lines that are so often cited today but so often misunderstood, "But where danger threatens / That which saves from it also grows," speak of both evil and its remedy, the escalation to extremes (divine promiscuity) and its opposite, reconciliation (the presence of God). This is the central apocalyptic intuition. To shift the historical positivity would be to show that this movement towards the worst is a negative trend that has a luminous obverse. Hölderlin is the martyr to this idea. Despite the pressure he suffers from fashion and his friends, the poet feels the truth: Dionysius is violence and Christ is peace. I cannot think of a better way of putting what we are trying to say. It is said by a Christian whose rare utterances during the time of his retreat includes the statement "I am precisely on the point of becoming Catholic."[18] This anecdote interests me in that it provides an anthropological basis for Catholic *stability,* which is the only thing that can hold the world together after the shock of the Revelation. However, we have to be careful not to portray Hölderlin as too Christian. His nature was deeply mystical; that cannot be denied. But we also cannot deny that his Protestantism and piety closed the way for him to Catholic cheerfulness. Furthermore, we should not forget that he experienced the elation of the French Revolution as the insane hope of all peoples. He marched all the way to Bordeaux; he believed in the Revolution.

Hölderlin is a kind of Clausewitz in his own way. He is also fascinated by France. He understood Hegel's naïveté to a greater extent than any of Hegel's modern adversaries, who have not had the strength to return to Christianity as he did. He understood that it is impossible to achieve reconciliation in the form that his friends imagined, and that history cannot be a battle leading to the heights, that the dialectic of violence cannot have a positive outcome.

One cannot escape from bipolarity unless one undergoes a conversion, which involves reversing time. This perspective is the only thing that could have enabled humanity to avoid the worst. There is now no guarantee that it will manage to do so. Some people pass through all this without seeing anything. They are not wrong, in a way, because the destructive capacity is, in the end, nothing. It exists only in relation to our world. It does not affect the real world, which is beyond, but also at the heart of human contradictions. The two worlds do not bespeak each other or if they do, it is in silence, in something left unsaid of which Hölderlin showed the importance. Destruction concerns *only this world,* not the Kingdom.

RATIONAL MODELS AND MIMETIC MODELS

BC: Does this not mean that, in opposition to the escalation to extremes, there is a "uniting ideal" that leads us back to precisely what you want to avoid?

RG: That ideal is not mine. Up to a certain point, we might be in a state of positive undifferentiation, in other words, *identified with others*. This is Christian love, and it exists in our world. It is even very active. It saves many people, works in hospitals, and even operates in some forms of research. Without this love, the world would have exploded long ago. We should not say that there are no legitimate, healthy political actions. However, politics is in itself powerless to control the rise of negative undifferentiation. It is more than ever up to each one of us to hold back the worst; this is what being in an eschatological time means. Our world is both the worst it has ever been, and the best. It is said that more victims are killed, but we also have to admit that more are *saved* than ever before. Everything is increasing. Revelation has freed possibilities, some of which are marvelous and others dreadful. The Scriptures thus announce a historical necessity and this is very important.

BC: But the atomization of individuals, each withdrawn upon his or her own model, indicates a breakdown, the failure of the movement towards reconciliation that was launched by Christianity and of which modern society is the heir. You seem to feel that the apocalyptic perspective cannot be avoided. Yet we still need to find ways to avoid the worst, and those ways can only be *individual*. This is why Bergson speaks of "saints and heroes" as exceptional individuals who are able to open their groups to the universal. In order to renounce war, the possibility of it occurring has to remain real. The real hero is thus the one who prepares for the worst, not the one who makes it happen.

RG: Your heroism is a response to my dilettantism. I kept jumping from one level to the other, from violence to reconciliation. Unlike what I thought for a while, you are forcing me not to linger on the duel, but to pass through it.

BC: Then it would in fact be from within reciprocity that the relationship would open up, what you call the good transcendence. However, we could speak instead of "peaceful reciprocity."

RG: I grant that we have to analyze the internal mutation of the mimetic principle, which consists in renouncing of the autonomy of our desire. I feel like saying that heroism is only a literary theme, and that it should remain so. It belongs to what could be called a *rational model*. The rational model tries to oppose the *mimetic model,* which is always stuck on a single figure who has become a rival or an obstacle. The rational model cannot thwart mimetism. Mimetism's law is implacable, as Clausewitz constantly reminds us. The distinction between the two models shows that we have definitely gone beyond external mediation and entered internal mediation. This explains why the

French Revolution and Napoleonic total mobilization correspond to the shift
from one era of imitation to the other. Clausewitz immediately identifies the
sudden acceleration with the concepts of the duel, of reciprocal action and the
trend to extremes, which mean the same thing. It was because France and
Germany were furiously imitating each other, and because each saw the other
as an obstacle that had to be eliminated, that the trend to extremes occurred
in Europe.

However, the rational model is not outdated. It allows us to think about
what lies beyond the duel, which I call the Kingdom. It corresponds to what
Pascal called the order of the spirit, the necessary passage towards the order
of charity. It is absolutely powerless to change the course of events, even
though it makes it possible to understand them. The mimetic model constantly forces us back into the hell of desire. We have to abandon all optimism: mimetic violence cannot be integrated into a dialectic. Great writers
have understood this law, but at what a price. These are strange experiences,
which I would classify, like that of Hölderlin, with religious experiences.
Proust is a kind of saint from this point of view, as well as Stendhal and
Cervantes. A few exceptional individuals have been given the gift of enlightening people about their behavior. However, we should never minimize our
inability to recognize this reality. Our miserable autonomy is more important
to us than anything else.

BC: Between mimetism of the order of bodies and the *imitatio Christi,* we
therefore have to think of a temporary release from mimetism, which belongs
to the order of the spirit in Pascal: that of philosophical concepts, mathematical models, and characters in novels?

RG: Absolutely, but let's not forget two things: on one hand, the model
has an opposite meaning depending on whether it is mimetic or rational,
and on the other hand, in the era of internal mediation that we have entered,
the mimetic model will always prevail over the rational model. Clausewitz is
in a mimetic relation to Napoleon, though he could have been in a rational
relation to Frederick II. The "god of war" is dangerous because he is too close.
Frederick II was more distant. He could have stimulated theoretical reflection,
if the French Revolution and Napoleonic era had not shaken Europe. In a
way, Antiquity and its sacrosanct respect for transcendent models ended in
the eighteenth century. The *exempla* no longer exist in the modern world. We
will soon see how Clausewitz's rational model was powerless to resist the
Napoleonic model.

The mimetic model is a means to an end. I cannot move towards an
object without moving towards the mediator, who inevitably competes

with me for it. My way is thus blocked. The mediator becomes what I call a "model-obstacle," whose *very being* I will try ever more violently to acquire. What I would like to call heroic temptation is a form of hypnosis, of mimetic obstruction, of fixation on a model: a blockage of the identification process that, in order to function, should move very freely from one model to the next. The movement is natural if one has met the right models during one's formative years. It is not at all so if one has missed the crucial stages. This is a true misfortune that no psychoanalysis or psychotherapy can ever change. Clausewitz was a standard bearer when he was 12 years old. He was too immersed in the culture of heroism to be able to resist the magnetism of the Napoleonic model after Jena. As we have seen, that is the great tragedy of his life. Remember his famous phrase concerning the events of the "recent wars" that shook the strategic balance in Europe.

Given the inevitability of mimetic models, it seems very difficult to describe a model that would remain rational. From this point of view, it is vain to try to imagine infallible procedures to prevent us from succumbing to imitation. No philosophical thought will master the shift to charity. Pascal writes: "There is nothing is so conformable to reason as this disavowal of reason."[19] Given the extent of its growing control, escaping from mimetism is something only geniuses and saints can do. Thus we would place in the order of charity a person who went from heroic temptation to sainthood, from the risk of regression that is inherent to internal mediation to the discovery of a form of mediation that we have to call ...

BC: Innermost?

RG: Why not. "Innermost mediation" (in the sense of Saint Augustine's *Deos interior intimo meo*), in so far as it supposes an inflection of internal mediation, which can always degenerate into bad reciprocity. "Innermost mediation" would be nothing but the imitation of Christ, which is an essential anthropological discovery. Saint Paul says, "Be imitators of me, as I am of Christ."[20] This is the chain of positive undifferentiation, the chain of identity. Discerning the right model then becomes *the* crucial factor. We imitate Christ less than we identify with the one who, in the apocalyptic texts, *will have been* Christ. To imitate Christ is to identify with the other, to efface oneself before him: "Truly I tell you, just as you did it to one of the least of these who are members of my family, you did it to me."[21] Identification supposes a special aptitude for empathy. This explains the constant reminder in these texts of the danger of Antichrists, the danger that they will increasingly present, for Christ alone enables us to escape from human imitation.

BC: Pascal had a great metaphor for expressing the leap from the order of bodies to that of charity. He talked about the distance you need to be from a painting to see it properly: neither too far nor too near. The "exact point which is the true place"[22] is nothing other than charity. Excessive empathy is mimetic, but excessive indifference just as much. Identification with the other has to be envisaged as a means of correcting our mimetic tendencies. Mimetism brings me too close to or too far from the other. Identification makes it possible to see the other from the right distance.

RG: But only Christ makes it possible to find that distance. This is why the path indicated in the Gospels is the only one available now that there are no longer any *exempla,* now that transcendence of models is no longer available to us. It is up to us to re-establish transcendence by resisting the irresistible attraction that others exercise upon us, and that always leads to violent reciprocity. Hölderlin was sublime in this respect. The ceremonious way that he received visitors in the tower in Tübingen consisted precisely in putting them at the right distance. To imitate Christ by keeping the other at the right distance is to escape the mimetic whirlpool: *no longer imitate in order to no longer be imitated.* Napoleon had to be a very fascinating model for Clausewitz to have been so vague when speaking of heaven in his letters to Maria von Brühl.

BC: In relation to that, Raymond Aron cites a letter dated April 4, 1813, in which Clausewitz, who was in the midst of war against Napoleon, wrote to his wife:

> I am in good health and the days are full of happiness; this is essentially the news that I have for you. To be part of a delightful little army with my friends at its head, to cross magnificent countryside in the summer months, and for such a goal, is just about the ideal longed for in earthly existence (if you consider it transitory and as a path to other existences).[23]

RG: What could have been the "other existences" that the future general was thinking of? Surely not Nietzschean super-humanity. Yet we have seen that he was touching on something archaic and absolutely fundamental. I imagine him as a good Protestant who went to church on Sunday and wrote tender letters to his wife while dreaming of glory, without imagining that his "ideal longed for" would lead to the end of Europe. This explains the "delightful little army" that very gradually began to replace his wife. If he knew how we are treating him and how we have now encircled his thought within an apocalyptic perspective, which he did not share, he would probably want to strangle us. However, this view of him is essential. The apocalypse appropriate for our time is perhaps no longer Saint John at Patmos, but a Prussian general riding with his friends along the roads of Russia and Europe.

What could have been the "other existences" of which he spoke except humanity finally at peace, the humanity of which all religions have dreamed since the beginning, since there have been humans and they have been at war? This suddenly makes me think of a Veda myth that I have never used: the one about *Purusha*, the archetypical man who is a little larger than the universe and is put to death by a crowd of sacrificers. Since he is the primordial man, we wonder where the crowd could have come from. It is from this murder that all of reality emerges. This is truly a founding myth, but violence is curiously absent from it. It is probably so old that the violence has faded out of the picture. This is the absolutely peaceful Vedic conception of things. It is very strange but I have never used it as I should have. It is perfectly consistent with what we have just proposed.

CHAPTER 6

Clausewitz and Napoleon

THE NAPOLEONIC ANTI-MODEL

Benoît Chantre: In Clausewitz's writings we have seen the twilight of a historical literature based on the *exempla*, even though he thought of himself as a little like Plato writing *The Republic*, and would have liked to have been able to reform the Prussia that had resulted from the humiliation by Napoleon. His rational model nonetheless remained very abstract. Clausewitz's real model was a historical figure, and he could not prevent himself from clinging to it. His conception of heroism suffered in consequence, since it was unable to resist this magnetism.

René Girard: Indeed, we constantly see a mimetic model in Clausewitz opposed by a rational model that is powerless against it. Clausewitz thinks over against Napoleon; he thus tries to construct a counter-model, and for that he looks to the mythical figure of Frederick the Great. His ploy was doomed to failure at the outset.

Let us look at Frederick for a moment. The musician-king had been forced by his father to undergo a military education that repelled him. He preferred to engage in correspondence with Voltaire and to read French philosophers. Mimetism, as always. He dreamed of being a "philosopher-king" and developed a contract-based philosophy that would eliminate divine right. In fact, Frederick II was really thinking of Louis XIV. However, he ended up continuing his father's domestic policy and forgetting about Voltaire and the code that was supposed to promote justice in Prussia. There was nothing unusual in all that. His foreign policy, in contrast, broke completely with that of his father: Frederick the Great went off to fight Austria without even declaring war on it. This adventurous policy weakened his overall achievement: the country underwent considerable development, but there was excessive centralization and authoritarianism, which fell apart like a house of cards at Jena.

Of course, Clausewitz does not speak of these contrasts. His dream—for he was never given the means—is to reform his country. However, Prussia has nothing equivalent to the French tradition, in particular the royal mythology, into which Napoleon was forced to integrate himself. Clausewitz tinkered, a little like a sorcerer's apprentice. He uses Plato, perhaps, and some Kant and Frederick II surely, but especially a lot of Napoleon, even though he refuses to admit it. He thus claims that Frederick was both a head of state and a military leader, capable of audacity but never adventurism.

BC: Frederick "controlled" the military leader who, in turn, "controlled" popular passions, just as politics "controls" strategy, which "controls" tactics. At least, this is what Clausewitz would like to believe, though he always leaves open the possibility that political ends could be contaminated by warlike means.[1]

RG: Clausewitz wants to see war from an aristocratic point of view, but at the same time the Revolution's influence is clear. The fact that in his theory passion belongs only to the people simply contradicts this ideal. It is proof that he could not find a way to link the parts together consistently. War is no longer aristocratic, but it was not yet democratic. Defining command by intelligence is thus not sufficient. Clausewitz gets carried away with his formulas. Because he has his "trinity," he wants to keep it, but in fact everything was contaminated. A leader needs more than intelligence and probability calculations.

Look at Clausewitz's description of engaging the enemy, for example. It gives the impression that he is a novelist or film maker. The commander is on the hill, more exposed to danger than anyone else. He is thus not pure intelligence: the leader is caught up in popular passions. This is Napoleon, not Frederick II. Napoleon was deeply committed as a leader. Naturally, he had a revolutionary side because he was neither the king, nor the people, but he led the people. Being carried into battle by the rabble is always less dangerous than forcing the rabble to fight. Voltaire saw this very clearly at the beginning of *Candide,* when the hero is dragooned into the Prussian army by recruiters who get him drunk. At this point I always used to say to my students, "Aren't you surprised? The king does not have the power to draft Candide.

The recruiters are forced to get him drunk to have him sign up! Conscription was not possible at the time. Democracy is the author of that little invention, the power to draft people!"

French voluntarism is a unique innovation, very different from Spanish partisanship, contrary to what Clausewitz thought. However, French soldiers were not respectful because they thought they were carrying out the Revolution. The recruiting officer is a mythical figure in France, never questioned. Now, what Voltaire is already referring to is violation of individual freedom. Those subjected to military service never rebelled. In the play of doubles, there is something that traps people. In fact, the republic is rivalry among all, whereas we used to be beaten by the king, who was alone responsible for battles. This was infinitely less humiliating and made real negotiations possible. Peoples used to face one another, but then believe the arguments designed to persuade them to put down their arms and walk away singing.

General mobilization is pure madness. Fortunately we can see this today with the United States' quagmire in Iraq. Bush is going to lose the war because he will no longer be able to find volunteers to sign up. The King of Prussia may have been a tyrant, but he did not have the power to conscript. Napoleon took care of procuring that for him. The failure of Clausewitz's amalgam is this shift to modern warfare, which his work helped to produce. Since Clausewitz dreams of war conducted by Spanish peasants, of whom the least we can say is that they were not democrats, he heralds the advent of totalitarianism.

BC: This is why Pascal provides us with such a convincing analysis of the "half-clever," the reformers who cause catastrophes by striking at the established powers. After having destroyed the existing models, they always end up suggesting that we should imitate them, like Stavrogin in *The Possessed*.

RG: Indeed, tinkering in such cases can prove fatal. The problem is that, in a world of internal mediation, we can only tinker, substitute one thing for another. This is what Napoleon did with his parody of the imperial coronation, but the model that he constructed was nothing but a bogus institution. He aggravated the forces that he was supposed to control: now everyone is going to think they can be Napoleon. This is why an *a priori* definition of heroism is contradictory, in the sense that Napoleon caused the heroic model to implode. He was more aristocratic than the aristocrats, and more vulgar than the most vulgar. He is able to say: "What a novel my life has been!" Thus, if there was a genius of the Revolution, it was he. He took the model of heroic wisdom, violated it, sullied it, and rendered it more perfect than ever before. He was both the odious sovereign and the absolute conqueror because he was stronger than either.

The Red and the Black is a very uneven book, but Napoleon's role in it is very important because the one who takes the emperor as his model is a little rascal who is more of a Trotskyite than anything else. Stendhal suggests this interpretation of the Revolution. He sees Julien Sorel as a certain type of ambitious man whom he considers politically dangerous. We have the impression that Dostoevsky could have read Stendhal because Raskolnikov is also a modern false hero, an abased hero. He is darker and has more complex ideas, but his is the same kind of post-revolutionary heroism. Raskolnikov imitates Napoleon, just like Julien Sorel. He is defined in analogous terms. Dostoevsky is anti-Western enough to sense that these sinister types come from the West, but he can nonetheless be considered perfectly consistent with Stendhal.

BC: So, do you suspect heroism of being a dangerous innovation? I feel like I am listening to a defender of the established order ...

RG: And you would be mistaken. As I have said before, there is no one more anti-Maurrassian than I. However, what you are saying with a smile certainly corresponds to criticism that could be directed against me. It is quite possible to see *Violence and the Sacred* as praising the efficacy of sacrifice as the only thing that can maintain social order. People forget that the model I was developing applies only to archaic societies, in other words, human groups that existed thousands of years ago and for which the return to order was a question of life and death. That conception of order was based on the hidden mechanisms of the mimetic violence at the origin of all institutions. The return to order meant the end of a fever that could have destroyed the group.

In this sense, there is no clear line to be drawn between a rebirth of the religious through a founding murder and each ritual undertaking. However, we have to identify a huge number of intermediaries between the ritual and the sacrificial crisis. The purpose of each rite is to stop a little crisis. Each rite imitates the original crisis, of course, but each rite's crisis is independent as such. The real "catharsis" occurs only because we introduce a little disorder into the rite so that something new will be produced. In other words, the more violence there is, the more "catharsis" there will be in the end. Every rite is thus a kind of founding murder, and every murder has a bit of a ritual aspect. Mimetism has to be thought of as both good and bad. In this sense, a society with no crises, entirely stabilized by the absence of violence, cannot have a history. The reactionary position consists in defending the existing order, which is absurd. This entails a deep positivism that does not take into account the unpredictability of the event. Moreover, the fact that human relations are never assessed through the lens of ritual, in other words, in relation to religious *instability,* is very unfortunate because it makes them harder to understand.

Christian revelation accelerated a trend to extremes by eliminating more and more sacrifices. The West's failing resides in its refusal to see the coming of Christianity as a liberating maturity, an anti-sacrificial education. In fact, poorly Christianized pagans (ever since Charlemagne used a battle axe to convert the Saxons) have acted from the beginning like Napoleon's mercenaries. The Crusades initiated the idea of having energy only for pillaging foreign nations. From this point of view, the Fourth Crusade was the most grotesque, loosing a band of antique hunters into the formidable accumulation of wealth that used to be Constantinople.

We cannot reduce Christianity to nothing but a venerable tradition to which we owe a message that is crucial for humanity's salvation. Christianity is also a historical current that finally led Pope John Paul II to an act of repentance during his visit to Yad Vashem and the Wailing Wall. It is a religion that very quickly returned to old sacrificial reflexes. In short, it has not lived up to its message, to the radically new information that it revealed: definitive knowledge of the mechanisms of violent foundations and radical demystification of the sacred, of the social organizations which it sanctions. Christ plunges us into knowledge of mimetic mechanisms. He thus indeed brings war not peace, disorder not order, because all order is suspect in a way: it always hides the one whose blood was shed in order to reconcile us. To denounce this, to chip away the paint of the "whitewashed tombs,"[2] was to disrupt the sacrificial mechanism forever. The death of Christ *will never have been* a founding lynching, and the resistance that people put up to the only possible model that He offers them will cause the acceleration of history of which they will be the first victims. Clausewitz is a steadfast witness of this blindness at the dawn of the catastrophes that are awaiting us.

BC: You were suggesting that Clausewitz imitated Napoleon. Thus he did not escape from the traps that you have called "metaphysical desire."

RG: Clausewitz is indeed completely caught up in his fascination with Napoleon. Here, we are dealing with a typically romantic way of thinking, caught in a passion that I call "underground": an attempt to acquire the model's being. In this, mimetic theory makes it possible to get a deeper grasp of the structure of Clausewitz's text. Let's not forget that Napoleon becomes a scapegoat right when Clausewitz begins writing his treatise, probably towards 1810. He was the enemy at bay whose strength his opponents were trying to steal for themselves. He was detested, for both good and bad reasons, at the same time that he was becoming the "god of war." Europe's hatred of the emperor shows us how the "unanimity minus one" phenomenon works. Europe is hoping to restore its balance, and Clausewitz is participating in the struggle against one of the primary authors of European disorder. He was baying with the pack to some extent.

"Identification with the acting person"

BC: Now that we are trying to identify the structure of Clausewitz's text, could you give a concrete example of a mimetic fixation on a single individual?

RG: The clearest example can be seen in the French Campaign. It lasted from January to April 1814, and in it Napoleon was trying to prevent the Sixth Coalition from entering Paris. The coalition included troops from Russia, Prussia, England, Sweden and Austria, along with soldiers from the kingdoms of Bavaria and Württemberg, which were former German allies of Napoleon. It is a model campaign, the most studied along with the first battles in Italy, which were the most "divine" campaigns on the strategic level, owing to Napoleon's relative weakness. The emperor succumbed at the very point when his genius became fully manifest.

The Austrians entered France through Switzerland, and the Russians and Prussians crossed the Rhine. Bernadotte, the emperor's former officer and Germaine de Staël's friend, raised an army of Swedish, Russian, Prussian and English soldiers, which came through Belgium. Napoleon demonstrated exceptional boldness, sometimes hacking his way through impasses his guard could not penetrate. He fought legendary battles at Champaubert, Montmirail and Montereau, but finally had to abdicate at Fontainebleau on April 6, abandoned by almost all. When they arrived in Paris, the allies themselves were disgusted by the cowardice of the French, who were so quick to switch sides. Yet their weariness was understandable. No dynastic tradition could survive him, despite the Duke of Vicence's efforts to get the allies to accept the idea of the regency of the King of Rome. As we have seen, nothing holds in a system of internal mediation; everything is affected and gets turned upside down. Politics scrambles to catch up to war, and can establish only momentary stopgaps, which fall apart almost immediately.

Nonetheless, all witnesses and historians have noted Napoleon's acute strategic intelligence. Like a hunted stag, he gave admirable fight to the armies of Bohemia (led by Schwarzenberg), Silesia (led by Blücher) and the North (led by Bernadotte). Clausewitz is watching all of this, and tries to learn from it. We have to linger for a moment on the "metaphysical desire" that attracts him to Napoleon, seen as the "god of war." Here we have an "Imitation of *Bonaparte*," whom Clausewitz, carried away by his hatred, never calls Napoleon or the emperor. Bonaparte is easier to imitate because he was no longer threatening, but was only a virtuoso—whose virtuosity one could calmly appreciate. Such imitation supposes that the theorist *follow his model step by step,* instead of passing freely from one model to another, that he re-experience his campaigns with him, in short, that *he become a Bonaparte.*

Clausewitz did not have the distance of a Cervantes or a Stendhal, who depicted characters imitating models. He does not know that the Napoleonic method, slavishly followed by Julien Sorel, will lead the hero to the scaffold. He resembles Napoleon's French critics, who tend to forget the emperor and remember only the first and last Napoleon. The young upstart and the defeated man make it possible to point out his virtuosity. Between those two extremes, victory can no longer be considered a "divine surprise." Napoleon's other battles were too huge, too massive: Wagram and Friedland resembled slaughters; they were too modern. In them, the exceptional individual is swallowed up in his great army.

Clausewitz gets closer to Napoleon, as if he has a zoom lens on a camera. The approach is less critical than cinematic. There is no way that he wants to give up the effects. There is a Leni Riefenstahl aspect to this aesthetic of fascination. However, it was Bonaparte who fascinates Clausewitz, not Napoleon: the winner of Campo Formio, not the loser at Fontainebleau. Clausewitz imbues the French Campaign with the memory of the Pont d'Arcole, and tries to appropriate Bonaparte's genius so that he can surpass Napoleon. This is striking. When, thanks to Bismarck, circumstances became favorable to *On War*'s return to prominence, Clausewitz's Bonaparte interests Ludendorff, as we have mentioned. The rigidity of the model constructed by Clausewitz, which does not have the flexibility and poetical nuances of Chinese treatises, is dangerous. He made a skillful attempt to escape his predecessors' sterile fascination with the "geometry" of war, but what was gained by going from mathematics to mimetism? This is the heart of the paradox: we have freed violence by understanding its mechanisms better. Losing control of our own violence enfeebles us, and prolongs our weakness.

Unlike Julien Sorel, Clausewitz had probably not read the *Mémorial de Sainte-Hélène.*[3] He wrote his treatise instead of that of the emperor. This of course reminds us of Dostoevsky and *Notes from the Underground.* Clausewitz is constantly seeking to resist the attraction that his model has over him, but he never succeeds. In the French Campaign, not long after Paris was taken, there was a time when Napoleon had considerable success against Blücher, the general at Waterloo. Clausewitz said that if Napoleon had continued to pursue Blücher, instead of beating him but letting him go and then attacking Schwarzenberg (whom Clausewitz did not consider a very able general, and this speaks of his disdain for Austrians), he would have pushed Blücher back to the Rhine and then the others would have panicked and withdrawn in fear. In Napoleon's shoes, Clausewitz would have won the French Campaign.

This is a formidable passage, incredibly romantic. There is a nod to the boldness of Frederick II, of course, so that not everything is attributed to Napoleon, but they do not have the same force. Clausewitz says that Napoleon was mistaken about Blücher, and that he had exaggerated the danger from Schwarzenberg. Destiny would have switched sides if he had persevered against Blücher—the essential enemy, the Prussian. Even if Schwarzenberg had gotten too close to Paris, Napoleon should not have paid attention to him. *He should have finished defeating the Prussians.* Napoleon had divided Blücher's army so that he could defeat it in separate sections. The Napoleonic and Clausewitzian genius would have been to continue this strategy, to dare to leave the rest defenseless. Success alone counted, and the prestige of this victory would have made all the allies retreat to Germany.

This more-Napoleonic-than-Napoleon Clausewitz is remarkable. We find this in Book 2 of the treatise, which contains the most interesting parts on the dramatic level. Retrospectively, Clausewitz becomes the advisor, replacement and substitute for Napoleon. He even says that it would not have mattered if Paris was taken, except that Napoleon had cared about it. This may have been truer then because capital cities are now formidable information centers; at Clausewitz's time they were less so. The French Campaign was strange in this sense. Napoleon demonstrated all his ability, but his forces were so much smaller that he was finally beaten. Carried away by his passion, Clausewitz said that Napoleon's mistake was to not have been Napoleonic enough. The subject is so close to his model that he no longer tries to acquire the model's property, but his being itself, his "luck" in Clausewitzian terms. Clausewitz thus set up a contrast between a very special kind of rationality and the pseudo-scientific method of the strategists of his time.

If the French Campaign had taken place in Italy in 1796, Napoleon would have pursued Blücher right to the end, just as he had crossed the Noric Alps and threatened Austria in the past. Napoleon agreed to make peace at Campo Formio for many different reasons. It was a negotiated peace. However, at that time he would have dared anything. Clausewitz placed extraordinary importance on that attitude: the young man did what the mature man would not dare. Thus, during the French Campaign, Napoleon returned to only some of his original qualities. Clausewitz was nostalgic for Campo Formio. The passages that speak of specific campaigns, which everyone was familiar with at the time, are sometimes interrupted by bits of theory, but in them the proportion of Napoleonic examples has to be three or four to one. Of course, there are examples that come from the Swedes, Gustavus Adolphus and the Thirty Years' War. Yet, in the end, only contemporary wars were important: according to Clausewitz, in the War of the Spanish Succession, guns had not reached the perfection of the Napoleonic campaigns. Classical examples were no longer up to date enough.

Like all subjects caught in mimetic desire, Clausewitz was sometimes swept away by the Napoleonic model, and sometimes switched to the completely opposite stance, that of hatred. This occurs suddenly in his writing, and when it does, the model of Frederick II appears as an effort to expel Napoleon. There is thus a passage where Clausewitz tries to make Frederick a Bonaparte. This is with respect to the conquest of Silesia, the great Prussian adventure. He stated that Frederick's march from one location to another could be considered quite daring, but also absolutely necessary. The King of Prussia could not save himself except through exceptional boldness and at the risk of his entire army and total defeat. Clausewitz tried to make Frederick the Great into a wiser Napoleon. He focused on the fact that he had huge manpower and resource problems. On the conceptual level, this model is stronger, but if we analyze the text using statistics, which is useful for defending the mimetic theory, we see immediately that there is a more complete endorsement of the Napoleonic model.

Note that the *Directoire* wanted to send Bonaparte to Italy because it was clear that he was dangerous. He was given an army of shoeless soldiers, yet he was able to achieve striking victories, in contrast with what was happening on the German front. The fewer means Bonaparte had, the greater his genius. For proud people like him, this is perfectly normal. There is no fear of failure when failure is what is meant to happen, when our enemies believe so and reasonable minds think so. In such cases, one becomes defiant and capable of anything. By contrast, when we are in an advantageous position, where our success is predicted, we make the worst mistakes and waste opportunities. Because we are expected to win, we have a fear of failing. Some people operate best only when absolute audacity is required. Clausewitz's admiration of Frederick II was real, but much less exciting. Here we see the internal combat in Clausewitz between the rational and the mimetic. However, on the literary level, the mimetic plays a much bigger role. I do not know whether many people have seen this, but we should highlight it. We need to use *literary* commentary to understand the way the author of *On War* criticized strategic writings because the essential occurs on this level. The fact that he has been interesting people for so long, and still does, is due to this attention to effects.

BC: This is the reason Clausewitz had recourse to what he called identification "with the person acting." He said that such identification is necessary but almost impossible: who "would lay claim to the talent of a Frederick or a Bonaparte?"[4] The military critic must thus try to take a "higher point of view," in other words, to integrate historical, geographical, psychological, etc. data that are not available to the army leader, who is too immersed in the battle. Distance enables the critic to avoid too much subjectivity and to circumvent arrogance, which could result from hindsight—knowledge of the success or failure of the "person acting." The only way to escape from such positivism (which Clausewitz called "judgment according to the result") is to get as close as possible to the views specific to the military genius. The argument is thus subtly circular. Clausewitz invites the critic to go from the specific to the global, and from the global to the specific. This to-and-fro is the only thing that can give us an idea of what we call "destiny" or "luck" for lack of a better term. Clausewitz is targeting nothing less, in effect, than to provide the critic with "access to the life."[5] He is trying to escape the rigid logical categories that prevail in strategy.

RG: This passage from the specific to the global and from the global to the specific is typical of polarization around a single model. This is not at all Pascal's "exact point," but a kind of focusing in which bipolarity comes into play, an essential oscillation. Clausewitz was both close to the "god of war" and rejected by him. To understand mimetism is to understand this circularity. Theorists of the eternal return understand only the return. Partisans of linearity grasp only the linear. Let's try to understand *both*. In that, we differ from Clausewitz, who was always on the way towards mimetic thought, in other words, a type of emotion that he sought to conquer using literary means.

It is clear that Clausewitz is reproving critics who take the liberty of blaming such and such general on paper and claiming to advance mathematical recipes for victory. It would be vain to say *a posteriori* that in 1812 the Russian Campaign was doomed to failure because it looked objectively like the Austerlitz, Friedland and Wagram campaigns. Clausewitz wrote, "the human eye cannot trace the interconnection of events back to the decisions of the vanquished monarchs."[6] This puts the arrogance of the armchair strategist back in its place. Clausewitz concludes, "There are times when the utmost daring is the height of wisdom."[7] Clausewitz admires the "military genius" too much to look down upon Napoleon. In contrast, he sticks to his model, after having moved away for a little while to understand what could have made the first campaigns successful despite the failure of the last ones. The critic's pleasure lies entirely in such moments, which, as we have seen, belong to the sacred:

> But it is obvious that the intellectual pleasure at success and the intellectual discomfort at failure arise from an obscure sense of some delicate link, invisible to the mind's eye, between success and the commander's genius. It is a gratifying assumption. The truth of this is shown by the fact that *our sympathy increases and grows keener as success and failure are repeated by the same man.* That is why luck in war is of higher quality than luck in gambling. So long as a successful general has not done us any harm, we follow his career with pleasure.[8]

Strong emotion is a gateway to bipolarity. Each battle could be Waterloo. There is a great deal of emotion involved in risking one's life, and he who takes such a risk is divinized. Clausewitz's emotion came from this very instability. Here we are touching on the genesis of modern humanity, in both its most unbalanced and most frightening aspects. Of course, Clausewitz would have liked to hold stability and emotion together, but that is impossible. He remains caught in the mimetic circle. He is more fragile and less arrogant than many other strategists, who did not have field experience as he did. He wrote that the critic should not push "himself into the limelight."[9] He was no positivist, and he was more realistic than many historians and strategists of his time, who were too quick to praise or criticize specific men of war. He also does not believe in a necessary sequence of events, but endeavors to take chance and unpredictability fully into account. There is arrogance in basing one's retrospective judgment of an action on its success or failure. Therefore the critic sometimes has to make use of his "greater knowledge, including as it does a knowledge of the outcome" and sometimes "ignore these things in order to place himself exactly in the situation of the man in command."[10] Such identification with the person is the only point of view from which one can "praise or blame." Yet it is rarely achieved. The critic has to go from the general point of view to the specific, from details to the overview, with as much care and sensitivity as possible.

> A critic should therefore not check a great commander's solution to a problem as if it were a sum in arithmetic. Rather, he must recognize with

admiration the commander's success, the smooth unfolding of events, the higher workings of his genius. The essential interconnections that genius has divined, the critic has to reduce to factual knowledge.[11]

Thus, Napoleon was right to engage in the Russian Campaign: it was not a mistake on his part, but a change in the conditions of war, a shift of conflicts towards Asia and thus towards the world. The emperor was like a fish out of water. He had not changed; it was the era. There is something in Clausewitz's critique that smacks of the aristocrat, or of the would-be aristocrat. For him, miserable critical reason did not really have any hold over military genius. The wellsprings of luck and genius will never be understood because both are part of a reality that is related to the sacred. Note that Clausewitz said that the critic has to "reduce to factual knowledge" "the essential interconnections that genius has divined." The reader is asked to enter into the elect through the ritual of the theory, itself finally provided with the right method. What Clausewitz is trying to do is thus deal with unpredictability, fit luck and hazard into his theoretical framework, and the latter is related to ritual. There is no recipe for victory in a world where reciprocal action reigns; it would be just as absurd to imitate Napoleon slavishly as to disdain him. One has to identify with him once one has obtained a general understanding of the situation. In a way, Clausewitz understands the attitude that he should have towards his model *if he were not his unique and only model*. It would then be simply one with the attitude of a historian drawing the portrait of a historical figure.

Yet in Clausewitz's writing there is, as we have seen, a clear fixation on Napoleon. The other models that would have been useful for balancing the analysis do not compare to the emperor. Everything comes back to Napoleon, in a way that can be compared to the process by which a victim is selected. However, Clausewitz was able to make this mechanism appear so clearly only because he was not entirely taken in by it. He therefore saw its true face, had an understanding of it in which the scapegoat mechanism was almost explicit. Evidence of this, if such were needed, is that he does not speak only about military relations: he put Enlightenment thought on hold, which allowed him to say essential things about human relationships. He knows that he is writing an indefinable masterpiece. Real literary criticism has to go beyond the limitations of literature. It is not through antimilitarism that we will do away with war, but by reading *On War* as closely as possible. Literary emotion is an elixir that demystifies in the most honorable way. To understand war completely is to no longer be able to be a warrior.

Only the logic of the sacred shows us the ambivalence of the theorist's point of view on the "military genius." Clausewitz values his prey, he admires it, and it fascinates him. His attitude towards the fallen emperor, who had become the scapegoat of Europe, is the attitude that all *unknowingly* adopted towards Napoleon, who was literally divinized after his exile. In a way, the victim is always the one who succeeds and fails at the same time. The victim wears contradictory badges. Its sacred nature comes from this very oscillation. Clausewitz tells us about the crowd's "vague feeling," in other words, the rationality that escapes the control of the mind. It is in this that "luck in war is of higher quality than luck in gambling."[12] Intellectuals amuse themselves, not warriors.

BC: Do we not have a case here of falling short of the order of the spirit, in a regression typical of internal mediation, in which one can go very quickly from the best to the worst, in which the audacity of the analysis can turn into fanaticism?

RG: Like all romantics, Clausewitz guesses but also overlooks something essential. This is solid proof that identification with the other very often leads to failure in a world of internal mediation. Instead of going from one model to the other, the subject gets stuck on the strongest model and starts competing with him to appropriate his being. This form of symbolic cannibalism is the symptom that the relationship has failed. Clausewitz, more than anyone else, takes "reciprocal action" into account, but he ends up falling into its trap. Once again, he is not alone, but he provides us with a lot of information on the feelings of the Europeans of his time, who were watching Napoleon and were also impressed by his effectiveness, though they did not pardon the pillaging and taxing by the French army. While Napoleon's virtuosity inspired admiration, his troops' behavior was scandalous. Hölderlin is a good symbol of the great disappointment of German intellectuals, who initially saw every Frenchman as a liberator and not as a soldier. It is only natural that these ambivalent feelings would crystallize around Napoleon. Indeed, the temptation to imitate him is only increased by the thought that he could be surpassed: there is always a partial basis for nationalistic delusions.

Let us go back to the point of maximum polarization, in other words, to the ultimate and prodigious virtuosity of the hunted stag, who fascinated all the generals in Europe at the very time when the net was tightening around him. Clausewitz is the prime contemporary here:

> The world was filled with admiration when Bonaparte, in February 1814, turned from Blücher after beating him at Etoges, Champ-Aubert, Montmirail,

and elsewhere, to fall on Schwarzenberg, and beat him at Montereau and Mormant. By rapidly moving his main force back and forth, Bonaparte brilliantly exploited the allies' mistake of advancing with divided forces. If, people thought, these superb strokes in all directions failed to save him, at least it was not his fault. No one has yet asked what would have happened if, instead of turning away from Blücher, and back to Schwarzenberg, he had gone on hammering Blücher and had pursued him back to the Rhine. We are convinced that the complexion of the whole campaign would have been changed and that, instead of marching on Paris, the allied armies would have withdrawn across the Rhine. We do not require others to share our view, but no expert can doubt that the critic is bound to consider that alternative once it has been raised.[13]

Clausewitz adopts Napoleon's point of view; he imagines he is Napoleon's advisor, as he was apparently Kutusov's in real life. What does he suggest if not that, even in their reflections on Napoleon's battles, critics are not daring enough. He was the only one who was really Napoleonic, super-Napoleonic even, in the French Campaign. His Blücher strategy is admirable, and perhaps he was right. Perhaps Napoleon might have won if Clausewitz had been there to encourage his genius. Remember all the passages in *On War* in which Clausewitz analyzed the weakening of an army that has marched too much. The effects are so terrible that in a few hours a superb army can be transformed into a pathetic herd. Here are the reasons Clausewitz gives to support his thesis:

> Suppose ... we ... wanted to prove that the relentless pursuit of Blücher would have served Napoleon better than turning against Schwarzenberg. We would rely on the following simple truths:
>
> 1. Generally speaking, it is better to go on striking in the same direction than to move one's forces this way and that, because shifting troops back and forth involves losing time. Moreover, it is easier to achieve further successes where the enemy's morale has already been shaken by substantial losses; in this way, none of the superiority that has been attained goes unexploited.[14]

He always highlights the importance of "moral" values. This supposes a concentration of the warlike mind in a single direction, in order to force the adversary to capitulate. The military genius is he who finds the weak spot:

this is where the bludgeon comes in, the pinnacle of Napoleonic tactics. Here, the synthesis of the "remarkable trinity" operates very well in Clausewitz's mind. The military genius knows how to channel the energy of his army towards a single goal. We know that only this polarization of all against one, in this case against the designated adversary, makes it possible to fuse the group into an effective whole.

> 2. Even though Blücher was weaker than Schwarzenberg, his enter-prising spirit made him more important. The center of gravity lay with him, and he pulled the other forces in his direction.[15]

Schwarzenberg was too timid to march on Paris and would have quickly withdrawn behind Blücher rather than stand in front of him. The idea that there is a center of gravity, an Achilles' heel where one has to strike, is an essential theoretical contribution. We can feel that Clausewitz regrets that the confrontation did not take place: to attack Blücher would have been to attack Prussia. All of Clausewitz is summed up in this combination of Napoleonism and Prussianism. Imitation of the adversary and the phenomenon of undif-ferentiation are working at full throttle.

> 3. The losses Blücher suffered were on the scale of a serious defeat. Bonaparte had thus gained so great a superiority over him as to leave no doubt that he would have to retreat as far as the Rhine, for no reserves of any consequence were stationed on that route.
> 4. No other possible success could have caused so much alarm or so impressed the allies' mind. With a staff which was known to be as timid and irresolute as Schwarzenberg's, this was bound to be an important con-sideration.[16]

Success would have been complete. In the French Campaign, as revised and corrected by Clausewitz, Napoleon triumphs. Clausewitz finally succeeded on paper in the military career that he failed in real life. Who knows what he thought of his superiors? We should always keep in mind the context in which the writer was living. When he wrote his treatise, Clausewitz was not living the life of a conqueror but of a defeated man. His colleagues probably never forgave him for being right *from the Prussian point of view* to have abandoned the Prussian army and king, who were allied with Napoleon, and to have joined the Tsar's armies. Thus, his defiant and Napoleonic side came from the fact that he was in exile for the wrong reasons, *like Napoleon*. Clausewitz ends up experiencing exactly the same fate as his model. Here, imitation is total, though it should be nothing more than a game, a temporary identification. Clausewitz is not playing; *he believes* in the "god of war" and finally ends up in a situation that is parallel to that of Napoleon. In some ways, *On War* is his *Mémorial de Sainte-Hélène,* a text that matured in exile. The cage is golden, but it is still a prison for the man who wants to reform his country.

Clausewitz failed to leave his mark on history because he was too good at what he did. It is like those institutions where everyone is in agreement to prevent the best from succeeding. Few officers did what Clausewitz did: he left his country to join the Russians. Almost all of his colleagues remained around their king. Thus they must have resented him terribly. If he had failed, if Napoleon had won the Russian Campaign, they would have demonstrated the magnanimity of conquerors. However, they knew that Clausewitz was right all the time. Clear thinking is rarely forgivable. Of course, it was said that the King of Prussia's strategy, which involved encouraging Napoleon to try to conquer Russia and provide him with support to get him to make that decision, was destined to drive the emperor towards a suicidal undertaking. But that justification is not convincing. The reactions of Clausewitz's colleagues, the coldness with which he was probably received when he returned from Russia must have demoralized him. He was considered a traitor. This is the small-mindedness of the *esprit de corps,* and I think it is one of the reasons for Clausewitz's melancholy.

While people like Scharnhorst and Gneisenau considered him to be one of their own, they probably did not have the power to protect him from their subordinates, who were hostile. Clausewitz had a scapegoat aura that is very tempting to "normal" military circles. Thus he had to be very discreet. He had such a sense of duty that he was able to keep his mouth shut when his colleagues tried to humiliate him. It is obvious that the people of Berlin saw things from Clausewitz's point of view, and not from the army's. The army must have held a grudge, and been out of step with the rest of society. Germaine de Staël provided a telling picture of the divide between the Prussian army and the rest of the country, but she did not see the danger that lay in reducing the distance: the policies of the Prussian reactionaries eliminated the hope for reform carried by Clausewitz, Scharnhorst and Gneisenau. In order to understand this phenomenon, we have to think of the Algerian War, and the difference between the soldiers who were ready to accept withdrawal and those who were not.

Here we are dealing with identification that regresses into imitation. This explains the strange magnetism of Clausewitz's text and the singular pleasure we take in reading phrases like "the losses Blücher suffered were on the scale of a serious defeat. Bonaparte had thus gained so great a superiority over him as to leave no doubt." Who is speaking? Bonaparte or Clausewitz? Both because *here, imitation is absolute,* whereas it should be relative to work properly and pass from one model to the other. Napoleon's resurrection in his critic's text has no consequences for us. Yet Clausewitz's unchanging identification with a single model has a captivating power, and Clausewitz's unfinished text becomes more and more fascinating. An inattentive reader might very well say to himself that if Napoleon had returned towards the Rhine at that point ...

BC: Yet the English would never have given up.

RG: The English are not fascinated by Napoleon. It is their advantage, in fact. England's insularity is good for trade, but also puts a brake on mimetic contagion. This is an advantage of maritime imperialism over continental imperialism. No one has focused on Clausewitz's very novelistic passion for his model. It is the same as in French Napoleonism, but in France it is completely open, free of complexes, because Napoleon is our champion. Liddell Hart, in contrast, is completely uninterested in Clausewitz's fascination. This is very English; it is their reasonable and boring side. Julien Green has perspicacious things to say about this because he admires England yet at the same time he said that there is nothing more boring than the English because they are not at all passionate. This is why in politics they are lucid about the mimetism of others and do not participate in it. Remember Churchill, who said to de Gaulle, "each time we must choose between Europe and the open sea, we shall always choose the open sea."[17] By contrast, Clausewitz's novelistic passion is a formidable textbook case of mimetism. Yet his treatise does not show a shift from fascination to hostility. Clausewitz manages to admire his rival. All armchair strategists are a little like that.

BC: Clausewitz is not a novelist. Thus, he never experienced the interior liberation that you call "novelistic conversion," even though he made excellent use of some literary devices in his text. If the mimetic model is so dominant at this point in his thought, can we still speak of a rational model?

RG: I think so. I continue to see Clausewitz as a skillful, profound writer, even though he is constantly endangered by his enthusiasm. It is not impossible to imitate a rational model. I even think it can be quite real and sincere. It would not be interesting to say that Clausewitz "does not believe" in Frederick II as a model; that would be a kind of psychoanalysis. On the contrary, he endorses Frederick II with every atom of his soul, and these two sides of him are not really contradictory. One is the aggravation of the other, in a way.

Clausewitz does not dare say to himself: "If Frederick II and Napoleon were a single man." That is not possible, he lives in the real world. The only thing he suggests is that, in our day and age, it is sometimes better to act like Napoleon to win a battle. France remained an unsurpassable model for this Prussian. Thus, we have to say that his rational model guides him inexorably towards his mimetic model. The shift is almost unconscious, and it shows how difficult it is to escape from this kind of neurosis. Clausewitz knew very well that France had been on the verge of succeeding at what Prussia was in the process of creating, namely, a single army under centralized control. Compulsory military service is what managed to unify France. Clausewitz saw French unification as already achieved by the centralization wrought by its kings. Tocqueville saw this as only negative with respect to the future, and he was perfectly right. Clausewitz instead gauged the immediate strength that this gave Napoleon: the French system brought him, as on a platter, an army that was four times stronger than any other army in the world. He was able to conquer all of Europe.

Thus, we have to see the "remarkable trinity" as a conjunction, but not as a synthesis, of two models. Clausewitz sometimes *understands* this as a rational model, sometimes *experiences* it as a mimetic model. While he always leans more to one side, that does not mean that the other side did not exist. Clausewitz is haunted by Napoleon and he is not haunted by Frederick II. The King of Prussia is, as it were, the heavy artillery that he uses against the emperor. Frederick II exists in a very powerful way for him, but less than the emperor, even when he was beaten. We can see now that Clausewitz reproaches Napoleon for having been a risk-taker because he would have liked to have been one himself. Clausewitz's life was not like a novel, and he sought to appropriate that of Napoleon.

We need to emphasize the fact that Clausewitz *never really managed to write his book*. If he had not imitated Napoleon to such a degree, he would have been able to distance himself from him and compare him with others. However, Clausewitz's life must have been hard. Anyone writing a novel about him in order to explain his fascination with Napoleon, would focus on the time when he was a standard-bearer in the army at the age of twelve. If he was at Valmy, he must have seen incredible things. Goethe also saw Valmy and wrote the famous phrase: "From this place and from this day a new epoch in world history begins."[18] He saw the era changing. There is thus no reason to exclude a little lyricism with respect to our author. It must have been thrilling for a child of twelve who already adored the military. That must be where he contracted the "disease." We are dealing with a great writer on resentment, perhaps one of the first modern writers where this is concerned. Since every-thing was written from the point of view of the adversary, his narrative of the French Campaign is more accurate than many others. Resentment often provides more realistic analyses than our vaunted "historical objectivity."

We should closely examine the passages where Clausewitz spoke of hatred because of the importance he placed on that widespread feeling in war. He was the first to focus on this. Nobody could have cared less what the common soldiers thought, but this was the paradoxical point of view that this latter-day aristocrat took. The military genius absorbs and channels the energy of the people. In terms of my theory, this is called the point of view of the crowd converging against a third party. It is very difficult to reconstitute this attitude when we are dealing with myths, but Clausewitz's text makes up for this because he unveiled such ancient mechanisms at the very point when war was crumbling as an institution. Clausewitz thus insisted on one funda-mental event with respect to the Revolution: compulsory military service. His resentment enabled him to construct his system, to show what military theo-rists did not see: the fact that there was no longer any aristocracy, that modern war was no longer an art or game, but in the process of becoming a religion. Clausewitz thus described the phenomena of reciprocal action whereby he is miles away from the heroic lyricism of his contemporaries, Hegel, Fichte and Schlegel. His imitation of Napoleon was profound enough to make him produce analyses of this sort.

Imagine for a moment the little Corsican entering the military academy, where he could not be kept down because he had too much talent. He must have undergone terrible experiences, of which he never spoke. Clausewitz was like Napoleon: he was not considered to "really" belong to his country. His nobility was very problematic. At the end of his life, thanks to his fine career, he was made a nobleman, but in an artificial manner. This was another reason for his colleagues to treat him as if he were "not really Prussian," just as Napoleon was "not really French." However, Clausewitz must have had a solitary temperament, judging by his life and the book he left unfinished. Perhaps he had too many scruples.

CHAPTER 7

France and Germany

The Voyage of Germaine de Staël

Benoît Chantre: In the course of our discussion, Clausewitz has appeared to us as a writer who went beyond the boundaries of his discipline. His treatise relates to more than the military, and at times touches on literature and anthropology. The way *On War* focuses on Napoleon places us at the heart of the European problem: French-German relations. Stylistic questions, while they interested Clausewitz, did not prevent him from falling into what you call "romantic lies," namely, unavowed imitation of a single model. We have thus situated Clausewitz in a history of desire, intensification of mimetism as the driving force behind human behavior. The growing danger is simply one and the same thing as what we more generally call the escalation to extremes. In the face of this peril, it is clear that there is an urgent need to resist mimetism. By this alternate route, you have clarified the goal that has been driving your research from the beginning.

All of your work was germinating in *Deceit, Desire, and the Novel,* which you published in French in 1961. The book describes a double conversion: to novelistic truth and to Christian truth. It was against the "falsehood" based on the supposed autonomy of our desires that you defined novelistic genius, which alone can flush out the hidden mediators of such desires: I desire a given object only because another desires it or *could* desire it. If the other is far away in time and space (and perhaps even merges into the surrounding culture), then my desire will be peaceful, almost "natural." However, if the other is nearby and becomes a real or possible rival, I will become wild with desire: I will hang on frantically to my difference. Institutions take root in the duel, and their role is nothing other than to control violence. However, history shows how this "human nature" is eroding: mythological falsehood, revealing its own secret, has become over the centuries a "romantic falsehood" by allowing resentment to appear. This is the great discovery of the nineteenth century. Clausewitz belongs to the period when the mechanism that produces culture is revealed in all its violence.

In the course of our discussion, you have shown how close you were to romantic sensibility: you said that you read *On War* out of love for Chopin. You are thus grateful to that feverish period for having shed light on "things hidden since the foundation of the world." The paradox of your position lies in this attraction and rejection. At the heart of an extremely unstable world, you seize the opportunity of what needs to be "intimate mediation," when violence is turned upside down and into reconciliation. So we have to talk about romanticism as a historical movement, and no longer as a metaphor for mimetic desire. For you, it is simply one with the ambivalence of France's relations with Germany. An exceptional woman incarnated that ambivalence at the dawn of the nineteenth century: Germaine de Staël. Her essay *De l'Allemagne,* published in 1813, helped to launch not only romanticism in France, but also the idea that only French-German dialogue could save a Europe that was torn apart by the Napoleonic adventures.

René Girard: The first ten years of the nineteenth century are fascinating. They contain the seeds of everything that was going to happen, namely the crumbling of Europe around the French-German nexus. Why did Hölderlin go to Bordeaux? Because he was more sensitive than anyone else to Germany's provincialism. Yet he brought nothing back from France. He, who was naïve enough to believe in the French Revolution, suffered greatly from the absence of dialogue between the two countries. He rapidly returned to Tübingen, where Madame de Staël could have met him in 1806, when she was visiting Goethe, Fichte, Schiller and Schlegel for her research. He is the one she should have met, but that did not happen.

Exiled by Napoleon, Germaine de Staël went to Germany to marshal forces for a literary and political war. However, she misses Hölderlin, who had chosen to remain silent for the reasons that we have tried to explain. And so the misunderstanding begins. We know that *De l'Allemagne* launched romanticism in France, but could it have established real dialogue between the French and the Germans? Hölderlin's silence casts doubt on this. Germaine de Staël wanted to get beyond the ravages caused by Napoleon in Europe, and she felt that they would have the worst consequences in Germany. However, she rekindled the hatred by playing the great German writers against French classicism. Do not forget that Napoleon tried to maintain classicism for purely political purposes. Thus it is indeed Germaine de Staël whom we have to investigate in order to see what kinds of relations there were between the two countries at the heart of the escalation to extremes that was to destroy Europe.

I have never written about her. You know, she published really poor novels. However, Robert Doran put me on to her talents as a literary critic. She seems to have understood literature in a very mimetic manner. So, I took a closer look, and found that, from this point of view, there are indeed utterly extraordinary remarks in *De la Littérature*. First, we have to remember that Germaine de Staël invented the literary and social essay. She tried to diagnose Europe's problems in a particularly difficult period of its history. She brought literature into the cultural, political and social debate. In short, she invented comparativism and the interdisciplinary approach. This freedom of tone and movement evidently led her to discover emulation while studying the reciprocity of human attitudes.

There are many profound intuitions in her approach to peoples and cultures. For example, what she felt about the fundamental role of religion was very new. If French classicism is opposed to German romanticism, if "northern" literature contrasts with "southern" literature, then we have to think about these differences. Beyond French-German reciprocity, Germaine de Staël sought to define a relationship between two cultures, the bridge that Hölderlin and his compatriots failed to build. She thus embodies the best of Montesquieu: a singular way of seeing the grain of truth in national clichés. She saw that the French-German relationship contained the essence of Europe: to fight for the reconciliation of the two countries would be to save Europe from denying its cultural heritage, not to speak of self-destruction. Germaine de Staël spoke both languages and had intimate knowledge of both countries. If anyone had a cultural idea of Catholicism before Baudelaire, it was she.

Germaine de Staël was the daughter of French statesman Jacques Necker, and lived in Geneva, the continental refuge for those threatened by the conflicts in Europe. She thus had the advantage of a distanced position from which she could observe the events that were tearing Europe apart. She focused her attention on Germany's imminent response to France, which thus meant she was looking at very sensitive issues. Napoleon may have felt a form of mimetic irritation with respect to her. He did not want to let her charm him; on that level, he did not share Benjamin Constant's weakness. She may very well have written *De l'Allemagne* uniquely as an attack on the emperor. That would resemble modern responses, media reactions, propaganda. Indeed, Napoleon understood that the Empire's interest lay with classicism, in opposition to German and English romanticism, which were the two models that the French were to choose after the Congress of Vienna. We will soon be coming to gothic novels. This is why Napoleon encouraged all the scrubby old classical fans who were still reading Voltaire's tragedies. They were typical of the Napoleonic intellectual world. The emperor had seen that France incarnated classicism in opposition to romanticism. By contrast, the intellectuals did not grasp this idea, but they followed along. They were given good positions, and they were well paid. Thus, classicism was well protected.

The story of *De l'Allemagne* is in itself eloquent. The French version of the book came out in July 1813, one year after Napoleon's abdication and Germaine de Staël's return from London to Paris. Her years in exile were crucial, and not just for French literature. Germaine de Staël had met the leading figures in Germany. When she returned to Paris, she received an impressive number of political and even military leaders; for example, Bernadotte attended her salon. It was *over against Napoleon* that she was writing and acting. She thus received special attention from the emperor; we find proof for this in all the police measures that were taken against her and her forced exile. She was larger than life, straight out of a novel, a woman who frightened Napoleon, had many domestic rows with Benjamin Constant and gave birth to children by other men. The fact that she is always described as ugly and mannish inevitably makes me think of the fantasy images that people had of Marie-Antoinette. Benjamin Constant hurt Germaine de Staël deeply when he published *Cécile,* in which he took revenge for the way she dominated him. She finally drew down on herself veritable persecution stereotypes: her generous sexuality became monstrous, her great intelligence made her androgynous. Parisian salons surely saw her as a traitor sold to the enemy, a new example of "l'Autrichienne," as Marie Antoinette was called. These factors probably weighed in her anti-Napoleonic hatred.

I see Germaine de Staël as belonging to the great feminist lineage dating back to Célimène's satire of intellectuals. What Molière glimpsed, Germaine de Staël incarnated. At the dawn of French intellectualism, *The Misanthrope* is the most powerful criticism of all; Molière defined it as the pure spirit of contradiction dreaming of distinguishing itself. Indeed, in France the spirit of contradiction generates excitement that seems to be the summit of "creativity" and "innovation." What Molière immortalized in his play was the decomposition of a specific intellectual lifestyle that would soon be called "classicism" or "the salon spirit." Negative thought was already at work in the seventeenth century, and Alceste was at the forefront. We have seen this negativity at work in Hegel, and we have also seen that the "negation of negation" did not lead to the happy ending of the old movies. Deconstructionism, and its denial of the referent or reality in its thesis that "everything is language," will have been the ultimate avatar of this spirit.

Following Célimène, Germaine de Staël discovered the truth about intellectuals, which is the same thing as the truth about salons. La Rochefoucauld's *Maximes*[1] are the misanthrope's handbook, and *La Princesse de Clèves* is one of the great novels of misanthropism. In Molière's play, there is a crucial duel between persons who have distinguished themselves and those who have failed, between those who have understood the rules of society and those who claim to be their victim. Célimène has discovered Alceste's secret, and will suffer as a result at the end of the play. The core of the lesson is contained in a few lines:

> Because he loves to make a fuss.
> You don't expect him to agree with us,
> When there's an opportunity to express
> His heaven-sent spirit of contrariness?
> What other people think, he can't abide;
> Whatever they say, he's on the other side;
> He lives in deadly terror of agreeing;
> 'Twould make him seem an ordinary being.
> Indeed, he's so in love with contradiction,
> He'll turn against his most profound conviction
> And with a furious eloquence deplore it,
> If only someone else is speaking for it.[2]

Such was the obsession with innovation that already held sway in France in Molière's time. It is because he cannot distinguish himself from others that Alceste pretends to disdain their company. The salons were the worst. Célimène is the only one who points out Alceste's resentment. *The Misanthrope* was written a century before Germaine de Staël's accusations against French classicism, and already describes the disintegration of a salon, of which Célimène suffers the consequences since she ends up in a convent. The denouement of the play is literally a lynching. Because she is the most spiritual,

Célimène pays the price in a world of conversation that goes to extremes and that contains a bitterness that follows a movement towards greater violence in society. As soon as it stops being superficial, the conversation explodes into violence. Alceste is not a scapegoat: he has failed to distinguish himself but he does not want to admit it. He is already a creature of resentment. Likewise, Germaine de Staël was the Célimène of the Napoleonic salons. What she described as the spirit of imitation in France and classicism's distrust of any form of distinction merged into the phenomenon of unanimity that must have been a prelude to her exile. Only the mistress of a salon, who understands the rules of the game *because she has been a victim of them,* could so clearly describe it as a mimetic system and see that it is from within imitation finally acknowledged as such that something new can emerge.

This is why Germaine de Staël's first action when she returned to France after Napoleon's fall is to re-open a salon. She is nostalgic for the Enlightenment thinkers, for the last sparks of the spirit of conversation. She simply hoped that the taste for imitation was no longer a misunderstanding of exceptional people, but the condition for producing new ideas. It is in this spirit that she tried to establish real dialogue between the French and the Germans, between the spirit of imitation and that of innovation, a marriage between the best of the Enlightenment and the best of romanticism. What this emissary victim of the French mind tried to do in post-Napoleonic France was to open the way to a *Catholic modernity:* that of dialogue between France and Germany. What she glimpsed at the heart of the dialogue was the finally articulated difference between the Christian and the archaic, to which Catholicism holds the key. We will soon come to Baudelaire and his admiration for Wagner. It is interesting to note that it was at the time when the Holy Roman Empire finally collapsed, with Napoleon and Bismarck, that these figures appear.

BC: Everyone will appreciate this unadorned portrait that you have just painted of French intellectuals! We have to get back to the question of religion and the fundamental distinction that you make between the Christian and the archaic. For the moment, I would like to focus our attention on the French-German dialogue. Could you describe in greater detail the comparative approach that Germaine de Staël took to these two cultures?

RG: She defined French literature as social, in contrast with German literature, which she discovered was a literature of solitary individuals. Hölderlin's withdrawal only proves her right. We have to think of his exile, at the same time as that of Germaine de Staël, as a kind of Manichaeism. This is why I see Catholicism as a stable point in the midst of all the fluctuations of the romantic period. Indeed, it involves much more than a simple attachment to a particular religion. We will see that Germaine de Staël's works lean in this direction, which is what makes them special.

In Lausanne in 1796, she publishes a treatise entitled *De l'influence des passions*. I cannot resist such titles. Open *De l'Allemagne* and you will find how clearly this author grasped that passions are essentially mimetic. Because Germaine de Staël understands the laws of what we could call German conformism and French mimetism, she is at the heart of the duel that was to destroy Europe. France was imitating old models and the Germans thought they had to imitate France. The French cling to their outdated classicism, and the Germans were humiliated by the Napoleonic empire. Germaine de Staël wanted to prevent this, of course, and there is tension throughout her book owing to the French-German *relationship* that she tried to revive behind the warlike *reciprocity* of the two countries. However, as soon as she returned to Paris, she quickly realized that Germany's revenge, which she had hoped for in her resentment of the emperor, was humiliating France in turn.

Basically, Germaine de Staël began by attacking Voltairianism: the irony, elegance and quickness characteristic of the French mind, which the Prussians, Saxons and Bavarians *imitated in vain,* with their good nature and the essential slowness of their syntax. This criticism was first applied to Frederick II, of whom she painted an unflattering portrait that Voltaire could have endorsed:

> One has to study Frederick II's character in order to understand Prussia. A man created that empire, which nature had not favored at all and which became a power only because a warrior was its master. In Frederick II there are two quite distinct men: a German by nature and a Frenchman by education. Everything that the German has done in the German kingdom left lasting marks; nothing the Frenchman has attempted took root in a productive manner.[3]

See how much the portrait of the same man can differ depending on whether it is painted by a Swiss novelist or a Prussian general. The man who was for Clausewitz the model of heroic wisdom and a statesman holding war in check was for Germaine de Staël an imitator forced to deny his own nature. Frederick II was dominated by Voltaire, as the Prussians were by Napoleon. Clearly, Germaine de Staël's explicitly mimetic analysis is more accurate than Clausewitz's. De Staël does not create a myth; she describes a divided soul. Indeed, why imitate the French whose "antique colour" clashed with the "ancient colour"[4] of the Germans, who were fascinated by the Middle Ages, by the spirit of chivalry and not by Greek and Roman classicism? French *imitation* of models from Antiquity was in complete contradiction with German *innovation,* or rather the innovation of a few individuals who distinguished themselves from a people too quick to obey and too ready to submit to authority.

However, Germaine de Staël's distanced point of view is nonetheless consistent with Clausewitz's violent nationalism, which shows that opinions are never innocent. These exceptional writers prepared a German *response* to the arrogant triumph of Voltairianism. Germaine de Staël was so involved in the situation, so absorbed by her hatred of Napoleon, that she did not see the risk inherent in the German awakening. What we glimpsed with Clausewitz appears implicitly in very astute remarks, and the author does not suspect their consequences for a moment. In a chapter entitled "Of the German Language in Its Relationship with the Spirit of Conversation," she wrote,

> The Germans see a kind of charlatanism in brilliant expression, and prefer instead abstract expression because it is more scrupulous and nearer to the very essence of the truth. However, conversation should not be difficult to understand or to engage in. As soon as the exchange does not concern shared interests in life and enters the sphere of ideas, conversation in Germany becomes too metaphysical. There is not enough intermediary space between the vulgar and the sublime, and yet it is in that intermediary space that the art of conversation is employed.[5]

Germaine de Staël's thesis can be summarized briefly: on one hand, she pointed out the German's self-conscious distrust of French wit, which is quick to target *similarities* and regard those who deviate from them with suspicion; on the other hand, she showed the German language's capacity for abstraction, which is paradoxical given the German people's leaning towards conformity. Note also the absence of mediation in German culture, between "the vulgar and the sublime." Germaine de Staël was quick to see her error after Napoleon's fall, when she had to deal with the patriotic ardor of her friend Schlegel. Indeed, ten years later, what achieved the impossible synthesis of the vulgar and the sublime, if not just that conquering individualism whose features we have glimpsed in the heroism of *On War?* The military (and Prussia) is going to play the role of the French Revolution, creating unity where division used to reign. Without realizing it, Germaine de Staël guessed the dangers of such military Hegelianism when she wrote that "Prussia has two faces, like Janus: one military and the other philosophical."[6] However, her intuition fails here when, a few pages later, she expresses the hope that the "warrior spirit" would take on a "national scope."[7] This point is absolutely fundamental. See also her definition of French courage in war:

> This social need to think like everyone else was used during the Revolution to explain the contrast between courage in war and pusillanimity in civil life. There is only one way to look at military courage, but public opinion can be led astray with respect to the way one should behave in politics. Criticism, solitude and abandonment threaten you if you do not follow the leading party, whereas in the army there is only the alternative between death and success, which is a charming situation for the French, who do not fear the former and passionately love the latter. Place fashion, in other words, applause, on the side of danger, and you will see the French face it in all its forms; … for in a country where conversation has such influence, the noise of talk often drowns out the voice of conscience.[8]

What Germaine de Staël is denouncing here is the mixture of conversation and courage, of imitation and audacity that constituted France's *rhetorical power,* skillfully merging Voltaire with Napoleon, irony with power, and making French culture an overwhelming model for the Germans, who are forced to imitate their oppressor. We have already cited Clausewitz's words expressing his fear of the return of France, "a nation which is homogenous and undivided as well as well situated, warlike and full of spirit."[9] Note that the French would soon be saying the same about the Germans. Nationalism is essentially mimetic: what it criticizes about others concerns it also, so it criticizes itself. National pride is always host to complexes of this kind. We have to think about it as revealing national rivalries in which boasting is the surest symptom of self-hatred. Here we again find bipolarity, the oscillation characteristic of an unstable world, and the essence of romantic falsehood. His use of "homogenous" in reference to France is thus quite extraordinary because it means Clausewitz was complimenting the Revolution. He said that the Revolution made it possible to engage in war better, by making everything homogenous. Everyone into the regiment. The invention of compulsory military service. Incredible.

At the same time, Clausewitz is mistaken: Napoleon exhausted France, which went downhill from then, especially on the demographic plane. He lacked a lucid vision because his hatred nourished belief in the adversary's advantages. We always see the adversary as more powerful than he really is. Clausewitz did not understand that things were starting to move towards the east, inevitably, because Europe was growing, getting bigger and becoming increasingly populous. He did not see this, or that there was something rotten called Napoleonic classicism. He did not see that desperate clinging to classicism, in other words, to the past, revealed a previously hidden weakness in French cultural domination. He was right to attribute imperial goals to Louis XIV and Napoleon; there is even a passage in which he said that, on the military level, Rome and France were equivalent in his eyes.[10] This worry fed the resentment of his last years.

The Germans, who were preparing to rise up at the time Germaine de Staël was writing about them, did indeed fall into a passionate nationalism identical to that of the French, who became romantics after 1815. A century and a half later, this resulted in the same exhaustion. Today, Germany's population is also declining. Germaine de Staël did not see that Germany's immense culture was threatened by the awakening of nationalism. Was it really, as has been said, the struggle of German "culture" against French "civilization?" I am not convinced. In fact, what I see re-emerging is "reciprocal action," in other words, an engine of undifferentiation, the opposition of two great cultures that almost disappeared in their very opposition. The dialogue that Germaine de Staël dreamed about has to be entirely rethought.

Therefore this was her singular mission: instead of helping to establish a French-German dialogue in the best Enlightenment spirit, she provided arguments and theses to feed the spirit of revenge. This woman who went to war against French classicism was overcome, like Clausewitz, by the "god of war," whose emergence she unknowingly accelerated. It is not surprising that when France was humiliated at the Congress of Vienna, it rushed into the breach opened by *De l'Allemagne*. Only he who hates himself can love himself, and, fundamentally, whether they are French or German, romantics are people who no longer love themselves. Why doesn't anyone ever say this? Germaine de Staël's victory over classicism was to be devastating, yet she would still be bitter. This is how I interpret the melancholy of her last years and her fairly unenthusiastic support of the Restoration. Yet she remained open to the possibility of a dialogue between the two countries. Her influence was enormous, in particular over French writers. I think that the renewal of a certain idea of Catholicism resulted from this resistance to national hatreds. Those who contributed to the renewal were those who understood that the essence of Europe resides in this dialogue.

BC: Do you think that Germaine de Staël's intuitions were similar to yours?

RG: We would have to look more closely, because the very fact of finding "mimetic" intuitions in her work would invalidate my theory! I have always said that only great novelists understand what is at stake in imitation, and that understanding mimetism is necessary to create a great novel. Germaine de Staël was more of a theorist than a novelist. She must have sensed the imitation at work in European salons, but she used it in the service of revenge. This shows the ambivalence of polemicists, who end up using their intuitions to promote "their" truth. But we will come back later to some of her ideas about religion, which seem to me to be related to awareness of mimetism. In that respect, I feel close to her analyses, of course. I think that she prefigures the human sciences. What she says about France, for example, that it is entirely attracted to the royal court, applies to all human societies:

> In France it seems that the spirit of imitation is like a social link, and that all would be in disorder if the link did not make up for the instability of institutions.[11]

This remark, which was made almost in passing, is of a rare depth. One might think it came from Tocqueville. It is perfectly consistent with everything we have said about the fundamental nature of imitation based on anthropological findings from the end of the nineteenth century. Germaine de Staël's views reach far forward. She said that conversation has become the last institution, and that all the others have collapsed. It is the institution of the end of institutions, in a way. While she saw that this is ridiculous, she also understood its effectiveness: imitation is at the root of innovation. In fact, conversation is the modality of a world of internal mediation, where glory does not last, but appears for an instant only to disappear a second later, where no heroic model can last because all *distinction* becomes suspect. Célimène is right, and the misanthrope and petty nobles are wrong. De Staël tells us that the "art of conversation," understood as an institution, is what occupies the space between the vulgar and the sublime in France.

What can we conclude from this except that conversation, typical of internal mediation, is flexible and vigilant enough to enable the French mind to avoid the heroic individuality that was then out of fashion? The mimetism of the French is universal. It therefore should have provided formidable protection against the purblind identification that produces myth, resentment and "heroic behaviour." Germaine de Staël was of course speaking about the French before Napoleon's time; she was nostalgic for the eighteenth century, when armies were less violent and "gentlemen's" war was an "armed conversation," as Clausewitz says. The model that she constructs is nonetheless very telling. It is the absence of this institution, the last one of all, perhaps, that characterized the Germans, who were, according to her, unable to find an intermediary between the sublime and the vulgar. The absence of mediation came from an absence of conversational culture. When Prussians were not at war, they were doing business; when they were not defending "sublime" interests, they restricted themselves to private concerns, even though such matters were "vulgar." We have seen that for Clausewitz, trade is a model for society. The Prussian he embodies is immersed in exchange and reciprocity, which are one and the same thing, differing only in degree. The exchange of ideas has no place between exchanging goods and trading blows. We have to imagine Clausewitz ripening his treatise in perfect solitude. The posthumous and unfinished nature of the writing is significant. Clausewitz did not spend much time in salons. This is the dark side of his withdrawal, full of sound and fury, in contrast to that of Hölderlin.

For Germaine de Staël, the issue of the absence of an intermediary state between the sublime and the vulgar no longer arose after 1815. This is the tone of a note added to the French edition of *De l'Allemagne:*

> Please note that this chapter, like the rest of the book, was written at the time of Germany's complete subjection. Since then, German nations have been awoken by the oppression, and have given their governments the strength they lacked to resist the power of the French armies. The heroic behavior of sovereigns and peoples has shown how opinion can affect the fate of the world.[12]

Of course, this note can be seen as an authentic profession of democratic faith. Yet in what Germaine de Staël calls the "heroic behavior of sovereigns and peoples," we find all the components of the reform that Clausewitz wished for Prussia: a military meritocracy able to unify the country, which was divided between its French ideal and its nationalist spirit. The reform required the establishment of a heroic model, which as we have seen was the purpose of *On War.* We have also seen that the model could unleash unpredictable powers. We are now forewarned against such dreams.

Germaine de Staël was like all romantics who, because they love the future, prove unable to anticipate it. Such people are playing with resentment, which is like playing with fire. Each in his or her own way shows how very hard it is to think from within mimetism, from within a mediation that has become extremely unstable. As you know, I think that such vagueness, as magnificent as it can sometimes be, implicitly raises a major question, which only religion can answer. Germaine de Staël saw clearly the instinct for imitation, but what she offered was limitless romantic individualism and all its innovations. Her final call for German "enthusiasm" against the rigidity of French intelligence puts the mimetic intuition at risk. The passage from sacred to holiness, for example, is completely unrelated to that enthusiasm. Our idea of "intimate mediation" suggests something that is both more discreet and more real: a distance to which novelists are closer than are essayists and theoreticians, who are too quick to fall victim to the illusion of autonomy. Stendhal, who was also very critical of Napoleon, would never have called for a German "national awakening."

The European Entente

BC: Novelists are more disinterested than polemicists. Yet the latter's commitment allows them to glimpse essential things. Germaine de Staël made political mistakes, but what do you think her decisive intuition was?

RG: As I have said: a specific idea about Catholicism. Here we are touching on the ambivalence of the romantic spirit, its dark side and its light side. On one hand, there is glorification of individuality, and on the other a better intuition about the social role of religion. Exceptional individuals understand what is lacking in the social contract. They see that the contract can be saved only through a new understanding of religion. Germaine de Staël is perhaps most convincing when she sincerely regrets Germany's division between Protestantism and Catholicism. She sensed that Germany is the country where the two traditions are more or less associated with intelligence and faith, but also have the greatest chance of being reconciled. She writes that Germany is not a country of religious wars, but one where religious differences can be found around common respect for reason. When Germaine de Staël wrote

> When man comes out of an ordeal more religious than he went in, it means
> that the religion is invariably founded. This is when there is peace between
> it and brilliant minds, and when they use each other.[13]

she corroborated everything we have just said. Germaine de Staël acknowledges Protestant free thought as the source not only of Germany's intellectual strength, but also of scientific knowledge of religion: "While French philosophical wits made jokes about Christianity, Germans made it a topic of scholarship."[14] Of course, historical and critical methodologies have since shown their limits, but they were nonetheless the prelude to the birth of the human sciences.

The chapter on Catholicism is very informative from this point of view. First, because, according to Germaine de Staël, "the Catholic religion is more tolerant in Germany than in any other country."[15] She did not feel in it the traces of French wars. Next, because the need to "believe" and the need to "examine"[16] were reconciled by some Catholics who came from Protestantism. Thus, she writes of Count Friederich Stolberg that "he has just published a history of the religion of Jesus Christ designed to win the approbation of all Christian communions."[17] I do not know that work, but I find what Germaine de Staël says about it extremely interesting:

> We find in this book a perfect knowledge of the Holy Scriptures, and very interesting researches into the different religions of Asia, which bear relation to Christianity. ... Count Stolberg, in his publication, attributes to the Old Testament a much greater importance than Protestant writers in general assign to it. He considers sacrifices as the basis of all religion, and the death of Abel as the first type of that sacrifice which forms the groundwork of Christianity. In whatever way we decide upon this opinion, it affords much room for thought. The greater part of ancient religions instituted human sacrifices; but in this barbarity there was something remarkable, namely, the necessity of a solemn expiation. Nothing, in effect, can obliterate from the soul the idea, that there is a mysterious efficacy in the blood of the innocent, and that heaven and earth are moved by it. Men have always believed that the just could obtain, in this life or the other, the pardon of the guilty. There are some primitive ideas in the human species which reappear more or less disfigured, in all times, and among all nations. These are the ideas upon which we cannot grow weary of reflecting; for they assuredly preserve some traces of the lost dignities of our nature.[18]

Germaine de Staël considered the idea that such "sentiments" apply to "truths about faith" to be an indisputable and eminently respectable fact. You have to admit that this is striking. Do not forget that she is interested in these topics at the same time that Joseph de Maistre is writing *Enlightenment on Sacrifices*,[19] which was published in 1810. Of course, the anthropology that was being sketched in this case was still in its infancy. It cannot grasp the revealing reversal of *Things Hidden since the Foundation of the World*. De Maistre's work contains an aborted meditation on sacrificing the other and sacrificing oneself: the victims are innocent, but at the same time the sacrifices have to have an expiatory function. Nonetheless, it was on this romantic loam that anthropology took root, and a science of religion beyond theological speculation became possible.

Germaine de Staël is not alone, but she offered an acute reading of her times. That her mimetic intuitions emerged at the heart of French-German interactions is also very significant. It is one of the most virulent seats of undifferentation in the history of Europe. We always have to keep in mind the fact that the rivalry ended up producing the monstrous sacrificial blunder of the Holocaust—a coldly calculated and organized attempted at extermination, a crime committed by a state, by which the very essence of the European idea has been stained. It is because he did not see that the *Aufhebung* was an avatar of *catharsis* that Hegel went so easily from dialectic to reconciliation. Dialectic is a conflict between adversaries, which Clausewitz said can lead only to extremes. Germaine de Staël probably also felt that the only possible outcome of this contagious imitation was sacrificial. However, she more vaguely felt that sacrifice was no longer useful because *victims are always innocent,* they are always paying for others.

In her intuitions about religion, Germaine de Staël rises above the French-German quarrel, though she remained trapped within it on other topics. With respect to religion, the opening was real, and defined by Catholicism. However, this is less the case when she speaks of enthusiasm than when she discussed the necessary reconciliation of knowledge and faith. There, she took a step further than Hegel and Clausewitz. This intuition proves that behind her war on Napoleon, Germaine de Staël was sincerely trying to *imagine a European culture.* The idea that German Catholicism was the most tolerant at the time interests me greatly, especially since it is rooted in strong, open respect for the Enlightenment in both France and Germany. Europe was *there,* not in the national wars that Napoleon kindled. This is what I find most stimulating here. The idea of going beyond all religious wars, of all the religions that are wars, utterly convinces me. The Napoleonic censor, whom the author cites at the beginning of the book, and who affirms that "we are not reduced to seeking models in the peoples whom you admire,"[20] did not see that the "German Catholic" model was the most subversive of all. Germaine de Staël did not see this either; she was too involved in her war against Napoleon to fully understand the model that she had built. However, it is crucial that she had this essential intuition and felt the need to create the model at the time when Austria no longer counted and the Holy Roman Empire was finally expiring.

BC: Could you give other examples of what you call the "German Catholic model," that would cut across the issues that Germaine de Staël was seeking to cover?

RG: This needs to be gone into more deeply than we can do here. However, we can identify a few avenues. The rational model that we are talking about is very complex. In the version proposed by Germaine de Staël, it seems bent on reconciling two sets of adversaries: the Catholics and the Protestants on one hand, and the Germans and the French on the other. It is political, literary and spiritual. Two events spring to mind: the first is the encounter of Baudelaire and Wagner, the second that of de Gaulle and Adenauer. They fit perfectly into the wake of Germaine de Staël and the space she opened. The first meeting was on the aesthetic and literary levels, the second on the political level. The third example that I would suggest is more recent, and fits perfectly into the chapter that we have just read. I mean the highly significant fact that a German pope was elected. This is crucial in the history of Europe and in the history of the world. Indeed, like his predecessor, Benedict XVI is incontestably a champion of the idea of Europe. These three examples are consistent with what could be called Germaine de Staël's "Catholicism," which is in her case a notion that is much more cultural than strictly confessional. These examples are logical consequences in the three levels to which they belong.

Let's begin with the political example. There was something great in the meeting between de Gaulle and Adenauer at Colombey-les-Deux-Églises in 1958, which was that they both saw that Europe had to be forgiven, in a way, for its sins. They found themselves together after the unprecedented upheaval of World War II, on the ruins of two countries that had imitated each other too much, and whose exacerbated imitation had led to the worst. This was an exceptional event. I cannot remember exactly where I was at the time of the *Te deum* at Reims on July 8, 1962, but I remember having experienced it with a great deal of emotion. Konrad Adenauer had ordered the best Bollinger and Heidsieck champagnes the night before in honor of the Champagne region, so close to the Rhineland, and then the next day we find him absorbed in his missal next to General de Gaulle. This happened in the cathedral where Joan of Arc had Charles VII crowned and which had received 300 German bombs in 1914. The Church organized the service, thereby consecrating the two countries' mutual wishes for forgiveness and their movement towards reconciliation. The French-German Friendship and Cooperation Treaty (the Élysée Treaty) was signed a few months later, on January 22, 1963. In his speech at The Hôtel de Ville, de Gaulle did not hesitate to say that "it was essential that the popular soul demonstrate its approval on this side of the Rhine." Adenauer more prosaically but just as accurately spoke of healing the rift between the two countries.

That meeting had a long history behind it. The two men had to renounce many prejudices before they could meet at Colombey. At the time, Adenauer greatly feared the meeting with de Gaulle, who had been portrayed to him as a rabid nationalist. It is true that de Gaulle was opposed to the establishment of a German army. I think that above all he wanted to neutralize the military issue in order to succeed in his operations in Champagne: it was perhaps more subtle than we think. I remember that their interpreter spoke of real "hand-to-hand combat" between the two men and said that "sparks flew" at each of their encounters. Today we do not realize that the reunion was a formidable political exploit; we do not acknowledge the heroic effort required for this *Aufhebung*. The French and German armies paraded in Reims where Clovis was baptized in 496. Why do you think Pope John Paul II chose to go to Reims to commemorate the 1,500th anniversary of the baptism? It was not to praise archaic Christianity. No one has really reflected on this. Everyone railed at the pope, as usual. No one wanted to understand that John Paul II was treating Europe and France in particular like a symbolic and spiritual game board on which one had to place one's pieces carefully. The fact that he chose the city where the two countries had decided to reconcile is something that has perhaps not yet really been analyzed. It is as if Europe's original sin, the evil that had to be treated, had taken place on the borders of the old kingdom of Lotharingia. It was both an anchor point and the site of a failure. We have seen this duel come back in Clausewitz's text. The papacy has been struggling with this conflict ever since Charlemagne and Pope Leo III. The real debate, the real war, is here.

Now for the second example, which belongs to the order of spirit because it is artistic. We have seen that Germaine de Staël's thinking was free enough to be above petty revenge. She opens the way for people like Fustel de Coulanges, Hugo and Tocqueville, and for "modernity," in other words, Baudelaire. For me, the great continuation of Germaine de Staël's work is Baudelaire's *L'Art romantique*,[21] which fits perfectly into the wake of *De l'Allemagne*. With Baudelaire, Germaine de Staël's approach, which makes comparative literature as well as European cooperation possible, takes on a musical meaning and leaves behind its warlike sense, thereby finding a magnificent confirmation. Of course, there is Hitler's vulgar appropriation of Wagnerism, and we cannot deny that a new form of neo-paganism was encouraged by this. However, on this issue Baudelaire has always seemed more convincing to me than Nietzsche, whose resistance to Wagner was too closely related to resentment. Baudelaire is not fascinated by Wagner; he admires him. One of the reasons for the distance perhaps comes from the fact that he discovered Wagner's genius in some bistro concerts in France. Baudelaire sees more clearly than Nietzsche because he interpreted Wagner's art as a dialogue between the archaic and the Christian, and not as a return of Dionysianism. He thus undeniably orients Wagner's influence in the direction of anthropological and religious mediation.

Baudelaire's two texts on Wagner are a letter to the composer dated February 17, 1860, and the famous essay, "Richard Wagner et Tannhäuser à Paris," which was published in the *Revue européenne* on April 1, 1861. These two writings should be reread from this perspective. Baudelaire is grateful to the composer for having oriented his aesthetics towards Greece, but the "resurrection" of Aeschylus and Sophocles involves a confrontation with Christianity:

> Although they show a genuine liking for classical beauty and a perfect understanding of it, [they] also have a strong admixture of the romantic spirit. They may suggest to us the majesty of Sophocles and Aeschylus, but they also forcibly recall to our minds the mystery plays of the period when Catholicism was dominant in the plastic arts. They are like those great visions that the Middle Ages spread out on the walls of its churches or wove into its magnificent tapestries.[22]

Baudelaire immediately felt that Wagner's genius participates in the dialogue between drama and music, the archaic and the Christian. He wrote that Wagner "could not help thinking on two planes, one of the two arts taking up its role at the point where the limits of the other stopped."[23]

This formal dualism is in service to a more essential dialogue, the fundamental struggle that, as we have seen, structures Christianity:

> *Tannhäuser* presents the struggle between the two principles that have chosen the human heart as their main battleground, the flesh and the spirit, hell and heaven, Satan and God. ... Languorous delights, lust at fever heat, moments of anguish, and a constant returning towards pleasure, which holds out hope of quenching thirst but never does; raging palpitations of heart and senses, imperious demands of the flesh, the whole onomatopoeic dictionary of love is to be heard here. Then, little by little the religious theme re-establishes its supremacy, slowly, by gradations, and swallows

up the other one in a peaceful, glorious victory, like the victory of the all-conquering being over the sickly and disordered being, of Saint Michael over Lucifer.[24]

This perfect definition of romantic desire and its "absorption" into the light of Revelation in no way resembles a Manichean struggle or any form of Gnosticism. Saint Michael "absorbs" Lucifer; he does not strike him down. It is a "peaceful victory" not a triumph. In the same way, Christianity sheds light on and reveals the archaic. All of the poems in "The Flowers of Evil"[25] should be reread in this light. How can we not see that Baudelaire identifies completely with Wagner, but precisely does not imitate him? He was not as close to the composer as Nietzsche was. Wagner could only be irritated by the latter, just as Goethe was frightened by Hölderlin. Nietzsche undeniably was out for vengeance. Hölderlin, in contrast, chose to stop speaking. As we have seen, his wish to "become Catholic" was accompanied by his awareness of the continuity and discontinuity, both essential, between Christ and the Greek gods. A text like *"Mon Coeur mis à nu"* should be studied in its relation to Hölderlin.

Baudelaire thus confirms the intellectual and spiritual Catholicism of Hölderlin and Germaine de Staël, a measure of a true European culture. Wagner was so furious with the Paris Opera that he did not see Baudelaire. Indeed, his anti-Semitism came in part from his hatred of the Parisian musical milieu. This in no way reduces Baudelaire's grandeur and *distance* when he saw while listening to Wagner that if archaic religion is fully understood, it is justified by Christianity. Christianity's relationship to archaic religion reveals the fact that there would have been no humanity without the latter. Baudelaire does not fall into the trap of self-denegation. He rejects the idea that the West should minimize its originality and bow down before the Greeks, who were so childish by comparison. European civilization is the first culture that addresses the whole world. The "struggle between two principles" that it incarnates restores the importance of the present as no civilization has done before, even though this has occurred in the midst of the greatest danger.

Baudelaire is thus indeed an apocalyptic poet who sees in Wagner the rise of the extraordinary tension of his time. We have to read the open letter to the composer while keeping in mind that, according to Baudelaire also, salvation grows in function of danger:

> Let me use a comparison borrowed from painting. I imagine a vast extent of red spreading before my eyes. If this red represents passion, I see it change

gradually, through all the shades of red and pink, until it reaches the incandescence of a furnace. It would seem difficult, even impossible, to render something more intensely hot and yet a final flash traces a white furrow on the white that provides its background. That, if you will, is the final cry of a soul that has soared to a paroxysm of ecstasy.[26]

It seems to me that our whole discussion is summarized here. This naturally brings me to my third example, which is consistent with the idea that there is an essential Catholicism in European culture. I am thinking about the first German pope and the Regensburg Lecture in September 2006, which was interpreted *solely* as Benedict XVI's declaration of war against Islam and Protestants. I see it instead as first a plea for reason. Everyone rushed to attack the pope, each for different reasons, reasons related to supposed differences. Considered to be a reactionary, the pope behaved like a defender of reason. I find it amazing that some consider this a paradox: as if Catholicism were not essentially rational. I like to think that Germaine de Staël unknowingly anticipated a figure who was to play a possibly crepuscular, though very symbolic, role in Europe and the world. It has been said that Benedict XVI is the "last European pope." I note that he was elected when the French-German "engine," which is essentially economic, was experiencing spectacular failures. Joseph Ratzinger's choice of a papal name is crucial in this respect. Benedict XVI, the first German pope, took the first name of the patron of Europe and chose to pray at Auschwitz. These are signs that call for lengthy meditation.

Think also about his predecessor, Benedict XV, whom he brought out of oblivion. Benedict XV was elected in 1914, and threw all his strength into trying to counter a war he considered absurd. He failed to gain acceptance for his peace proposals on August 1, 1917, was hated by both Germany and France, judged "anti-German" by the former and "anti-French" by the latter (Clemenceau called him a "Boche"), and was excluded by the Italians themselves from the Peace Conference. He was a pope obscured by a terrible war between two national idolatries. Now, go back one more Benedict, so to speak, and remember Benedict XIV, pope from 1740 to 1758. He was the pope of the reconciliation of Spain, the Two Sicilies and Portugal, who recognized the Kingdom of Prussia, the pope who defended progress in the historical and natural sciences, had the Index revised and corresponded with the greatest scientists of his time, thereby attracting the esteem of Protestants. Do you see a little better now why Ratzinger decided to be called Benedict XVI? He appeared on the balcony in Rome one year before the negative outcome of the French referendum on Europe. What did his *Urbi et Orbi* blessing mean if not that Europe urgently needed to unite in its disgust with the self-destruction that characterized the twentieth century. It meant that there is still hope, that all is not lost.

The issues arising out of the Regensburg Lecture thus become truly meaningful. In the lecture, the pope supported Greek rationality against the risks of "de-Hellenization." Declaring both Greek difference and Judeo-Christian identity at the same time is an essential philosophical and theological position. We will come back to it. This is what Hölderlin glimpses in poems like "Patmos" and "The Vatican." The papal chain is rich with meaning. We can see it as an eminent example of peaceful mimesis, which, throughout the history of the last two centuries, in the face of and against the sterile rivalry of the fundamentalists and the progressives, has maintained respect for a tradition founded on imitation of Christ. If the dogma of papal infallibility were explained to people in mimetic terms, they would get less upset. We should always seek the anthropological reality underlying the dogma. Christianity has been based since its origin on mimetic analyses. In this sense, we are simply translating Christian intuitions into theory. Being Catholic means identifying with the figure of uniqueness, the singular universal that is a pope. However, the identification that we are talking about here is not an intellectual game. It is part of a terrible war that has been going on against the empire for over a thousand years. Germaine de Staël only understood part of what she was doing when she wrote her praise of Count Stolberg, and yet she anticipated a world that has become our own. What if the French-German "engine" were in the process of becoming theological, global and reasonable? You have to admit that it would be a strange twist of history.

BC: Much more than simple "deceit," romanticism thus means to you the ambivalence of an unstable period when the best and the worst are side by side, the sacred and the holy, subjectivism and transcendence. Is this because romantic individuality is more mimetic than others, so it is also closer to religion, and more apt to grasp what Germaine de Staël called the "traces of the lost dignities of our nature"?

RG: Romantic individualism is "modern" in the sense that it is better able to grasp both the genesis of religion and the way to escape it. Schelling had splendid intuitions about mythology. And Nietzsche as well. However, they did not see, or did not want to see, that the Passion had completely transformed the sacred. This is the meaning of aphorism 125 of *The Gay Science*. Romanticism got a glimpse of the abyss of the foundation, the magma of undifferentiated crowds that all mythologies hide. It is thus both sublime and terrifying. Europe sank into the foundation madness that the French Revolution initiated. Napoleon continues on that path, and uses unheard-of violence to deal with the European continent as if it were a problem to be resolved. He slashed, parceled out, and enthroned people as things went on. Naturally, this is all fascinating, but the idea of empire, which was as old as Charlemagne, suddenly went off track.

I am not saying that we should have remained with Charles V. However, we have to think about the changes that occurred over those two centuries. In fact, to go straight to my point, I think that the idea of Europe took refuge in the Vatican, more than in Paris, Berlin, Vienna or Moscow. Between the papacy and the empire, it is the papacy that won. Because it has become a worldwide phenomenon since John Paul II, the idea of Europe is now spreading everywhere. This is why John Paul II consecrated human rights at the same time that he repented at Yad Vashem. The idea of Europe, in the form that the popes stubbornly advocate it today, means the identity of all people. However, attention has to be paid to the fact that this identity is strengthened by reason able to integrate *the divine that this identity supposes*. We have to hope that the Church will continue in this direction.

Remember that Napoleon, who understood many things, took Pope Pius VII hostage. This is when Catholics began calling him the Antichrist. In a way, he had become the Antichrist long before, and now we know why. However, Dante's old debate between the Guelphs and Ghibellines, between those who wanted the pope and those who preferred the emperor, began to reappear at that time. This is the file that we have to revisit. This traumatic event has been forgotten. It looks trivial, but in fact it is absolutely essential.

Countess de Ségur is an interesting example on this point. She was a Russian aristocrat who moved from Saint Petersburg to France in 1817, became a French writer, and passionately wanted Napoleon III to guarantee the Papal States. She did not understand that the suppression of all temporal power was the best thing that could happen to the papacy. Not only did Napoleon III not guarantee the States, but in 1870, owing to the occupation of France by the Prussians, the pope was again taken hostage, that time by the Italian government. These conflicts, which involved the papal Zouaves, in which the sons of the French aristocracy enlisted, were intensely interesting to her. Sophie Rostopchine, Countess de Ségur, saw the seizure of temporal control over the pope as a veritable catastrophe.

I think we could find many other examples of this kind of paradox. Why do you think there was an attempt to kill John Paul II in 1981? The USSR also had ideas about Europe. The counter-Reich that it had set up was falling apart at the seams. So it is not surprising that the papacy became so important at that point. Wherever the gunfire came from in this strange case, we cannot rule out the possibility that it was from the East. Paradoxically, the papacy was freed by the collapse of imperialism in Europe. European imperialism had been undermined by centuries of rivalry among the pope's and the emperor's various parties, and then among the various pretenders to the empire, then between France and Germany. This led to the definitive collapse of all imperial velleities in the escalation to extremes. The papacy's liberation gave rise to terrible resentment. This phenomenon is fundamental and recent, but who takes it into account? To tell the truth, a pope who is both German and European, who defends reason and who finally goes to Istanbul, is more persuasive to me than the "world spirit" passing under Hegel's windows in Jena.

This is why it is interesting to think about the two centuries during which these upheavals occurred, and about the French-German relations that partly structured the ambivalence of war and peace, order and chaos. This is the price of rebuilding the idea of Europe. This is what we have to fight for. There are strong taboos in France, many topics that get people angry and that we never want to talk about. We have already mentioned the crisis of military heroism, of which the Dreyfus Affair is for me the perfect symptom. Indeed, who would dare to say that Napoleon's tomb in the Invalides looks like Lenin's mausoleum? No one. Napoleon has literally been divinized, like Julius Caesar. However, his death established nothing; the French Empire died with him. So, his grand nephew rebuilt Paris to try to get people to forget him. The names Jena, Wagram, Austerlitz and Caulaincourt are more likely to make us think of avenues, rail stations and streets than the battles and generals that led France to ruin. Not long ago we still believed in the myth of "French greatness," in Louis XIV and Napoleon. de Gaulle embodied that myth in his own way. We are in a new era now, and this is probably a good thing. This shows a way out of national religion. The continuation of the best in Gaullism will require renouncing certain Gaullian myths, including that of a too narrow nationalism.

"The Strange Defeat" of 1940

BC: Everything you have just said is consistent with what Germaine de Staël was hoping for at the beginning of the nineteenth century. You have underlined clear shifts in the dialogue between the French and German cultures,

which are at the heart of the trend to extremes. However, the French nonetheless said no to Europe in the 2005 referendum. Was this the last flash of
national pride?

RG: Perhaps. I would like to believe so because that pride does not bode
well, but I will not join the chorus of lamenters; we should not give up on
France. The French have to believe in Europe, and this requires finally set-
tling their accounts with Napoleon. This should not be done in a shameful
manner, such as when we renounced commemorating the 200th anniversary
of Austerlitz, while commemorating Trafalgar with great pomp and circum-
stance. It is time to abandon the self-hatred that we are so good at. In a way,
Clausewitz can help us. We should learn to see our history through German
eyes; the Germans are better than us at thinking about all this. Some one
told me the *Arte* network had a television show on how Germans perceived
Napoleon at the time, which seems very interesting. At the beginning of the
nineteenth century, the Germans had the very strong feeling that the emperor
was accelerating the course of history. Of course, there were precedents, such
as the political mistakes of Louis XIV, the king who "loved war too much."
The emergence of the Napoleonic model was therefore not unforeseeable, but
in day-to-day life, everyone minds his own business. Napoleon was thus a
little like "the troublemaker who comes and bothers us nice, quiet, peaceful
Germans." There was not yet the climate of hostility for the very good reason
that Germany was not yet unified so it dealt better with the shocks it underwent and did not yet react too mimetically. France was imitated furiously in
Prussia, but not in Bavaria or Saxony.

This has nothing to do with French-German relations after the war of
1870. Curiously, we do not want to see this or even remember it. France has
not gotten over the conflict that linked it so closely to Germany for two centuries. The last *poilu*[27] will be buried with great ceremony. We want to keep
making heroes out of all those anonymous soldiers. We thus want to keep
seeing Germany with French eyes, whereas it is the French who should be
seen with German eyes. France should be able to look at itself in this mirror without shame. This is the price of mimetic history. We should therefore
reread and carefully study the texts that tell us about the beginnings of that
incredible confrontation, but we should make sure that we do not do this
from a nationalistic or unilateral point of view.

BC: Péguy wrote a revealing description of the situation before World
War I, the controlled hatred with which the two countries watched each
other, when it was still possible to temper "hostile feeling" and turn it into
simple "hostile intent," to use Clausewitz's terms. This is when, in the crisis of

Tangier of 1905, Kaiser Wilhelm II was strutting about in the Moroccan city of Tangier to provoke France:

> The two peoples recoiled before the event even as they were rushing into it. It was no longer a case of pitting a professional army against a national army. It was not a case of fighting oneself. Military service had become personal on both sides, so were two national armies, two peoples in arms going to attack each other? In truth, both were slowly backing away. The fear that had precipitated the Imperial drive was also the fear that pulled it back. The same feelings that had pushed the German forces forward were the ones by which they were finally withdrawn. This formidable adventure could have taken a bad turn: if there had been an accident or reversal of fortune, the whole victory would have crumbled ... the whole advantage of even the earlier victory could have collapsed in a totalizing disaster.[28]

This contains a perceptive analysis of politics' last stand against the imminent trend to extremes. Péguy wrote that Germany "gradually renounced its anti-revenge war" at the same time that France "gradually renounced its revenge war." This text is neither nationalistic nor unilateral.

RG: It is even an example of impeccable mimetic reasoning that shows that Péguy understood everything about reciprocal action. One army's withdrawal leads to that of the other owing to the play of reciprocity. Far from giving hope that the conflict will end, the fact of deferring it foreshadows what will happen later: the horror of Verdun, the battle of entrenched positions taken to its worst extreme. Europe's history has to be analyzed in light of such intuitions. We should never lose sight of mimetic doubles and mirror effects that give us a more accurate vision of history. The passage that you have quoted is essential for understanding what the relations between the two countries had become after the war of 1870. The incredible tension made people crazy on both sides of the Rhine, and in Germany relaunched a very perverse conception of heroism, against which Péguy resisted with all his strength. It is not wrong to say that Germany's Prussian violence had its foundations in disdain for international law. This is the position of thinkers such as Bergson and Durkheim. They were accused of being excessively patriotic, but they saw what Péguy saw: the Clausewitzian resentment that was to make Prussia one of the sources of inspiration for Pangermanism. The German resentment of the French increased again following Verdun and especially after the Treaty of Versailles, *kudos* this time passing to the French side.[29] Remember that the French army occupied the mining centers of the Ruhr in

1923 to force the Germans to honor the Treaty's clauses. At that point there were violent clashes between French soldiers and German workers supported by their government. All of this is known. However, we are too quick to forget that it was because of the 1914–18 disaster that no one dared to move when Hitler decided to invade the Rhineland in 1936. Hitler was almost nothing at the time, but would soon ask all his officers to carry a copy of *On War* in their bags.

France found itself in an impossible situation after World War I. This has to be kept in mind if we want to understand what Marc Bloch called the "strange defeat" of 1940.[30] When Germany re-armed the Rhineland in 1936, the radical socialist President of the Council, Albert Sarraut, quickly saw what it was all about. If he had entered Germany then with the French troops as they were, France would have been victorious immediately because the Germans were on horseback. Some did not even have guns. They would have retreated if France had gone into the Rhineland. In other words, Hitler was staking everything on re-arming the area. He was betting on the fact that the French would not enter the Rhineland, and they did not. Sarraut telephoned England, and England telephoned the United States. The answer was obviously no, a very firm no. If France had moved into Germany, it would have been seen as rejecting the Briand-Kellogg Pact of August 27, 1928 in which 57 countries had condemned war. There would never have been a Hitler, but no one would ever have known.

Sarraut nonetheless saw that the British and Americans, on whom France was dependent, would never have forgiven him for such an action. Remember that capitalists had large investments in Germany at the time. In the eyes of the rest of the world, France would have looked like the one that did not want to give up war. Sarraut, who almost entered Germany and could have reversed the course of events, saw that. He was more afraid of the future and understood perfectly that this would determine it. If we had to choose a point when everything hung by a thread, I would say this was it. Hitler entered the Rhineland almost unarmed, powerless, and no one did anything. This was the most decisive attack on the Treaty of Versailles, which collapsed an instant after the *Anschluss*. Hitler took advantage of the fact that the Germans were considered to be victims, exactly as his fellow countrymen had done in 1810. He undoubtedly frightened democrats. But his anti-Jewish rhetoric was considered very old fashioned, dated. It had been around for a long time. No one wanted to see the coming catastrophe.

This example validates our reading of the "remarkable trinity," which places the duel in time,[31] making the response all the more fearful for having been deferred. Intervening immediately would have made it possible to avoid war, but the intervention was impossible owing to France's alliances. The trend to extremes thus seems to unfold like fate. It is in this sense that warmongering and pacifism are mimetic doubles: they complement each other quite well. If two adversaries want war at the same time, they can neutralize each other: an example of this is nuclear deterrence. However, if one of the two *wants war more than the other,* the other may also have the tendency to *reject it all the more.* We saw this with Clausewitz, though such phenomena are unpredictable and elude our rational frameworks.

The primacy of defense over offense gives us one of the clues to the situation. The defender is the one who wants war. The attacking side wants peace. In the case at hand, in 1923 the French wanted to keep what they had acquired from victory in World War I: a precarious peace that they were ready to defend at any price and for which they would invade Germany. Their population was already dropping and they became warmongers out of pacifism. Hitler was then in a strong position because he was invaded first. He did not "invade" the Rhineland by re-arming it, but "responded" to aggression against his country. Re-arming the Rhineland was his first counter-attack, and it was to prove decisive.

It was thus the French *desire for peace* that caused the new trend to extremes. Without realizing it, they perpetuated the absurdity of Verdun. They continued building their monuments to the dead, without really thinking about what had just taken place; their arrogance as petty victors could only exasperate their adversary. *France was continuing to act like Napoleon,* who had invaded Germany to maintain peace. It had not understood anything. Hitler did not understand anything either when he redirected his offense to the east after his brilliant victory over France, and in time he was to make the same mistake as Napoleon. This is a perfect example of what I call *misapprehension.* The more I want peace, in other words, the more I want to conquer, then the more I seek to assert my difference, and the more I prepare a war that I will not control but that will control me instead. This is how undifferentiation becomes worldwide, how mimetic violence grows behind the backs of those involved. This is much more real than the Hegelian "ruse of reason," and much less abstract than Heidegger's "enframing of the world by technology." Clausewitz is the key to understanding this.

The mimetic hypothesis helps us to grasp the phenomena that we do not want to see. What I find striking is that so far in France there has never been a reflection on World War I. This is because that war cost us too dearly, and victory was too precious and too fragile for anyone to dare to touch it. In his father's footsteps, Admiral Philippe de Gaulle noted an interesting thing: the Germans were much better organized in World War I. They suffered only 900,000 casualties, whereas the French had 1,300,000 and the English nearly 600,000. Thus, the Germans made peace even though they knew they were victorious. They had only supply problems; they were forced to retreat, but they were not beaten on the battlefield. This is why the French, after the occupation of the Ruhr that the English and Americans decried, fell into an insurmountable political trap. How could they have escaped from it? If they had entered Germany in 1936, the English and Americans would eventually have cozied up with the Germans after a year or two. From that point on, if there was a World War II, France would have been beaten. This is a political dilemma that few people recall. The French could no longer respond to what had become a simple counter-attack by Hitler. World War I had begun again, but with increased violence because France did not have the right to counter Hitler in 1936. It placed itself in an even more impossible situation by not doing so. *Thus, the French felt responsible for not having prevented the war,* for not having stopped Hitler when there was still time. They were secretly ashamed of having acted like Napoleon, of having been led into a trap that prevented them from acting.

The Rion Trial in 1942, when an attempt was made to convict those held responsible for the defeat, was a vulgar propaganda ploy ordered by the Vichy regime: everything had begun in 1923. Thus, the "strange defeat" of 1940 was not caused by the left-wing Popular Front, but by a fatal mistake, a *misapprehension of reciprocal action.* If Hitler had failed in 1936, he would have lost all prestige. This is an especially interesting case: there was only one man, Albert Sarraut, who could have intervened in a decisive manner, but he was prevented from doing so. I realize that this may be a somewhat hypothetical point of view. Naturally, other "accidents" could have occurred, and the conflagration could have happened in another way. However, that was France's inextricable situation. It has suddenly become impossible to speak about it. That is why I am insisting on it so much. The French have to escape the shackles of that tragic point in their history. An irony of fate is that my first academic work at Indiana University concerned this issue, or more specifically the way that American public opinion saw the 1940 defeat.[32] You are letting me bring my work full circle. However, of course it is only now that I understand what was really at stake.

There is also, in this "strange defeat," a phenomenon of inertia that belongs literally to a kind of social physics, thus to mimetic mechanisms that need to be studied much more closely than I am doing right now. Here too,

Clausewitz is essential. His treatise contains surprising anticipation of 1940, the great time of national paralysis that affected everyone. We have already cited the following passage in Chapter 1, but we need to go back to it:

> The political object ... [can] provide the standard of measurement ... only in the context of the two states at war. The same political object can elicit *differing* reactions from different peoples, and even from the same people at different times. We can therefore take the political object as a standard only if we think of *the influence it can exert upon the forces [die Massen] it is meant to move. The nature of those forces therefore calls for study.* Depending on whether their characteristics increase or diminish the drive toward a particular action, the outcome will vary. Between two peoples and two states there can be such tensions, such a mass of inflammable material, that the slightest quarrel can produce a wholly disproportionate effect—a real explosion. ... Generally speaking, a military objective that matches the political object in scale will, if the latter is reduced, be reduced in proportion; this will be all the more so as the political object increases its predominance. Thus it follows that without any inconsistency wars can have all degrees of importance and intensity, ranging from a war of extermination down to simple armed observation.[33]

This is a text we need to study alongside that of Péguy. It tells us about the possible explosion of war, but also about the possible delay of that explosion, and the fact that politics cannot do much about it. What can rise to extremes and towards a war of extermination can also descend into simple armed observation. This is a strange and fascinating pendular movement that escapes all reason. "We can therefore take the political object as a standard only if we think of *the influence it can exert upon the forces [die Massen] it is meant to move. The nature of those forces therefore calls for study.*" This sentence is impressive. The "nature" of the opposing masses determines the outcome of the conflict. If the goal (or political reason) is weak, the act of war will be weak, but if it is strong, the act will be strong. *However, what determines the importance of the goal is the "nature" of the masses.*

The "political object" is only the relative standard, in other words, the relationship between the masses. Thus, it is not the political goal that influences the masses, but the nature of the masses that influences the political goal. The political "motive" is not what decides the outcome of the conflict, but what can suddenly provoke it, just as a spark can make gunpowder explode. The political factor is decisive when the masses are indifferent; it is trivial when they are no longer so. It is clear that we have gone beyond eighteenth century reasoning. Here, Clausewitz is foreshadowing Durkheim and sociology. Thus, if the laws internal to the opposing masses lead one of them not to act, they will encourage the other either to take action (the escalation to extremes) or not to act (armed observation). It was because the French misapprehended this form of reciprocal action that they did not want to see the direct interaction between what they were doing and what Hitler was going to do, between their pacifism and his warmongering. *They did not want to see that Germany had the upper hand in propaganda.* They had a very deep desire, which was to keep the improbable victory of 1918 at all costs and to never return to chaos. This inertia gave rise to an opposite force, which is proof that the law of the escalation to extremes always prevails. It is by trying to avoid a new Verdun at any price that they were led back to it. Hitler's rejoicing under the Eiffel Tower proves that he was only trying to vanquish France, that he was fundamentally a man of 1914.

What Clausewitz calls "armed observation" is a good description of what was called the "phoney war" in France. There are many things that correspond to that: all the symptoms of this rejection of war, of the "weaker form" of war to which the French aspired, for example. We can thus show that Clausewitz said it all, that he announced the French defeat of 1940. The passages on the "weaker form" of war point to the concept of inertia, but there is the possibility of a contradiction in the use of this term. In other words, where we might expect action, there is inaction, thus something that, strangely, is in opposition to war. This is the definition of the force of inertia. The translator of the French edition of *On War,* Denise Naville, never uses this expression. Instead, she employs all sorts of other things, such as "moderating principle." Yet "inertia" has a physical meaning that is easy to define, but on the psychological level it covers a kind of contradiction that is interesting. The less a people wants war, the more it will strengthen its "armed observation," its means of surveillance, its fortifications and containment measures that actually do not work and in fact provoke conflict.

A strengthened political objective, which supposes enormous means, thus becomes the spark that unleashes the worst. At the same time that it translates a very deep movement, that of a people that no longer wants war, it unleashes in the adversary of that people a movement that is just as deep, but contrary to it. The refusal of one leads to the desire of the other. Armed observation is thus not at all a containment of warlike violence, but what will unleash it in an unpredictable way. Refusal to fight does not appease the other party, except in the rare cases when the masses are "indifferent."

We have understood this phenomenon with respect to aggression: there is a way of not responding to the other that is in itself aggressive. To strengthen peace is to unleash war. In Clausewitz's terms, we would say that purely political "hostile intent" unleashes the "hostile feeling" that comes from the masses, in this case a nation galvanized by propaganda. In this regard, the political objective does in fact influence the masses, but not in the sense that Raymond Aron wanted. Hostile intent is French General Gamelin; hostile feeling is Hitler, the man who, precisely because he was not an aristocrat in the Cornelian sense of the term, channeled the mimetic energy of his people, and turned it back against France with the odious slogan of *Lebensraum* ("living space").

This makes it easier to understand the difference in context between 1905 and 1939. What Péguy described as an ebbing, a collateral retreat of both powers, was no longer possible in 1939 for a very simple reason: before the cataclysm at Verdun, politics still had relative control over events. But even in 1905 it was already less a case of politics than of what Clausewitz described as a descent into armed observation, a state of relative indifference of the opposing masses:

> But it is contrary to human nature to make an extreme effort, and the tendency therefore is always to plead that a decision may be possible later on. As a result, for the first decision, effort and concentration of forces are not all they might be. Anything omitted out of weakness by one side becomes a real, objective reason for the other to reduce its efforts, and the tendency toward extremes is once again reduced by this interaction.[34]

Everything changed in 1939. There was the Ruhr crisis and the invasion of the Rhineland. Against de Gaulle's recommendations, a strategic plan was adopted in French headquarters: it was that of General Gamelin's "invisible" Maginot Line, and then the interminable wait. Gamelin's inertia did not lead to German inaction. Quite to the contrary. I would say that the equivocation of the former led to the imprudence of the latter. Clausewitz's treatise makes it possible to explain this phenomenon, proof that *On War* is one of the keys to understanding the French-German conflict. We could use the type of reasoning that we have just sketched out to decipher, over a longer period, the symmetry of behavior on either side of the Rhine. The Prussian withdrawal in 1806 incontestably contributed to reviving the escalation to extremes by enabling Napoleon to invade Russia. Likewise, it was the French withdrawal in the 1930s that permitted Hitler to take the road to Moscow, thereby exacerbating the tensions that had been undermining Europe for over a century. Inertia, far from resisting violence, instead revived it. Those who withdraw are all the more surprised: what they did not want becomes a reality that is all the more violent because they thought they would be able to defer the conflict. Unilateral perspectives always result in the worst. To adopt mimetic reasoning would thus be to escape the old French-German logic and, perhaps, finally lead to the discovery of Europe.

BC: What memories do you have of this period?

RG: I remember 1937, 1938, 1939, the little white paper leaflets of partial mobilization that fell in total silence. I was still a child. I was captivated by the mysteriousness of the prospect of war. I thought I was fascinated by politics, but at the same time I could feel that there was something very strange going on, something Kafkaesque. My father was very clear-thinking. I will always remember the morning when he told me: "We will be beaten." Very few people dared to think that. "There is no doubt that France will be beaten; it is impossible to start over again," he told me. "France is the weakest partner in the English-American-French coalition." He was right. France was neutralized by its allies. We cannot blame them for their policy: in their position, we would have done the same thing. The inability to respond to Hitler came from the fact that we did not want to return to the conditions of 1916. All aspects of modern war went to extremes in 1914, and France was the first victim of this, militarily, politically, psychologically and spiritually. This is why my father's generation never spoke about the war. It was taboo. In 1939, we were at almost the same point as in 1919, and 1919 is what we had hoped to maintain in 1923. Pacifism and the poor military decisions that followed came from the fact that *the French wanted peace as much as Hitler wanted war.* However, in the meantime they had lost all possibility of action. Nobody said anything; routine life recommenced as if nothing had happened. We were the winners, we had killed war. No one wanted to hear about it anymore. Then it came back in greater force, with an unanticipated surge of violence. In this sense, the 1940 defeat still needs to be examined. The collapse was unimaginable: Jena to the nth power. I was still a child, but I understood in a way.

I remember the mobilization of the horses in the little village in Auvergne where I spent my vacations. It was like in 1914. We had the impression of a mixture of outdatedness and catastrophe at the same time, of a sinister déjà-vu and a powerlessness to conceive the political resources that were needed. The Americans seem to have wanted France to repeat what it had done at Verdun: absorb the main thrust of the German army without collapsing. They were unable to understand why we could not do it again. Their only dramatic historical experience up to that point had been the Civil War, which was much more present in their minds than World War I, which for them was only a political affair. They thought they had lots of time. It was impossible. It was clear that Stalingrad was not going to happen at Verdun. Stalingrad was the Verdun of World War II. The French knew that they would not be able to withstand a German attack. It was finished. France was out of the game. The French army's defensive strategy, which de Gaulle had the audacity to reject, was based on the gigantic losses of 1914.

Was de Gaulle's thesis that tanks would have changed everything correct?[35] Would war have returned to chivalry and nobility? De Gaulle's reasons were both humane and strategic. However, the truth was that the old warrior spirit was no longer there at all. History had become implacable. In fact, the French also had the idea that the German spirit was essentially warlike, that this was henceforth their culture, that this was the energy that had vanquished unemployment in Germany. But it was no longer the culture of the French. We have to think of this situation as the exact opposite of that in 1806, which made Clausewitz and Germaine de Staël think that the warriors *par excellence* were the French. Indeed, the French acknowledged in 1940 that the centuries of French predominance were behind them, that they were going to witness the return of the Germans and the empire. When the culture of war changes sides, the vision of history also changes. Clausewitz has enabled us to see the rising power of French militarism for what it was, but he did not see that the Revolution and the empire had killed the warrior spirit of his adversaries.

We in turn did not want to see that the 1870 defeat was the collapse of our warrior spirit; the flame was extinguished. This is why the France of the Second Empire, and especially that of the Third Republic, was built on a Napoleonic myth that literally finished the country by forcing it to live beyond its means. Our denial of reality grew as German resentment increased, but it is always the declining power that lives beyond its means. In 1806, it was Prussia; in 1940, it was France, but the proportions were obviously not comparable because the escalation to extremes had progressed. In the same way, Germany and Russia lost the warrior spirit after Stalingrad. The Russians exhausted themselves in Chechnya, as they did in Afghanistan. There also, it is finished; something has snapped. One by one, every European country has been crushed by this means. This is what America has trouble understanding. I always have to say to Americans: "You do not understand anything about the present situation in Europe, after two world wars that were the most gigantic, the most terrible in history." However, in a certain way, Clausewitz did not see this either. In the end, the French knew very well that they were not going to stop the apocalypse, but they no longer wanted to take an active part in it.

BC: Doesn't your "by the masses" argument, which forces you to take a long-term, apocalyptic view of history, make you minimize the values of the Resistance, which played an essential role in reviving the idea of Europe?

RG: I do not at all minimize that form of heroism, especially since it has been implied throughout our discussion. I admire de Gaulle for having gloriously escaped this spirit of resignation. This is what the right-wing French criticized him for: he completely accepted secularism. He had spoken of the future of France with the Count of Paris, and the latter had understood that he was not fit to govern. As soon as he returned to France, de Gaulle pointed out that the far-right monarchist *Action française* movement was terribly Third Republic and part of the country's general decadence. However, at the same time, de Gaulle himself said that France had not followed the Resistance, that the Resistance had not been able to unite the French.

We should not forget that people like Maritain saw him as an aspiring dictator. Later, Maritain suffered so much guilt about this that he felt obliged to accept the position of Ambassador to the Vatican. Clearly by sending him to the pope, de Gaulle had ulterior motives regarding a Catholic France. At the time, Maritain incarnated the best of French Catholicism, but many Catholics were against him because they saw him as a leftist. These were the precursors of what was to be Vatican II. In 1926, Maritain had taken the pope's side against the *Action française*. This is when he became a democrat. He is well remembered at Princeton. If any aspects of Catholic culture are European we see them here. There is no ambiguity with respect to the right-wing monarchist Maurras or its opposing, leftist progressivism. This is why I do not at all minimize what you call the "values of the Resistance." Here, despite his detractors, Péguy triumphs over the antiquated, stale *Action française*. This is indeed why those in favor of the Vichy regime did everything they could to claim him as one of their own.

De Gaulle had no illusions about the Resistance, which, owing to internal dissensions, was somewhat inefficient. Instead, he adopted a lofty vision of France, and invited Konrad Adenauer to Colombey. He wanted to act as if the European engine could restart, as if it were possible to annul the two world wars and begin all over again. His determination was extraordinary: he decided that we would not make the same mistakes and would no longer imitate Napoleon. He innovated by recommencing dialogue with Germany, and succeeded where Germaine de Staël had failed. We have lived for 40 years on the hope that came out of the Reims meeting.

However, demographics are unfortunately an accurate indicator. France, which used to have the largest population in Europe, collapsed since the 1870 defeat. Under Louis XIV, there were 25 million inhabitants in France and only four million in England. However, Napoleon caused a million deaths. When he said, "One night in Paris will fix that," it was odious and not at all true. Why has no one ever thought about these things? I think that the one who came closest to doing so was de Gaulle, but he chose not to talk about it. He was betting on a new beginning; he was placing all his stakes on it. The strength of his position came from this extreme tension, from his prodigious willpower, which succeeded in the end, on the personal, national and international levels, and for at least 25 years. However, de Gaulle's political successes were too large for France's real stature, and the French did not understand the almost miraculous success of his policy. They no longer had the means to do so.

I do not think that de Gaulle was entirely Clausewitzian. He was more of a politician than a soldier, though he was undeniably a great soldier during World War I. His military skills did not prevent him from engaging in politics all his life. Even during the time when he focussed on the army, he was already doing politics. He had premonitions about France's military disaster, but still believed in the primacy of politics over the military. This is what made the Resistance utopist, though I do not in any way minimize the greatness of the movement. Indeed, this is why de Gaulle won over Paul Reynaud, who was immediately interested in de Gaulle's strategic and military writings: *The Edge of the Sword* (1932) and *The Army of the Future* (1934).[36] At the time, de Gaulle thought France could beat Germany. We know about his difficult relations with Pétain, who first saw him as a protégé and then suddenly realized that he was not one at all. However, I am not very familiar with his relationship with the French chiefs of staff. At the military academy, he was rejected as a risk-taker. De Gaulle believed that one should be all the more audacious when one had nothing left to lose. France collapsed in 1870, after the Battle of Sedan. If de Gaulle's strategy had been adopted, perhaps things would have turned out quite differently. Perhaps the vacuity of Nazism would then have become clear? The role of chance is considerable in all this. However, generals like Gamelin did not listen to him; he was preaching in the desert. His only real reader was Heinz Guderian, the German general who created the *Panzerdivisionen*, the Wehrmacht's primary offensive force in 1939; he was a commander in the Ardennes in 1940. Both men had read each other's work. They shared the same ideas about motorized, armored divisions. They clearly shared the same doctrine.

Moreover, the rare French counter-offensives, at Montcornet and Abbeville in May 1940, were led by de Gaulle at the head of the 4th Armored Division. We must not forget these military exploits, which won him the position of Undersecretary of State for National Defense and War. However, his tanks were too big and not fast enough, though they were of excellent quality. The Germans were not much better off: most of their army was not really motorized. It was thus French Prime Minister Reynaud who made de Gaulle's career: if he had not appointed him to National Defense on June 6, 1940, four days before the 1940 armistice, de Gaulle would not have become the man he did. It was because he had political means to plead for the continuation of the war that the General was able to oppose those in favor of the armistice and continue his fight in London. This at least was needed, this slender thread to make June 18 into something, instead of nothing at all, even though no one heard the call. Reynaud made him a statesman. De Gaulle was able to launch his call on June 18 because Reynaud resigned on June 16 to make way for Pétain. This is where the beginnings of the General's legitimacy lie. He was the first to take a clear-eyed view of the situation. He was a military man, in a way, but he had neither troops nor a front, and could not go to where there was fighting because Roosevelt prevented him from doing so. Yet his tiny sliver of power was sufficient for him to turn France back into one of the Big Five. To say that de Gaulle rebuilt France with words alone is thus a covert Pétainist myth: for him, London was a rational choice, not at all based on a form of madness or literature.

Indeed, his taste for literature was a personal and political choice. It was the last thing that remained intact in France. De Gaulle had a deep love of literature, which he considered an institution. When he returned to France, the first dinner he held was with François Mauriac. He absolutely wanted Mauriac to have a meal with him at the Ministry of War. Later in Colombey, in 1948, he met with Georges Bernanos. When one's power does not match one's ambitions, politics become what Péguy, one of de Gaulle's models, wanted it to be: literature. Paradoxically, it was thus de Gaulle's total lack of military power that made him the hero he became. When heroism is literary or philosophical, it does not frighten me any more. Marc Bloch was undeniably a hero, and Jean Cavaillès also. In a way, heroism is an intellectual business. These were writers who refused to serve those in power, but whom events can force to become prophets. Remember Pascal's anger: "Unable to strengthen justice, they have justified might."[37] This anger shows a true refusal to collaborate. Weapons should be only a means to "strengthen justice" against those who "justify might." This is the heroic model, and there is no other. Here again we find in this the reciprocal intensification of violence and truth: truth that strengthens a violence that can do nothing, by contrast, against truth. I think that there is no other definition of resistance. It applies to each and every one of us.

This is also why de Gaulle was so wary about the Free French attempt to defeat the Vichy regime in Dakar, which was not his idea but Churchill's. He was reticent because he knew the people in Dakar would not abandon Pétain. This was one of the worst times for him. He anticipated failure, but could not oppose the operation because Churchill wanted to do something for the Free French after the British had destroyed much of the French fleet at Mers El-Kébir in order to prevent it from falling into German hands. Dakar proved catastrophic. The Free French were hanging by a thread at a time when Gaullism consisted only in Radio London. When Simone Weil spoke of "radio education," she was thinking about Maurice Schumann's Free French chronicles that were broadcast from London. A good third of France was Schumannist. I listened to Schumann religiously, and I was very moved to meet him later.

We thus have to stop saying that all French people were in favor of Pétain. Of course, all of France did not join the Resistance, but to say that no one did, as has been done since the film *The Sorrow and the Pity*,[38] is even more false. Historiography has allowed itself to be too influenced by this current and has fed the self-hatred that lingers in France. Every ideology that has failed to embody France has always ferociously held a grudge against de Gaulle because he succeeded. Everything that lowers the giant makes the dwarves taller and nothing is more mimetic than such jealousy. It would be much more accurate to say that there were many people who were passively Gaullist, who hoped. To think in terms of the Resistance and Collaboration is to remain within mythological frameworks, to be stuck on differences that were much fuzzier than one might think. In France as elsewhere, there were people who were cowardly and others who were courageous. Once again, heroism cannot be decreed. No one can claim to know the direction in which history is going. From this point of view, I greatly appreciate the fact that the "Justes de France," who risked their lives and those of their children in order to save Jews, were honored at the Pantheon on January 18, 2007. Listen to those who are still alive, and you will see that they were not trying to be heroes. They say that they did what had to be done, that's all.

CHAPTER 8

The Pope and the Emperor

THE LAST *INTERNATIONALE*

Benoît Chantre: In the realm of contingent wars in which we are immersed, there is thus an essential war: truth's war against violence. You say that truth has flushed violence out. To use Clausewitz to criticize Hegel, and Hegel to criticize Clausewitz, is to get closer to apocalyptic reason and see that the person whose "successful career" we need to watch is not whom we thought. He is not the "god of war" or the "world spirit" admired at Jena, but a ghostly figure that has for a time been hidden by the empire's darkness. I am of course thinking of Michel Serres' magnificent book *Rome: The Book of Foundations,*[1] and of his re-interpretation of Livy, which was in response to your ideas. In Serres' rereading, Alba the White is crushed by its rival city, Rome the Black; the victim is hidden, stoned to death by mendacious history. What this reading contains in potential form is now becoming real in a special way. You have just mentioned another phantom figure, who sits at the heart of Rome, a representation of the Unique, which the French Revolution concealed, and Napoleon humiliated, and Verdun smothered. It is an insistent and recurring figure, who did not fall under the bullets that probably came from the East and whom you consider to incarnate truth in its war against violence. You do not speak of the pope in your books, and yet you are deeply Catholic, which is something that always bothers the scientific community and people of faith.

René Girard: I am very sensitive to your praise of Michel Serres' book. As for the rest, I am a little tired of shuttling between those who believe in Heaven and those who do not, as if each had to remain in his corner and never talk with the other. All of my books have been written from a Christian perspective. My conversion is what put me on the mimetic path and the discovery of the mimetic principle is what converted me. It is unreasonable to say that my first two books are two halves of a whole (because I was relatively discreet about Christian revelation in them) and that all the others should be tossed out. Yet this attitude is quite common.

Even well-meaning readers still fail to follow me in my conviction that Judeo-Christianity and the prophetic tradition are the only things that can explain the world in which we live. There is a mimetic wisdom, which I do not claim to embody, and it is in Christianity that we have to look for it. It doesn't matter whether we know it or not. The Crucifixion is what highlights the victimary mechanism and explains history. Today, the "signs of the times" are converging and so we can no longer persevere in the madness of mimetic rivalries that we find on the national, ideological and religious level. Christ said that the Kingdom was not of this world. This explains why the first Christians were waiting for the end of the world, as we find in the two Epistles to the Thessalonians. We thus have to accept the idea that history is essentially finite. Only this eschatological perspective can give time back its true value.

BC: What role do you attribute to the Church in this revelation?

RG: A role that is both essential and relative. The Church is the guardian of a fundamental truth, but at the same time it is an institution and, like all institutions, it is immersed in history and subject to error. The Church was formed, then divided; it spread out and changed. It affirmed itself most in Catholicism, in particular that of the Council of Trent. The Council tried to restore the pope's power, which had become corrupted after the Babylonian Captivity of the papacy in Avignon and the imbroglios of Florence and Rome. From this point of view, the Jesuits were geniuses. Lord knows whether the miseries that they had to endure were related to the resentment against the papacy in Europe.

You are right to raise this topic. The papacy's gradual emergence in the struggle against the empire shows how the Spirit shapes history in ways unbeknownst to those involved. Hegel aped this idea with his dialectic. The Church has been falling and rebuilding itself for 2000 years, but it does not repeat the same mistakes. I have just mentioned the Council of Trent, but nineteenth century Catholicism also contained a decisive upheaval, and we have already looked at some of the players involved. Joseph de Maistre wrote that the strength of Catholicism, compared with Protestantism, is that it does not doubt. This expresses a special faith in history, which is in no way Hegelian.

De Maistre is someone we should mention at this point. He was a diplomat at Saint Petersburg, where as an intransigent Catholic he had to face the hostility of the Orthodox Church. He witnessed the disintegration of the empire into heterogeneous powers: Protestants (England and Prussia), Orthodox Christians (Russia) and Catholics (Austria), not to mention France, the object of de Maistre's saddened "considerations"[2] as it emerged shattered from the Revolution and the empire. As a baleful observer of the cruelty of war, which he considered "divine" because it was incomprehensible in its expansion, de Maistre had the feeling that the Church would not be able to survive such historical blows and that the Holy See was being criticized everywhere. He therefore decided to "show the pope to the world" by publishing a book, *The Pope*,[3] which was scandalous in 1819, both in the orthodox circles in which he moved and to the Gallican clergy. In it, he defended the pope's infallibility with arguments that reveal no resentment at all, but are nonetheless furious.

This insistence on the papacy's permanence in the midst of the political upheavals in Europe is essential for a political theoretician, especially since the argument in favor of the Church's permanence is related to the one concerning its leader's infallibility. Papal infallibility was not proclaimed (with respect to doctrine exclusively) until the end of the century. That proclamation is an essential event in the Church's history, for it freed the Church of compromises with temporal power. The intuitions of de Maistre and Baudelaire, and Claudel's powerful affirmations are related in one way or another to the emergence of the papacy. We have seen that Hölderlin also had intuitions about this stability. There are probably other people who lived at the turn of these two centuries and whom we should study. They would prove that "universal singularities" are possible, can be free of resentment and are aware of the radical truth that is in the process of emerging out of the general panic. The Enlightenment was the triumph of a certain kind of reasoning, and Catholicism after the Revolution promoted another. The clear culmination of this movement is Pope Benedict XVI's recent speech at Regensburg. The goal of mimetic theory is to bring this rationality to the forefront.

BC: What does that mean?

RG: I think, once again, that the world is caught up in an escalation to extremes and that people today do not see that it can be stopped. A pope cannot say that. His "infallibility" and his political position prevent him from doing so. He can intervene on questions of doctrine, and recommend dialogue when it has been interrupted. However, the audience that is now his shows clearly that an essential message is being conveyed: that of the absolutely *urgent need* for reconciliation. The urgency is eschatological, even though the pope does not want to say so as bluntly as we have in these discussions. His reluctance stems from the fact that he is the head of the Church and also a head of state.

BC: In what way is apocalypse a new idea in Europe and the world?

RG: In that the truth can gradually appear to people only through a veil of lies. The urgency of the Christian message has become clear because of the disintegration of the Powers and Principalities, in other words, through the collapse of the idea of empire. However, the empire tended to hold back the rise of violence: as we have seen, attackers *want peace*. They want to dominate, in other words, pacify: *pax romana, pax sovietica, pax americana*... The truth appears only once this falsehood has exhausted its last subterfuges.

Christianity reveals the central role of religion in the genesis of culture. Christianity truly demystifies religion because it points out the error on which archaic religion is based: the effectiveness of the divinized scapegoat. The Revelation *deprives* people of religion, and it is this deprivation that can increasingly be seen around us, in the naïve illusion that we are finished with it. Those who believe in the defeat of religion are now seeing it reappear as the product of that very demystification, but what is being produced is something sullied and demonetized, and frightened by the revelation of which it was the object. It is the loss of sacrifice, the only system able to contain violence, which brings violence back among us. Today's anti-religion combines so much error and nonsense about religion that it can barely be satirized. It serves the cause that it would undermine, and secretly defends the mistakes that it believes it is correcting; it frightens religion without managing to control it. By seeking to demystify sacrifice, current demystification does a much worse job than the Christianity that it thinks it is attacking because it still confuses Christianity with archaic religion.

People thus have to be immersed in untruth in order to have a little peace. This relationship between falsehood and peace is fundamental. The Passion brings war because it tells the truth about humanity, and deprives it of any sacrificial mechanism. Normal religion, which creates gods, is the one with scapegoats. As soon as the Passion teaches people that the victims are innocent, they fight. This is precisely what scapegoat victims used to prevent them from doing. *When sacrifice disappears, all that remains is mimetic rivalry, and it escalates to extremes.* In a way, the Passion leads to the hydrogen bomb: it will end up exploding the Powers and Principalities. The apocalypse is nothing but the incarnation of Christianity in history, which separates the mother from the child. In the Gospels, even miracles cause fights. Look at the great apocalyptic scenes in *The Possessed* by Dostoyevsky: you find there everything but syrupy reconciliation.

If the Kingdom is absolute peace, relative peace will be less and less possible owing to this growing empire of violence. Humanity cannot face its own truth without falsehood: this is the implacable truth of Christianity. The truth is now coming, and it is destroying everything by depriving us of our enemies. There will no longer be any good quarrels. There will no longer be any bad Germans. Total loss of sacrifice will necessarily provoke an explosion because sacrifice is the political-religious framework that sustains us. Without this elementary peace and all the ensuing justifications, humanity will be led to the apocalypse.

BC: Since you think the escalation to extremes is unavoidable, what do you think the Catholic Church's role is?

RG: Since he comes after a Polish pope, Ratzinger proves that the papacy has now been "internationalized." Catholicism has grown out of its childhood, and become the last *Internationale*. Even as he defends Western reason, that of Aristotle and Saint Thomas, Benedict XVI revives the papacy's struggle for Europe and against the empire. However, we now know that the battle does not resemble the fight for acquisition that it was for centuries. The papacy's struggle against the empire has been transformed into the battle of violence against its own truth, which it cannot refuse to acknowledge because to do so would lead to an apocalypse. The pope will never say that. All he can do is warn us about the dangers of our narrow rationalism by affirming that reason's battle against faith exposes us to a more frightening return of faith against reason.

That a pope defending "broad thinking" would warn about "de-Hellenization's" threat to culture in the city of Regensburg, where Hölderlin meditated on poems like "The Only One" and "Patmos," is what I would call a sign of the times. Western reason has everything to lose from this amputation, which it imposes on itself owing to some incomprehensible masochism. It urgently needs to reintegrate the divine as its essential dimension. Only this kind of rationality can deal with the returns of the corrupted sacred, which are attacks on reason. We urgently need to rethink the articulation of reason and faith. If Vatican II did one essential thing, it was to assert religious freedom, for if there is one single thing that Christianity cannot violate, it is the freedom to reject Revelation.

BC: You are thus placing irrationality on the side of the empire and reason on the side of the Church?

RG: This is indeed now the paradox we are witnessing. The empire wants peace, in other words, domination. It is thus based on exclusion. However, we know, thanks to Clausewitz, that this position is weak: the one who wants war is the one who will win. The popes thus *wanted war* against the empire, and we have to acknowledge that, on their level, they have won momentarily. However, the struggle is ongoing, and will increase in violence because the empire today is no longer the Holy Roman Empire or Europe or the United States or Russia or even the Latin Empire that Kojève described in 1945 in his "Outline of a Doctrine of French Policy."[4] It is the empire of unmasked violence, which panics all the more as Christian truth becomes absolutely compelling.

Of course, for several decades we have been witnessing a return of the papacy on the world scene. However, the pope is not Christ; he is only Peter's successor. Christ's return means something completely different, as we have seen. This is why sanely apocalyptic positions are situated beyond doctrinal refinements. We have to try to understand the great derailing in progress. The papacy's triumph, freed of all temporal ties, is one sign among others of this derailing. We must not be afraid of interpreting these signs. Mimetic theory is one of the interpretations. Since it sheds light on the processes of hominization, which perhaps took place at the dawn of humanity, it explores a theory about the "completion" of hominization, and discovers that it will be catastrophic.

In another way, we could say that the papacy's victory has revived Europe's essence at the very point when Europe may be disintegrating. From this point of view, the history of the Church is significant. We can understand retrospectively why, ever since Charlemagne and Othon the First, emperors have always wrestled with the papacy for control in Europe, and how this struggle has finally given the popes the spiritual importance that they have today. What happened in the Western Roman Empire did not occur in the Byzantine Empire, where the temporal managed, for profound, complex reasons, to take over the spiritual. By contrast with Orthodox patriarchs, Western popes have always resisted the empire. However, I would also agree that the empire has been able to resist the popes. Nonetheless, the war has been over since the worldwide papacy of John Paul II.

It has taken over a thousand years of friction to wear away the imperial model and establish the universality of Christian truth. John Paul II's repentance is an unheard-of event and absolutely unpredictable. It may have been partly an action against the Curia in Rome. We now know that John Paul II did whatever he wanted. That repentance alone has made pontifical infallibility a new idea in Europe because it turned the pope into the unpredictable representative of the idea of Europe. Who would have thought that in 1945? Kojève had glimpsed it, as did the three Catholics who reinvented Europe: Konrad Adenauer, Robert Schuman, and Charles de Gaulle. Let's not forget that it was Schuman who made France give up control over the Ruhr and opened the path that, ten years later, led to the meeting in Reims.

BC: That does not diminish the fact that the clashes between the pope and the empire were wars like others.

RG: Indeed, the recent popes' openness towards the world should not make us forget the nature of the papacy's war against the Powers and Principalities in the ninth century. Of course, that war was not always glorious, and naturally temporal concerns played a part in it. However, we have to understand it with a view to John Paul II's action, which closed the second millennium of the Christian era. When I say that the papacy won, I am thinking immediately of this repentance, by which the papacy triumphed over itself and acquired worldwide significance. Before our eyes, it succeeded in expelling all imperial ideas, at the very point when its temporal power disappeared. It has thus indeed been a struggle in which both sides put everything on the line, and the empire lost. The present "expansion" of Europe, without any imperial pretentions, therefore inaugurates a new period that is our only credible future, even though it is extremely precarious. This is the new face of the continent, in both its fragility and its strength. The idea that is being tried out in Europe and in every country where this idea is spreading is that of an identity of all people. When the pope took up this idea, he unceasingly and stubbornly reminded us of the divine nature of that identity.

A THOUSAND YEAR WAR

BC: As a former student of the École des Chartes, perhaps you could enlighten your readers about the medieval struggles that everyone has forgotten. As you have just noted, this is a way to show the other side of the escalation to extremes. Could you give us a few key dates in the war that the papacy fought against the empire to the benefit, according to you, of the idea of Europe?

RG: If you wish, even though I may make some mistakes. A "strange and tedious war" occurred between the popes and the empire. Note that such a war did not occur in the Byzantine Empire. It is a characteristically Western war.

The rivalry between the two powers began with Charlemagne, who decided to Christianize Europe and "imperialize" Christianity. Charlemagne was thus crowned in Rome by Leo III in the year 800. However, instead of observing the Byzantine ritual and kneeling before the emperor, the pope placed the crown on Charlemagne's head, thereby ensuring that he was seen as the one who had created the emperor. This event was probably the beginning of the empire's strange resentment of the papacy. At the other end of this story, we have Napoleon, who deliberately reversed Leo III's action and crowned himself before Pius VII, who was reduced to powerlessness. We have seen how the Church was able to take advantage of its powerlessness. Between these two coronations, that of a humiliated emperor and that of a self-proclaimed emperor, there are a thousand years of European history. A thousand years of quarrels, in which emperors forced popes to crown them, and popes excommunicated emperors.

Charlemagne was crowned emperor of the West, to reconnect with the Roman Empire after the spread of the Barbarians. After his death, the empire was divided between his three grandsons in the Treaty of Verdun in 843. Charles the Bald received the Western Frankish Kingdom, which later became France under Philip II Augustus; Louis the German received the Eastern Frankish Realm, the core of the future Holy Roman Empire of the German nation; and Lothair I received the Middle Frankish Kingdom, later known as Lotharingia, which extended from Friesland to Italy, and united the empire's two capitals, Aix and Rome. The rule of primogeniture made Lothair I the powerless emperor of a territory that his two brothers would try to take over. The Oaths of Strasbourg, which were the first in both the Old High German and Gallo-Romance languages, were between Louis the German and Charles the Bald, and concerned their alliance against Lothair I's imperial rights. Of course, we should avoid the approach adopted by nineteenth century historians, Michelet in particular, and not be too quick to place a national framework over the parceling out, in which vassal relations predominated. But we cannot fail to see the oaths as the origins of the fratricidal rivalry that was to tear Europe apart. The French-German duel over the Lorraine (whose name is derived from Lotharingia) probably has ancient roots in this.

Lothair's dynasty was quickly extinguished. It was thus not until the 962 coronation of Otto the Great, Duke of Saxony and King of Germany, that a Holy Roman Empire is reborn, encompassing Germany, Lotharingia and the Kingdom of Italy. The emperor appointed the bishops himself, and they played an essential role in the empire. When it came time for the Holy Roman Empire of the German nation, every king newly elected by the German princes took the road to Rome to be crowned emperor. The popes did not really have any choice. There were placed before a *fait accompli* and exploited in the same way that Napoleon exploited Pius VII. Pretenders to the throne used them against other pretenders. All of this was as mimetic as you please, and should be studied in detail from the perspective that we have described. It would then be clear that the conflict between the pope and the empire is perhaps one of the essential foci and a foundation for most of the political rivalries in Europe.

Owing to its spiritual pre-eminence, the papacy has always been a sort of island in Europe. It has supported one side and then another, but has never belonged to anyone. The complex interplay can only be seen from an anthropological point of view. The pope and England have always acted as neutral third parties with respect to competing claimants to the throne. However, in the history of Europe, the pope's status is special. His untouchable nature, which has increased as the papacy's temporal control has declined, resulting in the total loss of all pontifical lands aside from the Vatican, explains in itself why there has been an effort to appropriate the pope, or even to kill him as in 1981. The reason for the growing hatred is mimetic because the pope's *autonomy* is in the process of being achieved. Napoleon could not stand this. The pope, even a weakling like Pius VII, is scandalous because he is independent. He then becomes all the more desirable as he increasingly defends the idea of Europe freed from the last partisans of the empire.

Today, there are hardly any countries that are not seeking a visit from the pope. Appropriating the inappropriable gives the one who succeeds in this a political advantage: look at how the Turks took over Benedict XVI's words in Istanbul. Of course, the papacy's temporal temptations have also been mimetic. The papacy has always tried to regain authority over the Christian world, and has used very political means to do so. However, we must see this policy as fierce resistance to imperial domination, from whatever the source. The papacy's mimetism has thus slowly been refined and purified in the heat of unceasing struggle. Today it offers us a model we can identify with safely. Remember what I said about the biblical prophet at the beginning of our discussions: prophetic speech is rooted in the truth of the consenting scapegoat, but it does not claim to incarnate that truth. The same goes for the pope. This cuts short any idolatry of the pope.

BC: Is there a key point in the struggle that was essential in Western history?

RG: There must be several. However, there was in particular the point when the empire began to lose ground. In 1076, Pope Gregory VII, overcoming the autonomy acquired by the German kings, required every elected king, bishop, and abbot to obtain Rome's consent. The resulting Investiture Controversy led to the pope's deposition by Henry IV of Germany, and in return Henry IV's excommunication by the pope. The emperor later dressed in penitent's clothing and went to ask for the pope's pardon in Canossa (a fortress in the Apennines where Gregory VII had taken refuge). In some European languages, the expression "to go to Canossa" has come to mean "to do penance," which proves how deeply this struggle between the two powers is rooted in European memory. The emperor was nonetheless excommunicated. The Concordat of Worms, which in 1122 produced an agreement on the election of bishops and abbots, finally acknowledged the pre-eminence of ecclesiastical authority over lay power. The empire thus began to withdraw, and became a purely state entity that was so weakened that it never managed to unite Germany.

I am not going to reel off every significant event in this war because it lasted over 1,000 years. I have to make leaps in time, over the fourteenth century and the Avignon Papacy. The crisis of Imperial legitimacy, combined with the religious wars that forced the Holy Roman Empire of the German Nation to accept different sects in its states, forced the emperor to take refuge in Austrian lands after the Peace of Westphalia in 1648; it forced Francis II to abdicate, under pressure from Napoleon, in 1806. We have seen what happened to Napoleon himself after he laid hands on the pope.

French troubles will increasingly resemble those of Austria if we are not careful. Continuing to see Napoleon as a fetish without really analyzing the reasons for worshiping him is to condemn France to become a second Austria, to similarly narrow its attention to domestic quarrels. The famous "French arrogance" is nothing but a denial of reality. Only Europe can save it from this dead end, and make it finally hear John Paul II's question in the town of Le Bourget in 1979: "France, eldest daughter of the church, are you faithful to your baptismal promises?" The pathological adversaries of Catholicism have seen the pope's question as the beginnings of a fresh conquest, when in fact it was a new blow to the Napoleonic model. Other attacks followed. The troubles seem to have had deep roots. At the time, few people understood what was happening. I would not have described it as I do now, if I had not witnessed it, as have others.

BC: Let us go back for a moment to the fourteenth century, which you have just skipped over. Dante can help us sum up what has come out of our discussion. Few people know that you talked about the author of *The Divine Comedy* early in your work. We have never discussed *De Monarchia*, which is the political treatise the poet wrote in 1311, a few years before his death.

This was when Holy Roman Emperor Henry VII came into Italy and laid siege to Florence. Dante, who was in exile with White Guelphs and Ghibellines hostile to Pope Boniface VIII, bet on the empire against the papacy's temporal power. Was this not also an essential point in the war between the two powers vying for Europe?

RG: In any case, it was a point that was intense enough to give birth to the greatest poem in all of Catholicism. We need to go back to Dante if we want to get some idea of what a pope should incarnate. When I speak of "metaphysical hell" in *Deceit, Desire, and the Novel*, it was obviously in reference to *The Divine Comedy*. In 1963, two years after that book, I published an article that I am still proud of: "De *La Divine Comédie* à la sociologie du roman."[5] We have mentioned it before. In it I tried to show, through the torments of unconscious identification by Paolo and Francesca with the model of Lancelot and Guinevere, that the hell of desire is contained entirely in our refusal to see imitation. In fact, the poet's descent from circle to circle consists in describing a change that occurs at the heart of mimetism itself. We have to acknowledge our mimetic nature if we hope to free ourselves of it. I concluded by saying that the structure of *The Divine Comedy* is identical to that of novelistic truth. We have called such mediation "intimate" during our conversation in order to suggest that it transforms mimetism and opens the door to the other side of violence.

It was because he was exiled by Pope Boniface VIII that Dante took the empire's side and held Ghibelline positions. However, he would be delighted today to see the papacy's autonomy achieved, which the proclamation of his infallibility consecrated. Dante was constantly separating the temporal and the spiritual in order to better link them together. He defended both the pope (because he was a Guelph) and the empire (because he was a White Guelph, as opposed to a Black Guelph). However, he was not a Ghibelline in the strict sense. In his mind, the empire was thus only a temporary construction, that of an immanent human nature in which Grace *might* be expressed. For him, popes had only the power to bless, which is no small thing. Their role is to testify to the fact that the Revelation is following its course and that human awareness of human violence is progressing. Human reconciliation is a prerequisite for the Kingdom, which explains the importance of the idea of empire in Dante's work.

Dante had the feeling that Rome had finished something in history, and that wars no longer established anything. He was just as naïve as Hegel in thinking that people had to agree to stop fighting and trying to dominate. In this sense, Henry VII was Caesar's heir. Rome won in a legitimate manner.

This is the strength, but also the limitation of the idea of empire in Dante's writing. This great European did not see the precariousness of his idea. Like Hegel, he lacked a lucid vision of violence's possible ravages. His political and philosophical theory cannot explain the struggles among pretenders to the imperial throne. That requires a more radical anthropological analysis: the one that Clausewitz, not Hegel, provides. Dante hoped that history was ending because he believed that pretenders could lead only to the worst. However, history goes on. The dreaded duel has taken place, and it has led to the final explosion of Europe in the twentieth century.

BC: Paradise can no longer be envisioned today?

RG: It is, like the Kingdom, the opposite of the escalation to extremes: "Where danger threatens / That which saves from it also grows." Heidegger said that god appears amidst fear. We have to have the courage to look archaic religion in the eyes, somewhat as the papacy faced the empire long ago. However, the struggle has become much more violent, much more decisive.

THE REGENSBURG CONTROVERSY

BC: So, unlike some French Catholics, you do not think that Benedict XVI made a blunder at Regensburg?

RG: Benedict XVI said what a pope has to say, and he did so with courage. He said that, if we are not careful, the war of reason against religion will follow that of religion against reason. Why should we not wholeheartedly applaud such remarks? We have to re-examine the Regensburg lecture from a different point of view. It was delivered by a German pope who was redefining the intangible values of Europe before travelling to Istanbul. What, essentially, does he tell us? That the separation between faith and reason, which reduces faith to practical reason, is now exposing us to

> pathologies of religion and reason which necessarily erupt when *reason is so reduced* that questions of religion and ethics no longer concern it.[6]

Christian truth is now facing two religions, which are all the more terrible because they are hostile to each other: rationalism and fideism. This resembles the defeatist and bellicose pair that we talked about in relation to 1940. The weakening of rationality results, according to Benedict XVI, from a triple reduction of reason in general, and thus of humanity itself: the reduction of reason to its purely practical side, its reduction to an empirical-mathematical conception of science, and finally the de-Hellenization of the Gospels in favor of their strictly Hebraic aspects. According to him, the de-Hellenization performed by historical and critical exegesis, which always seems to suspect the Greek of overshadowing the Hebraic, has weakened Western thinking. Look how close we are to Hölderlin here. Benedict XVI, a German Catholic pope, is alerting Europe to the loss of Greek culture, for only rational theology, "broadened reason," capable of integrating the divine, will make us "capable of that genuine dialogue of cultures and religions so urgently needed today."[7]

Personally, I think that the "dialogue of cultures and religions" is meaningless unless it contrasts Christianity to archaic religion as a whole. It is less reason that needs to face religion than one form of religion that has to face the other. Nonetheless, I entirely agree with the pope, who hopes that the dialogue between reason and faith will be a rational dialogue. The theological thinking for which he is hoping has to demystify rationalism and fideism. This is the war that is looming, and for which Christians have to prepare themselves. No one expected this "strange defeat" of reason.

The pope is alerting us to the fact that Greek reason is disappearing, and that its disappearance will leave the way open to rampant irrationality. He was putting his finger on an essential point. Rationalism's disdain of religion not only turns reason into a religion, but makes for a corrupted religion. We know about the war that reason waged against faith, and we have seen that it did not win, that faith still resists. However, we comprehend only the precursor signs of the "pathology of religion," which is the violent response of faith preached "by the sword." The debate with Islam thus cannot take place unless it has foundations that are both religious and anthropological. The only way of not returning to a crusade, of escaping from the violent reciprocity between these two worlds that everything brings together and divides at once, is to not give in to a certain form of rationality. The pope quoted Byzantine emperor Manuel II:

> God is not pleased by blood—and not acting reasonably (σὺν λόγω) is contrary to God's nature. Faith is born of the soul, not the body. Whoever would lead someone to faith needs the ability to speak well and to reason properly, without violence and threats … To convince a reasonable soul, one does not need a strong arm, or weapons of any kind, or any other means of threatening a person with death.[8]

The pope was praising the Septuagint, Alexandrian scholars from around 200 and 300 B.C., who, as they were translating the Bible into Greek, made

possible "an encounter between genuine enlightenment and reason." Then he
highlighted the enduring analogy between human and divine reason:

> The truly divine God is the God who has revealed himself as *logos* and, as
> *logos*, has acted and continues to act lovingly on our behalf.[9]

Here, Benedict XVI returns to both the Greek and the Jewish traditions,
both the rational and the monotheist origins of Christianity. He says it is
urgent to remedy the three episodes that he believed shook the foundations
of the original unity: the wave of Reform until Kant, which limited faith to
practical reason; the wave of liberal theology in the nineteenth and twentieth
centuries, which favored the empirical model and made Jesus "the father
of a humanitarian moral message"; and the current trend, which seeks "to
return to the simple message of the New Testament prior to that [Greek]
inculturation."[10] Yet the "New Testament was written in Greek and bears the
imprint of the Greek spirit, which had already come to maturity as the Old
Testament developed."[11] This explains why his lecture has a fundamentally
European dimension, which people have refused to hear. It was thus absolutely necessary that it be delivered a few months before Benedict XVI's visit
to Istanbul. Indeed, it was as if the pope intended to provide the only keys
possible for entry into Europe:

> Given this convergence [of the Greek and Jewish worlds], it is not surprising
> that Christianity, despite its origins and some significant developments in
> the East, finally took on its historically decisive character in Europe. We
> can also express this the other way around: this convergence, with the sub-
> sequent addition of the Roman heritage, created Europe and remains the
> foundation of what can rightly be called Europe.[12]

It is this transformation of the Greek heritage by Christianity that
resulted in Europe. This sheds light on the beginning of Benedict XVI's lecture, which created a scandal because many people wanted to see it as a rejection of Islam. The pope spoke about "the dialogue carried on—perhaps in
1391 in the winter barracks near Ankara—by the erudite Byzantine emperor
Manuel II Paleologus and an educated Persian on the subject of Christianity
and Islam, and the truth of both." The dialogue was transcribed during the
siege of Constantinople between 1394 and 1402. The pope noted the "star-
tling brusqueness, a brusqueness that we find unacceptable" with which the
emperor addressed the Persian:

Show me just what Mohammed brought that was new, and there you will find things only evil and inhuman, such as his command to spread by the sword the faith he preached.[13]

Let us note two things: one, this was a dialogue between a Christian and a Muslim, a dialogue that Benedict XVI said was absolutely necessary; next, the "brusque" and "unacceptable" nature of the emperor's statement is clearly criticized. Perhaps Benedict XVI saw himself as taking distance from the Byzantine tendency to hastily mix the spiritual with the temporal and to oppose one theocracy to another. He thus recommended respectful, firm dialogue with Islam. The pope was opposed to any "compulsion" in religion, and asserted in agreement with the Byzantine emperor's statement that "God is not pleased by blood—and not acting reasonably (σὺν λόγῳ) is contrary to God's nature."[14]

Rejection of sacrifice and a radically new approach to religion: have I ever advanced any other thesis? I thus wholeheartedly approve of this lecture, but I approve as well of its contextual implications. In it, the pope is undertaking a spiritual struggle, and he has Islamic terrorism in his sights, in other words, a completely new configuration of violence. Benedict XVI identifies the orders so as to later link them to a "broadened" reason. He is opposed to the "pathologies" of religion and reason, in other words, the situation that occurs when their powers are disturbed by a complete separation. The orders should neither be mixed up, nor separated, but *understood*.

BC: Do you thus include Islamic terrorism in the continuity of our analysis of Clausewitz's book?

RG: What have our discussions allowed us to glimpse if not that Clausewitz's *military religion*, which made ideological wars possible, also involves a confusion of orders? We criticized his conception of human relations as always potentially warlike. We have seen that the hidden structure of this theory operates like an imitation of the Napoleonic model. The consequences of the confusion, of which Clausewitz's treatise has informed us, have not tarried, and violence soon spread across and destroyed Europe.

On War does indeed have to be completed in order to see where it leads. The treatise works like a fascinating mirror of its time. In a more realistic manner than Hegel, Clausewitz showed the utter powerlessness of politics against the escalation to extremes. Ideological wars, monstrous justifications of violence, have led humanity to the stage beyond war where we are today. The West is going to exhaust itself in its fight against Islamic terrorism, which

Western arrogance has undeniably kindled. Clausewitz thought violence would continue to erupt in international conflicts in the nineteenth century. Nations existed to contain the revolutionary contagion. In 1815, the Congress of Vienna was still able to put an end to the War of the Sixth Coalition. That era is over. Violence can no longer be checked. From this point of view, we can say that the apocalypse has begun.

Epilogue

WHEN DANGER THREATENS

If we follow our line of reasoning right to the end, if we take our analysis of a now global escalation to extremes to its logical conclusion, we have to consider the complete novelty of the situation since September 11, 2001. Terrorism has raised the level of violence up a notch again. This phenomenon is mimetic and opposes two crusades, two forms of fundamentalism. George W. Bush's "just war" has revived that of Muhammad, which is more powerful because it is essentially religious. However, Islamism is only one symptom of a trend to violence that is much more global. It comes less from the South than from the West itself because it takes the form of a response of the poor to those who are well-off. It is one of the last metastases of the cancer that has torn the Western world apart. Terrorism is the vanguard of a general revenge against the West's wealth. It is a very violent and unpredictable revival of the Conquest, which is all the more terrifying because it has encountered America along the way. The sources of Islamism's strength include the fact that it is a response to the oppression of the Third World as a whole. The reciprocal theologization of war ("Great Satan" versus "the forces of Evil") is a new phase in the escalation to extremes.

In this sense, everyone knows that the future of the idea of Europe and thus also the Christian truth running through it, will be played out in South America, India and China, as well as in Europe. Europe has been playing a role analogous to Italy's during the wars of the sixteenth century, except worse. It has been the battlefield of the entire world. Europe is a tired continent that no longer puts up much resistance to terrorism. This explains the stunning nature of the attacks, which are often carried out by people "on the inside." Resistance is all the more complex because the terrorists are close to us, beside us. The actions are completely unpredictable. The very idea of "sleeper cells" corroborates everything we have said about internal mediation, the identity between people that can suddenly take a turn for the worst.

Atta, the leader of the September 11 group who piloted one of the two airplanes, was the son of a middle class Egyptian family. It is staggering to think that during the three last days before the attack, he spent his nights in bars with his accomplices. There is something mysterious and intriguing in this. Who asks about the souls of those men? Who were they and what were their motivations? What did Islam mean to them? What does it mean to kill oneself for that cause? The growing number of attacks in Iraq is impressive. I think it is strange that there is so little interest in the logic of these events, which dominate the world just as the Cold War once did. Since when? We are not really sure. No one could have imagined that we would be in this situation barely 20 years after the Berlin Wall fell. This disturbs our vision of history as it has been written since the American and French revolutions. Our vision of history does not take into account the fact that the entire West is challenged and threatened by this. We have to say "this" because we do not know what it is. The Islamic Revolution was revived during Bill Clinton's presidency with attacks on two embassies in Africa. Despite everything, we have not discovered what "this" is. Likewise, we do not even know whether Bin Laden is a real person. Do people really realize the kind of history they have entered and what kind of history they have left behind? I do not have much more to say from this point on because the situation is too unknown and our reflection has reached its limits.

In the face of this, I feel a little like Hölderlin looking into the abyss that separated him from the French Revolution. Even at the end of the nineteenth century, it would have been clear that something extraordinary was happening. We are witnessing a new stage in the escalation to extremes. Terrorists have conveyed the message that they are ready to wait, that their notion of time is not ours. This is a clear sign of the return to the archaic, a return to the seventh, eighth and ninth centuries, which is significant in itself. But who is paying attention to this significance? Who is taking its measure? Is that the job of the ministry of foreign affairs? We have to expect a lot of unexpected things in the future. We are going to witness things that will certainly be worse. Yet people will remain deaf.

On September 11, people were shaken, but they quickly calmed down. There was a flash of awareness, which lasted a few fractions of a second. People could feel that something was happening. Then a blanket of silence covered up the crack in our certainty of safety. Western rationalism operates like a myth: we always work harder to avoid seeing the catastrophe. We neither can nor want to see violence as it is. The only way we will be able to meet the terrorist challenge is by radically changing the way we think. Yet the clearer it is what is happening, the stronger our refusal to acknowledge it. This historical configuration is so new that we do not know how to deal with it. It is precisely a modality of what Pascal saw: the war between violence and truth. Think about the inadequacy of our recent avant-gardes that preached the non-existence of the real.

We have to think about time in such a way that the Battle of Poitiers and the Crusades are much closer to us than the French Revolution and the industrialization of the Second Empire in France. The points of view of Western countries are at most unimportant background features for Islamists. They think of the Western world as having to be Islamized as quickly as possible. Analysts tend to say that this is the attitude of isolated minorities cut off from the reality in their countries. They may be so with respect to action, of course, but with respect to thought? Despite everything, does such thinking not contain something essentially Islamic? This is a question that we have to have the courage to ask, even though it is a given that terrorism is a brutal action that hijacks religious codes for its own purposes. It would not have taken such a hold on people's minds if it did not bring up to date something that has always been present in Islam. To the great surprise of our secular republicans, religious thought is still very much alive in Islam. It cannot be denied that some of Muhammad's theses are active in today's world.

However, what we are witnessing with Islam is nonetheless much more than a return of the Conquest; it is *what has been rising since the revolution has been rising,* after the Communist period that acted as an intermediary. Indeed, Leninism had some of these features, but what it lacked was religion. The escalation to extremes is thus able to use all components: culture, fashion, political theory, theology, ideology and religion. What drives history is not what seems essential in the eyes of Western rationalists. In today's implausible amalgam, I think that mimesis is the true primary engine.

If we had said in the 1980s that Islamism would play the role it plays today, people would have thought we were crazy. Yet the ideology promoted by Stalin already contained para-religious components that foreshadowed the increasingly radical contamination that has occurred over time. Europe was less malleable in Napoleon's time. After Communism, its vulnerability has returned to that of a medieval village facing the Vikings. The Arab conquest was a shock, while the French Revolution was slowed by the nationalism that it provoked across Europe. In its first historical deployment, Islam conquered religiously. This was its strength and it also explains the solidity of its roots. The revolutionary impetus accelerated by the Napoleonic era was checked by the equilibrium among nations. However, nations became inflamed in turn, and destroyed the only possible means of stopping revolutions from happening.

We therefore have to radically change the way we think, and try to understand the situation without any presuppositions and using all the resources available from the study of Islam. The work to be done is immense. Personally, I have the impression that this religion has used the Bible as a support to rebuild an archaic religion that is more powerful than all the others. It threatens to become an apocalyptic tool, the new face of the escalation to extremes. Even though there are no longer any archaic religions, it is as if a new one had arisen built on the back of the Bible, a slightly transformed Bible. It would be an archaic religion strengthened by aspects of the Bible and Christianity. Archaic religion collapsed in the face of Judeo-Christian revelation, but Islam resists. While Christianity eliminates sacrifice wherever it gains a foothold, Islam seems in many respects to situate itself prior to that rejection.

Of course, there is resentment in its attitude to Judeo-Christianity and the West, but it is also a new religion. This cannot be denied. Historians of religion, and even anthropologists, have to show how and why it emerged. Indeed, some aspects of this religion contain a relationship to violence that we do not understand and that is all the more worrying for that reason. For us, it makes no sense to be ready to pay with one's life for the pleasure of seeing the other die. We do not know whether such phenomena belong to a special psychology or not. We are thus facing complete failure; we cannot talk about it and also we cannot document the situation because terrorism is something new that exploits Islamic codes, but does not at all belong to classical Islamic theory. Today's terrorism is new, even from an Islamic point of view. It is a modern effort to counter the most powerful and refined tool of the Western world: technology. It counters technology in a way that we do not understand, and that classical Islam may not understand either.

Thus, it is not enough to simply condemn the attacks. The defensive thought by which we oppose the phenomenon does not necessarily embody a desire to understand. Often it even reveals a desire to not understand, or an intention to comfort oneself. Clausewitz is easier to integrate into a historical development. He gives us the intellectual tools to understand the violent escalation. However, where do we find such ideas in Islam? Modern resentment never leads all the way to suicide. Thus we do not have the analogical structures that could help us to understand. I am not saying that they are not possible, that they will not appear, but I admit my inability to grasp them. This is why our explanations often belong to the province of fraudulent propaganda against Muslims.

We do not experience this reality; we have no intimate, spiritual, phenomenological contact with it. Terrorism is a superior form of violence, and it asserts that it will win. However, there is no indication that the work that remains to be done to free the Koran from its caricatures will have any influence on terrorism itself, which is both linked to Islam and different from it. We can thus put forward the tentative hypothesis that the escalation to extremes now uses Islam as it used to use Napoleonism and Pangermanism. Terrorism is fearsome in that it knows how to use the most deadly technology outside of any military institution. Clausewitzian war is an analogy that can make only imperfect sense of terrorism, but it certainly does foreshadow it.

In *Violence and the Sacred,* I borrowed the idea from the Koran that the ram that saved Isaac from being sacrificed was the same one that was sent to Abel so that he would not have to kill his brother: proof that in the Koran sacrifice is also interpreted as a means of combating violence. From this, we can draw the conclusion that the Koran contains understanding of things that secular mentality cannot fathom, namely that sacrifice prevents vengeance. Yet this topic has disappeared from Islam, just as it has disappeared in Western thought. The paradox that we thus have to deal with is that Islam is closer to us today than the world of Homer. Clausewitz allowed us to glimpse this, through what we have called his *warlike religion,* in which we have seen the emergence of something both very new and very primitive. Islamism, likewise, is a kind of event internal to the development of technology. We have to be able to think about both Islamism *and* the escalation to extremes at the same time; we need to understand the complex relations between these two realities.

The unity of Christianity in the Middle Ages resulted in the Crusades, which were permitted by the papacy. However, the Crusades are not as important as Islam thinks. The Crusades were an archaic regression without consequences for the essence of Christianity. Christ died everywhere and for everyone. Seeing Jews and Christians as falsifiers is the most irremediable thing. It allows Muslims to eliminate all serious discussion, any comparison among the three religions. It amounts to not wanting to see what is at stake in the prophetic tradition. Why has Christian revelation been subject to the most hostile and ferocious possible criticism for centuries, but not Islam? There is an abdication of reason here. In some respects, it resembles the aporia of pacifism, which as we have seen can be a strong encouragement for aggression. The Koran would thus benefit from being studied in the same way that Jewish and Christian texts have been studied. I think that a comparative approach would reveal that it contains no real awareness of collective murder.

By contrast, there is a Christian awareness of such murder. The two greatest conversions, those of Peter and Paul, are analogous: they are one with the awareness of having participated in a collective murder. Paul was there when Stephen was stoned to death. His departure for Damascus immediately followed that lynching, which must have affected him terribly. Christians understand that the Passion has rendered collective murder inoperative. This is why, far from reducing violence, the Passion aggravates it. Islamism seems to have understood this very quickly, but in the sense of *jihad*.

There are thus forms of acceleration in history that are self-perpetuating. We have the impression that today's terrorism is somehow the heir of totalitarianism, that terrorism and totalitarianism contain similar forms of thought and ingrained habits. We have followed one of the possible threads of this continuity, with the construction of a Napoleonic model by a Prussian general. The model was later taken up by Lenin and Mao Zedong, to whom Al Qaeda has apparently referred. Clausewitz's brilliance lies in his having unknowingly anticipated a law that has become worldwide. The Cold War is over, and now we are in a very hot war, given the hundreds, and tomorrow perhaps the thousands, of victims every day in the Middle East.

There is an indissoluble link between global warming and the rise in violence. I have repeatedly emphasized the confusion of the natural and the artificial, which is perhaps the strongest thing in apocalyptic texts. Love has "cooled down." Of course, we cannot deny that it works in the world as it has never worked before, that the awareness of the innocence of victims has progressed. However, charity is now facing the worldwide empire of violence. Unlike many others, I still think that history has a meaning, the one that we have never stopped talking about. The trend towards the apocalypse is humanity's greatest feat. The more probable this achievement becomes, the less we talk about it.

I have come to a crucial point: that of a profession of faith, more than a strategic treatise, unless both are mysteriously equivalent in the essential war that truth wages against violence. I have always been utterly convinced that violence belongs to a form of corrupted sacred, intensified by Christ's action when he placed himself at the heart of the sacrificial system. Satan is the other name of the escalation to extremes. What Hölderlin glimpsed was that the Passion has radically altered the archaic world. Satanic violence has long reacted against this holiness, which is an essential transformation of ancient religion.

It is thus that God revealed himself in his Son, that religion was confirmed once and for all, thereby changing the course of human history. Inversely, the escalation to extremes reveals the power of this divine intervention. Divinity has appeared and it is more reliable than all the earlier theophanies, but no one wants to see it. Humanity is more than ever the author of its own fall because it has become able to destroy its world. With respect to Christianity, this is not just an ordinary moral condemnation, but an unavoidable anthropological observation. Therefore we have to wake up our sleeping consciences. Seeking to comfort is always to contribute to the worst.

Notes

Introduction

1. Heraclitus, in *The Art and Thought of Heraclitus,* ed. and tr. Charles H. Kahn (Cambridge: Cambridge University Press, 1979), 66–67.

2. Carl von Clausewitz, *Vom Kriege* (Bonn: Dummler, 1973), 199.

3. See René Girard, "Literature and Christianity: A Personal View," *Philosophy and Literature* 23.1 (1999), 32–43; Girard, *La conversion de l'art* (Paris: Carnets nord, 2008), esp. "La conversion romanesque: du héros à l'écrivain," 187–200.

4. Friedrich Hölderlin, "Patmos," in *Friedrich Hölderlin, Poems and Fragments,* tr. Michael Hamburger (London: Anvil Press, 1994), 483.

Chapter 1. The Escalation to Extremes

1. Girard finds a covert tension in Clausewitz between (1) a notion of war's escalation slowed or reversed by "frictions" or by a reciprocal climbdown between antagonists, and (2) a near-apocalyptic recognition that modern war is becoming endless and uncontrollable. Naville and Howard/Paret follow Clausewitz's muted terminology of "Tendenz" (*Vom Kriege,* 8) and "das Streben nach dem Äussersten" (*Vom Kriege,* 199) by using "tendance" (Naville), "trend" or "tendency towards extremes" (Howard and Paret). *Achever Clausewitz* consistently uses "montée aux extrêmes" to emphasize the breakaway irreversibility of the reciprocal process towards extremes. We will follow Howard and Paret when quoting Clausewitz directly, but when the issue is this process as Girard understands it, we will translate Girard and Chantre's "montée aux extrêmes" as "escalation towards extremes."

2. Carl von Clausewitz, *On War,* ed. and tr. Michael Howard and Peter Paret (Princeton: Princeton University Press, 1984), 1.1.2, 75.

3. *La Violence et le sacré* (Paris: Bernard Grasset, 1972); *Violence and the Sacred,* tr. Patrick Gregory (Baltimore: The Johns Hopkins University Press, 1977).

4. Carl von Clausewitz, *De la guerre,* tr. Denise Naville (Paris: Les Éditions de Minuit, 1955).

5. Raymond Aron, *Penser la guerre* (Paris: Gallimard, 1976); *Clausewitz: Philosopher of War,* tr. Christine Booker and Norman Stone (Englewood Cliffs, NJ: Prentice-Hall, 1985). [RG/BC]

6. The translators have followed Naville (p. 51) as well as Howard and Paret (p. 75) who both translate "Zweikampf" (Clausewitz, p. 191) as "duel." Yet Bergson, in *Two Sources of Morality and Religion* (275–276) argues the obsolescence of duel for modern warfare and more recently Michael Waltzer in *Just and Unjust War* argues cogently against accepting the connotations of conflict governed by rule suggested by "duel" (New York: Basic Book, 2006), 22–25. Clausewitz's homely image of two wrestlers ("zwei Ringende," 191) in this passage suggests we should understand something like "hand-to-hand combat" for "Zweikampf" throughout. Interestingly, the *Oxford English Dictionary* suggests that "duel" derives from Latin "duellum," an ancient form of "bellum" (*The Compact Edition of the Oxford English Dictionary,* vol. 1 [Oxford: Oxford University Press, 1971], 705).

7. Clausewitz, 1.1.2, 75. [RG/BC]

8. Clausewitz, 1.1.3, 75. [RG/BC]

9. Clausewitz, 1.1.3, 75–76. [RG/BC]

10. Our emphasis.

11. Clausewitz, 1.1.3, 76–77. "... so gibt jeder dem anderen das Gesetz, es entsteht eine Wechselwirkung, die dem Begriff nach zum äussersten führen muss. Dies ist *die erste Wechselwirkung und das erste Äusserste, worauf wir stossen*" (*Vom Kriege,* 194). [RG/BC] German text footnoted in *Achever Clausewitz;* the phrase in the last sentence is emphasized by Clausewitz.

12. Clausewitz, 1.1.11, 81. [RG/BC]

13. Clausewitz, 1.1.8, 79. [RG/BC]

14. Clausewitz, 1.1.6, 78. [RG/BC]

15. Clausewitz, 1.1.7, 78. [RG/BC]

16. Clausewitz, 1.1.8, 79. [RG/BC]

17. Clausewitz, 1.1.8, 80. [RG/BC]

18. Clausewitz, 1.1.8, 80. [RG/BC]

19. Clausewitz, 1.1.10, 80. [RG/BC]

20. "Undifferentiation" is the term used in *Violence and the Sacred* to describe the state of a social group threatened by a "mimetic crisis": violence is so widespread in the group that all differences (social, family, individual) have disappeared. [RG/BC]

21. Clausewitz, 1.1.11, 80–81 [emphases in original]. [RG/BC]

22. Clausewitz, 1.1.11, 81. [RG/BC]

23. Clausewitz, 1.1.3, 76. [RG/BC]

24. Clausewitz, 1.1.11, 81 [emphasis in original]. [RG/BC]

25. Clausewitz, 1.1.11, 81. [RG/BC]

26. Here and elsewhere the translators will sometimes translate literally Naville's "action reciproque" (Naville, 57) for Clausewitz's "Wechselwirkung" rather than follow Howard and Paret's "interaction."

27. See *The Critique of Pure Reason,* III, §11 passim.

28. Clausewitz, 1.1.12, 82. [RG/BC]

29. Clausewitz, 1.1.13, 82. [RG/BC]

30. Clausewitz, 1.1.15, 83. In a zero-sum game, the victory of one side and the defeat of the other cancel each other out: they add up to zero. [RG/BC]

31. Clausewitz, 69. [RG/BC]

32. According to Clausewitz, tactics are *theoretically* the tools of strategy, and strategy the tool of policy. Tactics (the art of conducting battle) are the implementation of strategy (the art of designing maneuvers necessary for preparing for battle). Strategy is in turn the implementation of policy: it uses victory, acquired through tactics, as a means to political ends. In contrast, the "trend to extremes" implies that the means of war influence political goals. It thus reverses Clausewitz's famous saying according to which war is a "continuation of policy by other means." [RG/BC]

33. Clausewitz, 1.1.14, 83. [RG/BC]

34. Girard, *Violence and the Sacred,* 152–154. [RG/BC]

35. Clausewitz, 1.1.16, 84. [RG/BC]

36. Jacques Bainville, *Napoléon* (Paris: Gallimard, 2005); *Napoleon,* tr. Hamish Miles (Boston: Little, Brown and Company, 1933), 287. [RG/BC]

37. Clausewitz, 6.7, 377. [RG/BC]

38. Sir Henry Basil Liddell Hart, *The Ghost of Napoleon* (London: Faber and Faber Ltd., 1933). Hart was an English officer and strategist, and in his essay he blamed a Clausewitzian interpretation of Napoleon for the massacres at the Somme and in Flanders. [RG/BC]

39. Bainville, *Napoleon,* 282–283.

40. Ernst Nolte, *Der europäische Bürgerkrieg, 1917–1945* (Berlin: Propyläen Verlag, 1987); Ernst Nolte, *La guerre civile europeenne,* tr. Jean-Marie Argelès (Paris: Ed. des Syrtes, 2000). [RG/BC]

41. François Furet, *Le Passé d'une illusion* (Paris: Calman-Lévy, 1995); *The Passing of an Illusion,* tr. Deborah Furet (Chicago: The University of Chicago Press, 1999). [RG/BC]

42. Girard and Chantre give the following passages in a footnote, in Argeles's translation of Nolte, *Der europäische Bürgerkrieg.* Nolte's book has not yet been translated into English; our English translation has been checked against the German text. "But it was neither Germany nor Russia that entered into war on June 22, it was Bolshevik Russia and National Socialist Germany who, in a very different way, were for each other at once foil and model" (*Der europäische Bürgerkrieg,* 334; *La guerre,* 362–363); "But the Soviet Union served him [Hitler] during his political life as a foil and, at the same time, as a partial model" (*Der europäische Bürgerkrieg,* 456; *La guerre,* 493); "We shouldn't understand the expression

'exchange of characteristics' in the sense that the bolshevists had, during the course of the war, adopted the face of their adversary and where national-socialism, inversely, had adopted that of bolshevism. Nevertheless, in the two regimes one could see evolutions, tendencies that led to an internal reciprocal rapprochement between the two enemies. Hostilities between them didn't weaken, but rather reinforced this." (*Der europäische Bürgerkrieg*, 517; *La guerre*, 559).

43. Blaise Pascal, *Pensées*, ed. and tr. Roger Ariew (Indianapolis: Hackett Publishing, 2004), 37 ("Oppositions"). [RG/BC]

CHAPTER 2. CLAUSEWITZ AND HEGEL

1. Hegel to Niethammer at Jena on Monday, October 13, 1806: "I saw the Emperor—this world-soul—riding out of the city on reconnaissance. It is indeed a wonderful sensation to see such an individual, who, concentrated here at a single point, astride a horse, reaches out over the world and masters it." *Hegel: The Letters,* tr. Clark Butler and Christine Seiler with commentary by Clark Butler (Bloomington: Indiana University Press, 1984), 114.

2. *Hegel's Philosophy of Right,* tr. T. M. Knox (London: Oxford University Press, 1952), 10.

3. G. W. F. Hegel, *Phenomenology of Spirit,* tr. A. V. Miller (Oxford: Oxford University Press, 1977), 493.

4. Alexandre Kojève, *Introduction à la lecture de Hegel* (Paris: Gallimard, 1947); *Introduction to the Reading of Hegel,* tr. James H. Nichols Jr. (New York: Basic Books, 1969).

5. Hegel, *Science of Logic,* tr. A. V. Miller (London: George Allen and Unwin, Ltd., 1969), 138–40.

6. Hegel, *Phenomenology of Spirit,* §260, 158ff.

7. Hegel, *Phenomenology of Spirit,* §178, 111ff.

8. See Kojève, *Introduction to the Reading of Hegel,* 7.

9. Hegel, *Lectures on the Philosophy of History,* tr. E. S. Haldane and Frances H. Simson (London: Routledge and Kegan Paul, 1968), 397–398.

10. Clausewitz, 1.1.26. Girard and Chantre follow the French translation of Denise Naville throughout (*De La Guerre,* 68). We have in this case translated from Naville's French, which is closer than the standard Howard and Paret translation to "denn betrachtet man die Politik wie die Intelligenz des personifizierten Staates" in *Vom Kriege* (Bonn: Ferd. Dummlers Verlag, 1972), 211–212.

11. Johann Gottlieb Fichte, *Addresses to the German Nation* (New York: Harper and Row, 1968).

12. *Hegel's Philosophy of Right,* §358 (4), 222.

13. In Bainville, *Napoleon,* 211. [RG/BC]

14. In Bainville, *Napoleon,* 210. [RG/BC]

15. Clausewitz, 1.1.21, 86. [RG/BC]

16. Henri Bergson, *Two Sources of Morality and Religion,* tr. R. Ashley Audra and Cloudesley Brereton (New York: Henry Holt and Company, 1935), 149. [RG/BC]

17. Clausewitz, 1.1.23, 87 [our emphasis]. [RG/BC]

18. Clausewitz, 1.1.25, 87–88 [our emphasis]. [RG/BC]

19. Clausewitz, 1.1.26, 88. [RG/BC]

20. "The forty kings who made France" is the formulaic phrase for the royal grandeur that France set aside in the Revolution and which occurs in the membership oath (popularly attributed to Maurras) for the *Action française*.

21. Samuel Huntington, *The Clash of Civilizations and the Remaking of World Order* (New York: Simon and Schuster, 2003).

22. *Critique of Critical Reason* (London: Verso, 2009), passim.

23. With Jean-Michel Oughourlian and Guy Lefort, *Des choses cachées depuis la fondation du monde* (Paris: Bernard Grasset, 1978); *Things Hidden since the Foundation of the World*, tr. Stephen Bann and Michael Metteer (Stanford: Stanford University Press, 1987). [RG/BC]

24. Luke 18:8.

CHAPTER 3. DUEL AND RECIPROCITY

1. Clausewitz, 1.1.28, 89 [translation amended]. Howard and Paret translate "eine wunderliche Dreifaltigkeit" (213) as a "paradoxical trinity" (89); Naville, "une étonnante trinité" (69). "Paradoxical" suggests a more analytical comprehension of the trinity than "wunderliche." But Howard in *Clausewitz* (Oxford: Oxford University Press, 1983, 2002) uses "remarkable trinity" (21). We are following the later Howard.

2. Clausewitz, 8.2.2, 579. [RG/BC]

3. Clausewitz, 1.1.28, 89 [translation amended].

4. Clausewitz, 1.1.24, 87. [RG/BC]

5. Clausewitz, 8.6.B, 605. [RG/BC]

6. See chapter 7, "France and Germany." [RG/BC]

7. Clausewitz, 1.1.2, 75. [RG/BC]

8. Clausewitz, 1.2, 97. [RG/BC]

9. See Mark Rogin Anspach, *À charge de revanche. Figures élémentaires de la réciprocité* (Paris: Seuil, 2002). [RG/BC]

10. Lucien Goldmann, *Towards a Sociology of the Novel*, tr. Alan Sheridan (London: Tavistock Publications, 1975), 7; Goldmann, *Pour un sociologie du roman* (Paris: Editions Gallimard, 1964), 25. Girard discusses these passages from Goldmann in "The Mimetic Desire of Paolo and Francesca," collected in *"To double business bound": Essays on Literature, Mimesis, and Anthropology* (Baltimore: The Johns Hopkins University Press, 1978), 7.

11. Clausewitz, 1.1.28, 89. [RG/BC]

12. See Jean-Pierre Dupuy, *Pour un catastrophisme éclair* (Paris: Seuil, 2002) and *Petite métaphysique des tsunamis* (Paris: Seuil, 2005). [RG/BC]

13. Charles Péguy, *Oeuvres en prose complètes*, 126 [our translation]. [RG/BC]

14. See "The Concept of the Political," in Carl Schmitt, *The Concept of the Political* (Chicago: The University of Chicago Press, 2007), 19–79.

15. See Frédéric Gros, *États de violence. Essai sur la fin de la guerre* (Paris: Gallimard, 2006). [RG/BC]

16. Carl Schmitt, *Theory of the Partisan* (New York: Telos Press, 2007).

17. Schmitt, *Theory of the Partisan,* 4.

18. See Heidegger, "The Question Concerning Technology," tr. William Lovitt, in *The Question Concerning Technology and Other Essays* (New York: Harper Torchbooks, 1977), 3–35. "Enframing" occurs on page 18.

19. Clausewitz, quoted in Aron, *Clausewitz,* 17–18.

20. Emmanuel Levinas, *Totalité et infini* (Le Haye: M Nidjoff, 1961); *Totality and Infinity,* tr. Alphonso Lingis (Pittsburgh: Duquesne University Press, 1969). [RG/BC]

21. Bergson, *Two Sources of Morality and Religion,* 285. [RG/BC]

22. Bergson, *Two Sources of Morality and Religion,* 285–298. [RG/BC]

CHAPTER 4. THE DUEL AND THE SACRED

1. Charles Péguy, *Oeuvres en prose complètes,* vol. 3, pp. 1342–1343 [our translation]. [RG/BC]

2. See Paul Dumouchel, "Génocides et mimétisme" in *Cahiers de l'Herne/René Girard,* ed. Mark Anspach (Paris: Éditions l'Herne, 2008), 247–254. [RG/BC]

3. Blaise Pascal, *Pensées,* 37. [RG/BC]

4. Blaise Pascal, *Pensées: Provincial Letters,* tr. W. F. Trotter and Thomas M'Crie (New York: The Modern Library, 1941), letter 12, 498. [RG/BC]

5. Pascal, *Provincial Letters,* letter 12, 498. [RG/BC]

6. Pascal, *Pensées,* 6. [RG/BC]

7. Joseph de Maistre, "The Saint Petersburg Dialogues." [RG/BC]

8. Clausewitz, 1.3, 106. [RG/BC]

9. Clausewitz, 1.3, 106. [RG/BC]

10. Clausewitz, 1, 3 102. [RG/BC] Clausewitz uses the French term "coup d'oeil" in *Vom Kriege* I, 3, 237.

11. Clausewitz, 1.7, 120. [RG/BC]

12. Clausewitz, 1.8, 122. [RG/BC]

13. Clausewitz, 1.3, 104–105. [RG/BC]

14. Cited in Aron, *Clausewitz,* 31. [RG/BC]

15. Cited in Aron, *Clausewitz,* 38. [RG/BC]

16. Cited in Aron, *Clausewitz,* 39 [our emphasis]. [RG/BC]

17. Clausewitz, 1.8, 122. [RG/BC]

18. Victor Hugo, "The Expiation," in *Selected Poems of Victor Hugo: A Bilingual Edition*, 134. [RG/BC]

19. Pascal, *Provincial Letters,* letter 12, 498. [RG/BC]

20. Clausewitz, 1.8, 122–23. [RG/BC]

21. Clausewitz, 1.8, 123. [RG/BC]

22. Howard and Paret offer "combat experience" but Naville (which Girard and Chantre use throughout) translates Clausewitz's "Die Kriegsgewohnheit" (*Vom Kriege,* 265) more accurately as "l'aguerrissement" (*De la guerre,* 112). Instead of something like "habituation to war" the translators offer "combat-readiness."

23. Clausewitz, 1.4, 113–14. [RG/BC]

24. Clausewitz, 1.3, 105. [RG/BC]

25. Friedrich Nietzsche, *The Gay Science,* tr. Walter Kaufmann (New York: Vintage Books, 1947), 181; *Aphorism,* 125 [our emphasis]. [RG/BC]

26. Nietzsche, *The Gay Science,* 181; *Aphorism,* 125. [RG/BC]

27. Levinas, *Totality and Infinity,* 21. [RG/BC]

28. Levinas, *Totality and Infinity,* 222. [RG/BC]

29. Charles Péguy, *Oeuvres en prose complètes,* vol. 2, p. 124 [our translation]. [RG/BC]

30. See Girard, *I See Satan Fall Like Lightning,* tr. James G. Williams (Maryknoll, NY: Orbis, 2001); *Je vois Satan tomber comme l'éclair* (Paris: Bernard Grasset, 1999). [RG/BC]

31. Colossians 2:15. [RG/BC]

32. Levinas, *Totality and Infinity,* 21. [RG/BC]

Chapter 5. Hölderlin's Sorrow

1. Luke 21:24. The French Bible uses "temps des païens," but the source phrase is rendered "time of the Gentiles" in both the *King James* and the *New Revised Standard Version,* 1995, which is the version of the Bible used throughout. In this context, "Gentile" means both "non-Jewish" and "non-Christian."

2. Luke 18:8. [RG/BC]

3. Luke 21:23, 21:24. [RG/BC]

4. Pascal, *Provincial Letters,* letter 12, 498. [RG/BC]

5. Luke, 23:12. [RG/BC]

6. John 19:5. [RG/BC]

7. Hölderlin, "Patmos," 483.

8. "En brisant ce sceptre solaire" has been literally translated; it refers to Hölderlin's "und zerbach / Den geradstralenen, / Den Zepter," which Hamburger gives as "The straightly beaming, the sceptre" ("Patmos," 488–489).

9. *Der Spiegel,* May 31, 1976, pp. 193–219.

10. Hölderlin, "Hyperion," in *Hyperion and Selected Poems,* 32. [RG/BC]

11. "The Oldest Systematic Program of German Idealism," in *Philosophy of German Idealism,* ed. Ernst Behler, (New York: Continuum, 1987), 162 [mostly our emphasis].

12. Schelling, *The Philosophy of Art,* tr. Douglas W. Stott (Minneapolis: University of Minnesota Press, 1989), 76.

13. Hölderlin, "The Only One," in *Frederich Hölderlin: Poems and Fragments,* 467–471. [RG/BC]

14. Euripides, *Bacchae and Other Plays,* tr. James Morwood (Oxford: Oxford University Press, 1999), 52; see Euripides, *Bacchae,* ed. E. R. Dodds (Oxford: Oxford University Press, 1960), lines 302–304.

15. Girard and Chantre reference the Pleiade *Hölderlin, Oeuvres,* tr. Gustave Roux (Paris: Gallimard, 1967), 866–867. We have translated directly from "Der Einzige," Dritte Fassung, ll. 62–71 in Hölderlin, *Sämtliche Werke, Zweiter Band,* ed. Friedrich Beissner (Stuttgart: W. Kohlhammer, 1951), 163.

16. The second set of verses comes from another manuscript, cited in *Sämtliche Werke, Zweiter Band, Zweite Hälfte,* 752–753 [our translation from the German].

17. Hölderlin, "Patmos," 487. [RG/BC]

18. Jouve, *Poèmes de la folie de Hölderlin* (Paris: Gallimard, 1963), 130 [our translation]. Cited in the very fine article by Jean-Michel Garrigues, "Du 'Dieu présent' au 'Dieu plus médiat d'un Apôtre,'" in *Hölderlin, Cahiers de l'Herne* (Paris: L'Herne, 1989), 373. The present analysis is partly inspired by Garrigues' article. [RG/BC]

19. Pascal, *Pensées,* 272, 94. [RG/BC]

20. 1 Corinthians 11:1. [RG/BC]

21. Matthew 25:40. [RG/BC]

22. "So with pictures seen from too far or too near; there is but one exact point which is the true place wherefrom to look at them: the rest are too near, too far, too high, or too low. Perspective determines that point in the art of painting. But who shall determine it in truth and morality?" Pascal, *Pensées,* tr. Roger Ariew (New York: Random House, 1941), 381, 224. See on this topic Michel Serres, *Le système de Leibniz et ses modèles mathématiques,* (Paris: Presses universitaires des France, 1968), vol. 2, part 3, "Le point fixe," 647–810. [RG/BC]

23. Aron, *Clausewitz,* ix. [RG/BC]

CHAPTER 6. CLAUSEWITZ AND NAPOLEON

1. See Emmanuel Terray, *Clausewitz* (Paris: Fayard, 1999). [RG/BC]

2. Matthew 23:27. [RG/BC]

3. Count de Las Cases, *Mémorial de Sainte-Hélène.* (Napoleon dictated his memoires to Las Cases during his exile on St. Helena.) [RG/BC]

4. Clausewitz, ch. 5, 165. [RG/BC]

5. Clausewitz, ch. 5, 168. Naville, whom Girard and Chantre follow throughout, better translates "Eingang in das Leben" (331) as "accèss à la vie" (168) than Howard and Paret's "contact with its subject" (168). We have offered "access to the life" (translators).

6. Clausewitz, ch. 5, 167. [RG/BC]

7. Clausewitz, ch. 5, 167. [RG/BC]

8. Clausewitz, ch. 5, 167 [our emphasis]. [RG/BC]

9. Clausewitz, ch. 5, 166. [RG/BC]

10. Clausewitz, ch. 5, 164. [RG/BC]

11. Clausewitz, ch. 5, 165. [RG/BC]

12. Clausewitz, ch. 5, 167. [RG/BC]

13. Clausewitz, ch. 5, 162. [RG/BC]

14. Clausewitz, ch. 5, 153. [RG/BC]

15. Clausewitz, ch. 5, 153. [RG/BC]

16. Clausewitz, ch. 5, 153. [RG/BC]

17. Charles de Gaulle, *War Memoirs, III: Salvation,* tr. Joyce Murchie and Hamish Erskine (London: Weidenfeld and Nicolson, 1960), 56. [RG/BC]

18. *Goethes Werke,* ed. Erich Trunz (Hamburg: Wegner, 1948), vol. 10, 235. Cited in Nicholas Boyle, *Goethe: The Poet and the Age,* vol. 2 (Oxford: Oxford University Press, 2000), 128.

CHAPTER 7. FRANCE AND GERMANY

1. La Rochefoucauld, *Reflections; or Sentences and Moral Maxims.* [RG/BC]

2. Molière, *The Misanthrope* in *"The Misanthrope" and "Tartuffe,"* tr. Richard Wilbur (New York: Harcourt, Brace and World, 1965), 66. See "Le Misanthrope," in Moliere, *Oeuvres Complètes* (Paris: Éditions de seuil, 1962), vol. 2, part 4, 669–680 (p. 332) [RG/BC]

3. Germaine de Staël, *De l'Allemagne,* vol. 1, 127 [our translation]. [RG/BC]

4. Germaine de Staël, *De l'Allemagne,* vol. 1, 46 [our translation]. [RG/BC]

5. Germaine de Staël, *De l'Allemagne,* vol. 1, 112–113 [our translation]. [RG/BC]

6. Germaine de Staël, *De l'Allemagne,* vol. 1, p. 130 [our translation]. [RG/BC]

7. Germaine de Staël, *De l'Allemagne,* vol. 1, p. 135 [our translation]. [RG/BC]

8. Germaine de Staël, *De l'Allemagne,* vol. 1, p. 107 [our translation]. [RG/BC]

9. Aron, *Clausewitz,* 39. [RG/BC]

10. Clausewitz, *On War,* ch. 3, 101: "Possession of military genius coincides with the higher degrees of civilization; the most highly developed societies produce the most brilliant soldiers, as the Romans and French have shown us."

11. Germaine de Staël, *De l'Allemagne,* vol. 1, 106 [our translation]. [RG/BC]

12. Germaine de Staël, *De l'Allemagne,* vol. 1, 178 [our translation]. [RG/BC]

13. Germaine de Staël, *De l'Allemagne,* vol. 2, 244 [our translation]. [RG/BC]

14. Germaine de Staël, *De l'Allemagne,* vol. 2, 247 [our translation]. [RG/BC]

15. Germaine de Staël, *De l'Allemagne,* vol. 2, 254 [our translation]. [RG/BC]

16. *De l'Allemagne,* vol. 2, 257 [our translation]. [RG/BC]

17. Germaine de Staël, *De l'Allemagne,* vol. 2, 258 [our translation]. [RG/BC]

18. *De l'Allemagne,* vol. 2, 259. [RG/BC]

19. Joseph de Maistre, *Enlightenment on Sacrifices.* [RG/BC]

20. Germaine de Staël, *De l'Allemagne,* vol. 1, 39 [our translation]. [RG/BC]

21. Baudelaire, *L'Art romantique* (Paris: Flammarion, 1968). [RG/BC]

22. Baudelaire, "Richard Wagner and Tannhäuser in Paris," in Baudelaire, *Selected Writings on Art and Artists,* tr. P. E. Charvet (London: Penguin, 1972), 338. In *L'Art romantique,* 278–279. [RG/BC]

23. Baudelaire, *Selected Writings on Art and Artists,* 334–335, in *L'Art romantique,* 275. [RG/BC]

24. Baudelaire, *Selected Writings on Art and Artists,* 342, in *L'Art romantique,* 280–281. [RG/BC]

25. Baudelaire, *Les fleurs du mal.*

26. Baudelaire, "Lettre à Richard Wagner," in *Selected Letters of Charles Baudelaire,* tr. and ed. Rosemary Lloyd (Chicago: The University of Chicago Press, 1986), 146. [RG/BC]

27. *Poilu* is the French equivalent of "doughboy."

28. Charles Péguy, *Œuvres en prose complètes,* vol. 2, 121–122 [our translation]. [RG/BC]

29. "Le kûdos étant cette fois passé dans le camp français," *Achever Clausewitz,* 308. See the passage on kudos as sacralized violence in *Violence and the Sacred,* 152–154.

30. Bloch, *Strange Defeat,* tr. Gerard Hopkins (New York: Norton, 1968); originally published as *L'étrange défaite* (Paris: Société des Éditions Franc-tireur, 1946).

31. See chapter 3, "Duel and Reciprocity." [RG/BC]

32. René Girard, *American Opinion of France, 1940–1943.* [RG/BC]

33. Clausewitz, 1.1.11, 81 [our emphasis]. [RG/BC] Insertion of Clausewitz's "die Massen" (*Vom Kriege,* 200) by translators to clarify Howard and Paret's "forces."

34. Clausewitz, 1.1.8, 80. [RG/BC]

35. In 1940, de Gaulle, then still a colonel, wrote a memo entitled *L'Avènement de la force mécanique* in which he argued that the key to success in modern warfare was the combined use of tanks and planes.

36. De Gaulle, *The Edge of the Sword* (New York: Criterion Books, 1960); *The Army of the Future* (Philadelphia: Lippincott, 1941).

37. Pascal, *Pensées,* 299.

38. *Le chagrin et la pitié* (1969), directed by Marcel Ophüls.

Chapter 8. The Pope and the Emperor

1. Michel Serres, *Rome: The Book of Foundations,* tr. Felicia McCarren (Palo Alto: Stanford University Press, 1991). (Originally published as *Rome ou le livre des fondations* [Paris: Grasset, 1983].) [RG/BC]

2. Joseph de Maistre, *Considerations on France,* tr. Richard A. Lebrun (Cambridge: Cambridge University Press, 1994); first published as *Considérations sur la France,* 1797.

3. Joseph de Maistre, *The Pope.*

4. Alexandre Kojève, "Outline of a Doctrine of French Policy."

5. *Revue de l'Institut de sociologie* (Brussels: Institut de Sociologie, 1961), 263–269; "From the Divine Comedy to the Sociology of the Novel," tr. Petra Morrison, in *Sociology of Literature and Drama,* ed. Elizabeth and Tom Burns (London: Penguin, 1973), 101–108; "The Mimetic Desire of Paolo and Francesca," in Girard, *"To double business bound,"* 1–8.

6. Benedict XVI, "Faith, Reason and the University: Memories and Reflections" [our emphasis]. [RG/BC]

7. Benedict XVI, "Faith."

8. Benedict XVI, "Faith."

9. Benedict XVI, "Faith."

10. Benedict XVI, "Faith."

11. Benedict XVI, "Faith."

12. Benedict XVI, "Faith."

13. Benedict XVI, "Faith."

14. Benedict XVI, "Faith."

Index